A GUIDE TO
BIRD-WATCHING IN EUROPE

A Guide to
Bird-Watching
in Europe

EDITED BY

James Ferguson-Lees
Quentin Hockliffe, Ko Zweercs

THE BODLEY HEAD
LONDON   SYDNEY
TORONTO

ACKNOWLEDGMENTS

The Editors gratefully acknowledge the help given in the preparation
of this book by Dr Bruce Campbell, Dr A. Dyrcz, Dr Lars von Haartman,
Holger Holgersen, Major R. F. Ruttledge, B. L. Sage, Dr Finn Salomonsen,
Dr J. T. R. Sharrock, Dr Per Olof Swanberg and George Waterston.

Maps by Edgar Holloway
Drawings by H. J. Slijper

CONTENTS

CONTENTS

INTRODUCTION

It is sometimes the practice when introducing 'yet another' new bird book to apologise for producing it—and the editors of *A Guide to Bird-Watching in Europe* are well aware that almost every week new bird books, in most European languages, are offered to the public. But they believe that this guide does provide for the first time certain special information covering the whole of Europe in one manageable-sized book; and that it fills what they have found to be a very real gap in the practical ornithological literature of Europe.

The editors, each concerned with different aspects of field ornithology, have for some time been conscious of the need for a pocket guide which would provide essential and interesting information for the amateur bird-watcher on the Continent and for the Continental visitor to the British Isles—a practical reference book, which was not concerned with providing page after page of pictures of species, but which would quickly and clearly show the bird-watcher where in each European country are the places especially rich in bird life; where and in what season he would have a good chance of seeing species with which he is likely to be unfamiliar and which he is unlikely to see in his own country; the whereabouts and characteristics of nature reserves and of bird observatories; and the names—and briefly the scope—of the significant ornithological and nature conservation organisations. To this end, the editors invited leading field ornithologists to contribute concise descriptions under these headings for the countries of whose bird life they have special knowledge. Two aims have been kept in mind in the actual preparation of each contribution: to present as much scientifically accurate information as possible within the limits imposed by a book of this size; and to present this in a readable manner. For instance, scientific names have not been included in the text and species are given there only in the vernacular. We believe the tables at the end of the book will be found especially helpful. They show in simple form the status of all the birds mentioned in the text in the countries covered by the guide—twelve different symbols indicate commonness or rarity, summer or winter visitor, resident or vagrant. Both the scientific and English names are given for each species entry.

The maps accompanying the chapters have been prepared as background to the descriptions of the bird life of each country. For the sake of clarity, only the physical features which will help to orientate the bird-watcher are shown, such as mountain ranges and rivers, principal cities and towns, and some areas of particular ornithological significance. They do not pretend to be comprehensive: there is not room on such a small scale to include more than a few of the localities mentioned in the text and, in any case, the traveller will always want to buy his own map of the country he is visiting.

The maps are to different scales and in each case these are given in both miles and kilometres. After some deliberation, however, we have not used the metric system in giving distances in the text because we believe that the majority of British and American bird-watchers still find the English system of measurements much easier.

The contributors have indicated where information about the bird life in some parts of Europe is still restricted: frequently the amateur bird-watcher can contribute to our knowledge of the distribution of both the common and rarer species in these areas, and it is hoped that our readers will, by their reports, help towards this end. This particularly applies to the tables. Nor has the question of conservation and protection been overlooked, for each contributor has emphasised this vital matter and has shown where a species is increasing or declining, or is in danger for a variety of reasons.

Bird-watching and travel to other European countries become yearly more popular, easier and more extensive. *A Guide to Bird-Watching in Europe* has been prepared with the aim of giving factual help to the growing band of amateur ornithologists and adding to their enjoyment of watching birds in Europe.   J. F.-L.

Q. H.

K. Z.

England, Scotland and Wales

James Ferguson-Lees

Red Grouse

The oldest ornithological society is the British Ornithologists' Union (c/o The Zoological Society of London, Regent's Park, London NW1 4RY); it publishes a quarterly journal *The Ibis*, which is concerned particularly with biology and behaviour, and as much with Africa and other continents as with Europe. The British Trust for Ornithology (Beech Grove, Tring, Hertfordshire HP23 5NR) is responsible for the development and co-ordination of amateur network research and its many projects include the national ringing scheme, censuses, nest records, studies of estuaries and a host of shorter-term enquiries; among the last is the *Atlas of Breeding Birds in Britain and Ireland*, which is expected to appear in 1976 following field work carried out during 1968–72; the BTO also publishes a quarterly journal *Bird Study*. The third main bird journal is *British Birds* (Macmillan Journals Ltd, 4 Little Essex Street, London WC2R 3LF), an independent monthly on the birds of Britain and western Europe, concerned particularly with identification, status and distribution, migration, breeding biology, and occurrences of vagrants. Other journals covering limited parts of the United Kingdom are *Nature in Wales*, published by four Welsh naturalists' trusts (4 Victoria Place, Haverfordwest, Dyfed), and *Scottish Birds*, the journal of the Scottish Ornithologists' Club (21 Regent Terrace, Edinburgh EH7 5BT). The Scottish Centre for Ornithology and Bird Protection (same address as last) is glad to give advice to bird-watchers visiting Scotland. The Wildfowl Trust (Slimbridge, Gloucester GL2 7BT) runs several major waterfowl collections and reserves, and publishes the annual journal *Wildfowl*.

In the field of bird protection and conservation, the Royal Society for the Protection of Birds (The Lodge, Sandy, Bedfordshire SG19 2DL), which now has over 180,000 members and publishes the magazine *Birds* six times a year, as well as running a separate Young Ornithologists' Club for juniors with its own publication *Bird Life*, manages more than 50 important reserves; most of these are open to visitors, but some only by permit obtained in advance. Many other nature reserves, some of them of only limited ornithological interest, are owned or leased by such bodies as the government's Nature Conservancy Council (19 Belgrave Square, London SW1), by the network of county and regional naturalists' trust linked under the umbrella of the

Society for the Promotion of Nature Reserves (The Green, Nettleham, Lincoln LN2 2NR), and by the National Trust (42 Queen Anne's Gate, London SW1).

Britain is fortunately well-stocked with ornithological guide-books. Particularly recommended are *Where to Watch Birds* by John Gooders (André Deutsch), which details localities by counties with descriptions of the habitats, the birds to be seen, and how to get there, plus information on local societies and literature; *Collins Guide to Bird Watching* by R. S. R. Fitter (Collins), which includes a topographical guide by counties of habitats, special birds, reserves, societies and literature; and *A Regional Guide to the Birds of Scotland* by W. K. Richmond (Constable), which gives regionally grouped descriptions of habitats, tables of status and distribution, maps and lists of reserves and organisations. Also very useful, but now out of print and difficult to obtain is the *Shell Nature Lovers' Atlas* by James Fisher (Ebury Press), which has 32 pages of maps with reserves and other sites of interest plotted and described. Distribution maps for Britain and Ireland are currently available in *The Birds of Britain and Europe with North Africa and the Middle East* by Hermann Heinzel, Richard Fitter and John Parslow (Collins) and in *A Field Guide to Birds' Nests* by Bruce Campbell and James Ferguson-Lees (Constable). Sea bird colonies are mapped in *The Seabirds of Britain and Ireland* by Stanley Cramp, W. R. P. Bourne and David Saunders (Collins). Almost all English counties, and Wales and Scotland each as a whole, publish annual bird reports; and lists of the addresses concerned are given in *British Birds* each year.

The British Travel and Holiday Association (64–65 St James's Street, London SW1) and the Scottish Tourist Board (2 Rutland Place, Edinburgh 1) can provide information on travel.

Since this chapter was written, the boundaries and names of a number of English, Scottish and Welsh counties have been altered. As the old names are still in general use, however, we have considered it more helpful to retain these for the present.

ENGLAND, SCOTLAND AND WALES

England is a rough triangle with a base of 316 miles and sides of about 350 miles. To the west, the double peninsula of Wales is a maximum of 136 miles from north to south and varies in width from 90 miles in the south to only 37 miles in the centre. To the north of England, the shaggy head of Scotland has a greatest length of 274 miles and a width varying from as little as 26 miles to 154 miles. With the islands of Shetland and Orkney, the total length of the United Kingdom is some 600 miles, roughly between the latitudes of 61° N and 50° N. Shetland is on the same latitude as Oslo and Helsinki, while Land's End and the Isles of Scilly are south of the Netherlands. Thus there is much variation in daylight, temperature, and plants and animals. The climate is notoriously mixed, but Britain, being surrounded by sea, avoids the Continental extremes of heat and cold.

The list of birds recorded in Britain and Ireland (taken together as an ornithological unit) totals 480 species. At least 203 of these breed regularly and over 30 others have nested; apart from the regular breeders, 55 are regular visitors in winter or on passage, 40 more are annual stragglers and the remainder are rare vagrants. The indigenous fauna of the United Kingdom is the poorer as a result of the devastation of the Ice Age and the separation of this group of islands from the mainland just when the climate was becoming more temperate; this resulted in the loss of many of the larger mammals and in some bird families—the woodpeckers, for example —being rather thinly represented. England also suffers from a heavy human population and more urbanisation and agricultural development than many other European countries.

Nevertheless, the avifauna compares favourably with those of neighbouring countries and, in spite of recent decreases through the destruction of hedgerows and the effects of agricultural chemicals, the visitor is often surprised that small birds are more numerous than in many places on the Continent. This relative abundance is due partly to the persistence of a wide variety of suitable habitats, including woods, parkland and large gardens, and partly to the enlightened attitude of a public which generally encourages birds. An indication of the richness of the avifauna is given by preliminary results of the forthcoming *Atlas of Breeding Birds in Britain and Ireland* which is based on nesting distribution by 10 km squares of the national grids of the two countries: good 10 km squares with varied habitats in lowland England, even inland ones, may have 95 to 105 bird species breeding in them and some even up to 115; the corresponding figures in Wales are 80 to 90, and in Scotland 85 to 95 but with a remarkable 125 or more in one area.

To the visitor from the Continent the great sea bird colonies of the north and west are the outstanding feature of the British avifauna. Some are in Wales and a few in England, but the majority and largest are in Scotland, which therefore makes a good starting point. The Inner and Outer Hebrides total over 500 islands, four-fifths of them uninhabited. They combine moorland and mountain with lochs, bogs and marshes and some of the finest stretches of sand in Britain; most are almost treeless and there is little cultivation. Some have magnificent cliffs and offshore stacks, and it is these which hold the huge sea bird colonies.

The most famous Hebridean sea bird islands are the St Kilda group with the largest colony of Gannets in the world, the biggest colony of Fulmars in Britain, many thousands of Puffins, Guillemots, Razorbills and Kittiwakes, and smaller numbers of Manx Shearwaters and Leach's and Storm Petrels. There are, however, more colonies of Gannets and Leach's Petrels on Sula Sgeir and the Flannans, and Leach's on North Rona, while most of the other sea birds breed in large numbers on these islands and on, for example, Haskeir, the Shiants and Mingulay in the Outer Hebrides and on Canna, Rhum, the Treshnish Isles, and Colonsay and Oronsay in the Inner Hebrides.

Among other Hebridean birds, Red-throated Divers (and a few Black-throated) are a feature of the lochs, and Black Guillemots of the coasts; Arctic Skuas breed on Lewis, North Uist, Coll and Jura, and Red-necked Phalaropes erratically on the Uists, Benbecula and

Tiree. Greylag Geese nest on Lewis and the Uists, and the Outer Hebrides (notably the Monach Islands) are a major wintering area for Barnacle Geese, as are Coll and Islay in the Inner Hebrides. Small birds are few in species on most of the islands, but include countless Rock and Meadow Pipits, as well as Wheatears, Stonechats, Twites and Corn Buntings. There are also Corncrakes and abundant Rock Doves and, among larger land birds, Golden Eagles and Hen Harriers, as well as rock-nesting colonies of Grey Herons on Mull, Skye, Jura and Raasay and on low, scrubby islets in the Outer Hebrides.

Even the Outer Hebrides form a sizeable area, over 120 miles from north to south, and St Kilda and many other islands are difficult of access. The Uists and Benbecula, joined to each other by causeways and reachable by scheduled air and sea services, are probably the best for the visitor, who can base himself at Lochmaddy or Lochboisdale. Among the areas which should be visited are the RSPB reserve at Balranald (as many as 17 duck species seen in summer), Griminish Point, Wiay and the national nature reserve at Loch Druidibeg (stronghold of Greylag Geese). Fulmars, Kittiwakes and auks abound on the cliffs, and the moorland birds include Greenshanks, Golden Plovers and Dunlins. Contact the Western Isles Tourist Association, 21 South Beach Street, Stornoway, Outer Hebrides.

Orkney, with 67 islands, and Shetland, with over 100, are both rather treeless like the Hebrides, with magnificent cliff scenery on the western sides, but otherwise Orkney is very different in character. Hoy and Rousay are the only two Orkney islands with extensive heather and peat moorland, and most of the group are rather lower, flatter and, being very fertile, intensively farmed. Nevertheless, there are big sea bird colonies on the cliffs of Hoy, Marwick Head, Westray and Copinsay, and also Gannets on Sule Stack, while other breeding birds include Red-throated Divers, Manx Shearwaters, Storm Petrels, Great and Arctic Skuas (especially Papa Westray), Red-necked Phalaropes, and a notable and well-studied population of Hen Harriers.

Shetland, 74 miles from north to south, is a group of bare and rugged islands with extensive peat bogs and some very spectacular

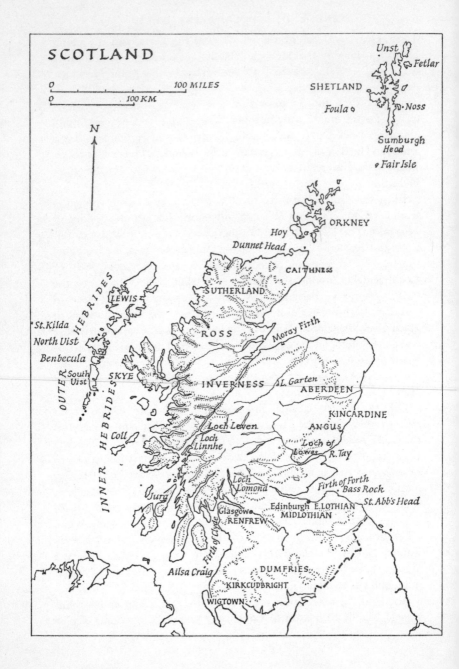

SCOTLAND

0   100 MILES
0   100 KM

N

Unst
Fetlar
SHETLAND
Foula
Noss
Sumburgh
Head
Fair Isle

ORKNEY
Hoy
Dunnet Head
CAITHNESS
SUTHERLAND
St.Kilda
North Uist
Benbecula
South Uist
SKYE
ROSS
Moray Firth
INVERNESS
L. Garten
ABERDEEN
KINCARDINE
ANGUS
Loch Leven
Loch of
Lowes
R. Tay
Loch
Linnhe
Coll
Loch
Lomond
Firth of Forth
Bass Rock
St. Abb's Head
Jura
Glasgow
RENFREW
Edinburgh E.LOTHIAN
MIDLOTHIAN
Ailsa Craig
DUMFRIES
KIRKCUDBRIGHT
WIGTOWN

OUTER HEBRIDES
INNER HEBRIDES
LEWIS
Firth of Clyde

cliffs where a large variety of sea birds can be more easily seen than almost anywhere else. There are Gannets on Noss and Unst (Hermaness), Manx Shearwaters on Foula and Fetlar, and Storm Petrels, Great and Arctic Skuas and huge cliff colonies of Fulmars, auks and gulls on these and other islands. For example, many Fulmars, Kittiwakes, Puffins, Razorbills, Guillemots and Shags, and small numbers of Black Guillemots, nest on Sumburgh Head not far from the airport. Snowy Owls now seem established on Fetlar and other breeding birds of Shetland include Red-throated Divers, Wigeon, Common Scoters, Red-breasted Mergansers, Golden Plovers, Dunlins, Whimbrels, Red-necked Phalaropes and Twites; Whooper Swans and Glaucous Gulls are regular winterers and odd ones stay through the summer. Hermaness, Noss, Fetlar, and Foula are the highlights and boat services are available, but almost all the islands are interesting. Even the biggest, Mainland, which tends to be forgotten, has such places as Ronas Hill, Weisdale and Whiteness Voes, Scousburgh, Spiggie and the Pool of Virkie, all worth visiting at different seasons. Then there is Fair Isle, midway between Shetland and Orkney and best known as a focal point for migration and rarities in both spring and autumn, though it too has many breeding sea birds; it can now be reached by air or sea. For the last, write to the Warden, Fair Isle Bird Observatory, by Lerwick, Shetland, but for Shetland as a whole contact the Shetland Tourist Association, Alexandra Wharf, Lerwick.

Apart from the islands, the visitor to Scotland is most likely to be attracted to the Highlands, which fill the north and west, and to the contrasting gentler slopes of the north-east and east from Caithness to Angus. The Highlands are the remains of an ancient plateau eroded into a complex of ridges, transverse valleys, river gorges and lochs. In the north-west the highest ground is found along the Atlantic coast, rising steeply from the sea to around 2000–2,800 feet and then sloping more gently down towards the Great Glen which runs diagonally through Inverness from the Moray Firth to Loch Linnhe; south-east of the Great Glen the scenery is more varied with evenly rounded summits of up to 3,900 feet. The coast of the western Highlands is heavily indented throughout by long, narrow sea lochs recalling the Norwegian fjords. By contrast, the north-eastern region is low-lying with a comparatively unbroken coast and the hills sloping gently down to the sea or ending in low cliffs.

In Caithness and Sutherland there are a number of sea bird colonies on or close to the mainland, including Duncansby Head, Dunnet Head, Berriedale, Clo Mor and the spectacular little island of Handa, now an RSPB reserve. Black Guillemots breed along the north and west coasts, Arctic Skuas in Caithness, and Grey-lag Geese there and in Sutherland. Red-throated and Black-throated Divers nest by lochs, along with Red-breasted Mergansers and Goosanders, large numbers of Wigeon and Teal, and a few Common Scoters and Pintail. The Highlands also hold Golden Eagles, Pere-grines, Ptarmigan, Capercaillies (mainly in the east), Greenshanks and Crossbills. Slavonian Grebes nest south to Inverness-shire, Wood Sandpipers and Redwings are increasing as breeding birds, Crested Tits are locally common (particularly in Strathspey and Strathnairn) and there are still a few nesting Snow Buntings. The Ospreys breeding at Loch Garten in Inverness-shire have, under the care of the RSPB, provided a remarkable tourist attraction since the 1950s, while another site, at the Loch of Lowes in Perthshire, now also has hide facilities under the protection of the Scottish Wildlife Trust.

Among the many other areas worth visiting in the Highlands and north-east Scotland, some of them profitable chiefly in the spring and summer (s), or in the autumn and winter (w), might be mentioned: Inverpolly (s), Invernaver (s) and Loch Fleet (w) in Sutherland; Beinn Eighe (s), Loch Carron (w) and the Dornoch and Beauly Firths in Ross; the Speyside area of Rothiemurchus and Abernethy (s) in Inverness; the Cairngorms (s); Loch Loy (s) in Nairn; Culbin, Findhorn Bay (w) and Loch Spynie in Moray; Troup and Pennan Heads (s) in Banff; Strathbeg, Collieston Lochs, Ythan estuary and Sands of Forvie in Aberdeen; the spectacular sea bird cliffs at Foulsheugh (s) in Kincardine; Caenlochan Glen (s), Lochs of Forfar (w), Montrose Basin (w) and Invergowrie Bay (w) in Angus; and Flanders Moss (w), Lake of Menteith (w), Loch Rannoch, Carsebreck (w) and Lochs Drumellie and Stormont near Blair-gowrie in Perth. But the adventurous visitor to Scotland will prefer to find his own localities. Of the hundreds of lochs, many are of limited interest but plenty of others are fascinating at one time of year or another: it is impossible to tell from the map which these are, but discovering them is half the fun of bird-watching.

The remainder of Scotland south of the Highlands comprises the distinct zones of the Central Lowlands and the Southern Uplands, the former a broad, flat area traversed by the valleys of the Tay, Forth and Clyde, and the latter rolling moorland rising to 2,700 feet. Both the Clyde and the Forth have Gannet colonies on Ailsa Craig and the Bass Rock respectively, while the Isle of May off the Fife coast has many sea birds in summer and migrants in autumn. Not far away, Loch Leven in Kinross is the most important loch in Scotland for breeding ducks, including Gadwall, Wigeon, Tufted Duck, Pochard and sometimes Pintail, and has large numbers of wintering geese. Of even greater importance to geese in winter, however, is the area of the Solway Firth, particularly such places as Caerlaverock (Barnacle and several species of grey geese) in Dumfries and Castle Douglas and Loch Ken (Greenland Whitefronts) in Kirkcudbright.

Other areas to visit in southern Scotland include the Morton Lochs, Tentsmuir, the Eden estuary (w), Cameron Reservoir (w), Fife Ness, and Kilconquhar Loch in Fife; Gartmor Dam (w) in Clackmannan; Grangemouth (w) in Stirling, and Loch Lomond on the border between that county and Dunbarton; Castle Semple and Barr Loch in Renfrew; Seafield (w), Duddingston Loch (w) and Gladhouse Reservoir in Midlothian, as well as the island of Inch-mickery; Aberlady Bay and Tyninghame in East Lothian; Hule Moss (w) and St Abb's Head (s) in Berwick; Portmore Loch in Peebles; the Lochmaben Lochs (w) and Priestside Bank (w) in Dumfries; Glentrool (s) and Mersehead and Carse Sands (w) and Southerness Point (w) in Kirkcudbright; and Castle Loch (inland Cormorant colony) in Wigtown.

Many other birds are quite widely distributed in Scotland. Breeding species include Shelduck, Teal and Eider in addition to the ducks mentioned; several more birds of prey (Buzzard, Sparrow-hawk, Merlin and Kestrel, with Hen Harriers also in the Highlands and the south); Ptarmigan and Red and Black Grouse; such waders as Oystercatcher, Ringed and Golden Plovers, Snipe, Woodcock,

Curlew, Common Sandpiper, Redshank and Dunlin; six species of gulls and five of terns (including Roseate); Barn, Short-eared, Long-eared and Tawny Owls; Great Spotted Woodpecker; Dipper; five thrushes apart from the Redwings, including Ring Ouzel and a few Fieldfares; Whinchat, Stonechat, Wheatear and Redstart; several warblers, among them Sedge and Wood; Siskin, Twite and Redpoll. In winter the scene is enriched by all three divers, many geese and ducks (including Scaup, Long-tailed and Goldeneye), Whooper Swans, such waders as Turnstones, Purple Sandpipers, Sanderlings and Knots, Glaucous Gulls, Bramblings and sometimes Waxwings.

Like Scotland, England with Wales is highest in the north and west, the western coastline is again very rugged and indented, and the land gradually flattens towards the east and south. The upland country in the north is mainly in the Lake District counties of Cumberland, Westmorland and Lancashire, in Northumberland and Durham, in the large county of Yorkshire, and in Derby.

The Lake District has peaks of 2,900 feet, a number of long and comparatively narrow lakes, and the highest rainfall in England. Cumberland has a good sea bird colony on St Bees Head (including Black Guillemots), big dune areas at Drigg Point, Grune Point and Ravenglass (large colonies of Black-headed Gulls and terns); coastal marshes at Rockcliffe and along the southern side of the Solway in general (many winter geese); and, of course, the various large lakes, which lead us into Westmorland where Haweswater and Sunbiggin Tarn are two of the most interesting water areas.

Where Lancashire descends to the Lune estuary there is an RSPB reserve at Leighton Moss with extensive reed-beds, pools and surrounding woodland, the breeding birds including Bitterns and Bearded Tits. Farther south in Lancashire, out of the Lake District, places to visit include Astley and Pennington Flashes (near Leigh), the Ribble Marshes, Freshfield, Formby, and Ainsdale (dune areas), and Walney Island where there is a huge colony of Herring and Lesser Black-backed Gulls and the southernmost British nesting Eiders: not far away at Foulney all five British tern species may sometimes be found breeding.

Going north again, Northumberland has many interesting spots, among them Holy Island, Seaton Sluice, Fenham Flats, Budle Bay and such lakes and reservoirs as Gosforth Park, Fontburn, Hallington, Seaton Burn and Capheaton. But one of the most important places in the north-east is the Farne Islands, with its colonies of Kittiwakes, Shags, Eiders, Roseate Terns and other sea birds. There are also sea birds on Coquet Island, Cullernose Point and Dunstanburgh, and a colony of Kittiwakes on warehouses at North Shields. At Teesmouth in County Durham the now largely reclaimed mudflats still attract waders and waterfowl and sea bird movements may also be watched.

Southern Teesmouth is in Yorkshire, which extends from there down to the Humber; apart from these estuaries, Yorkshire has many centres of interest, such as the reservoirs and other sheets of water at Eccup, Gouthwaite, Fairburn Ings and Hornsea Mere, but the best known are perhaps the sea bird cliffs at Bempton (a few Gannets included) and the bird observatory at Spurn Point (many migrants). North Derbyshire has some of the finest scenery in the Pennines, which form the backbone of northern England, and places to visit in south Derbyshire include Ogston reservoir and Egginton sewage farm.

These moorland counties hold Merlins (getting scarcer), Buzzards (in the west), Red and Black Grouse, Golden Plovers, Dunlins, Common Sandpipers, Short-eared Owls, Dippers, Ring Ouzels, Twites and, in the wooded dales, Pied Flycatchers. The north-west also has Red-breasted Mergansers, Wigeon and Corncrakes in suitable areas. Many of these birds are also found in Wales where, in addition, there is Britain's tiny remnant population of Red Kites.

Much of Wales is hill country intersected by deep valleys and rising to over 3,000 feet in the north. There are lakes and, in the east and south, the more rounded hills are interspersed with bogs. The north coast is low, but the south-west has rocky headlands, bays and islands. Places to visit in Anglesey include Newborough Warren, the marsh and estuary of Malltraeth and sea bird colonies on Holyhead Island. More sea birds breed on Bardsey Island (including Manx Shearwaters), St Tudwal's Islands and Great Orme's Head in Caernarvonshire, in which county there are also several estuaries and, in the north, Choughs. Other focal points in Wales include inland Fulmars near Abergele in Denbigh and inland Cormorants on the Bird Rock near Towyn in Merioneth; the Dovey estuary in Merioneth and

Cardigan; Tregaron Bog in Cardigan; the reservoirs of the Elan Valley in Radnor; and the Black Mountains and Talybont Reservoir in Brecon.

In Carmarthen and Glamorgan the Burry estuary is important for wintering Eiders, Black-tailed Godwits and Oystercatchers, and Glamorgan also has Kenfig Pool, Oxwich Ponds, the Gower dunes, and sea birds on Worms Head. But perhaps the most rewarding Welsh county is Pembroke with its samples of moor, marsh and estuary and especially its sea birds, including the great Gannet colony on Grassholm, the Puffins, Storm Petrels and Manx Shearwaters on Skokholm and Skomer, and the other auks there and on Ramsey; Choughs also breed on these coasts and islands. Skokholm and Caernarvon's Bardsey are bird observatories.

The belt of counties from Cheshire to Cornwall takes in much hilly country with the same upland birds. Cheshire also has Delamere Forest (Black-headed Gulls and inland Shelducks), Burton Marsh and such meres and lakes as Rostherne, Marbury, Tatton and Tabley (big colony of Grey Herons), as well as the estuaries of the Mersey and the Dee, shared with Lancashire and Flint respectively; in the Dee are the islands of Hilbre, where countless thousands of waders congregate at high tide. Shropshire sites include the Long Mynd (moorland), Ellesmere and Venus Pool. Hereford shares the Black Mountains with Brecon, and Gloucester the important Forest of Dean (Pied Flycatchers, Hawfinches and Wood Warblers) with Monmouth. Gloucester also has a number of gravel pits, such as Frampton, and the Severn estuary, notably around Slimbridge. There, in addition to the Wildfowl Trust's remarkable collection of ducks, geese and swans, many White-fronted Geese and Bewick's Swans spend the winter.

The south-western peninsula of Cornwall, Devon and Somerset has fine cliffs with indented bays, and some wild moorland on Exmoor (up to 1,500 feet), Dartmoor (up to 1,800 feet) and Bodmin Moor. Somerset also has several important reservoirs (Blagdon, Cheddar, Barrow Gurney, Durleigh, Sutton Bingham and especially Chew Valley), such estuaries and marshes as Bridgwater Bay (moulting Shelducks), Parrott, Porlock and Stert, and the upland country of Brean Down and the Mendips. Devon has the dune area of Braunton Burrows and Dawlish Warren, the estuaries of the Exe, Axe, Taw and a study centre at Slapton Ley, and sea bird colonies on the cliffs at, for instance, Berry Head and Martinhoe in addition to those on the island of Lundy.

In Cornwall many sea birds breed along the north coast, including Puffins near Newquay, Polzeath and Trevone, and also worth visiting are the estuaries of the Camel, Hayle and Tamar, as well as Marazion Marsh, Crowan Reservoir, Tamar Lake and Dozmary Pool. There are plenty of sea birds too on the Isles of Scilly, including Storm Petrels on Rosevear and Annet, Manx Shearwaters on Annet, and a few Roseate Terns; St Agnes, in particular, is also important for migration studies.

Another bird observatory where there are again cliff-breeding sea birds is Portland Bill in Dorset; not far away Chesil Bank has nesting terns and at Abbotsbury there is the famous colony, dating back to at least the fourteenth century, of several hundred pairs of Mute Swans. Other places of interest include Radipole Lake and Lodmoor near Weymouth, while the heathland around Purbeck and Poole Harbour is now the centre of the range of the Dartford Warbler in Britain; Poole Harbour itself has many ducks and waders.

The coastal counties from Hampshire to Kent and north to Lincoln form the last main section. Lincoln and East Anglia have generally flat coastlines, but there are some fine chalk cliffs in Hampshire, Sussex and Kent (though less notable for sea birds). In Hampshire a most striking habitat is the 90,000 acres of the New Forest: here are Dartford Warblers and a remnant population of Red-backed Shrikes, as well as Hobbies, Buzzards, Woodcock, Woodlarks, Stonechats, Firecrests, Hawfinches and Crossbills. Among important estuaries and marshes in Hampshire are Christchurch Harbour, Langstone Harbour, Titchfield Haven, Stanpit Marsh and the Solent from Keyhaven to Needs Oar; at these places there are many migrant waders, including Black-tailed Godwits, Spotted Redshanks and other scarcer species.

Sussex shares Chichester Harbour with Hampshire and among other interesting points on the coast are Thorney Island, Pagham Harbour, Pett Level and the shingle areas at Eastbourne, Rye and the Midrips; inland there are lakes and reservoirs such as Darwell

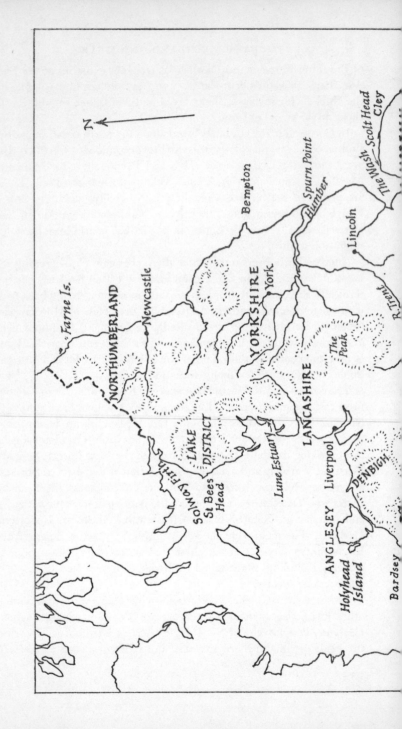

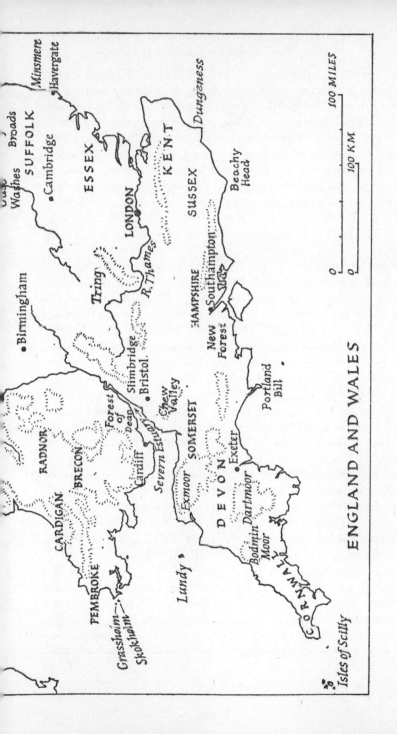

ENGLAND AND WALES

Minsmere
Havergate
Washes Broads
SUFFOLK
Cambridge
ESSEX
Birmingham
Tring
LONDON
R. Thames
KENT
Dungeness
SUSSEX
Beachy Head
HAMPSHIRE
Southampton
New Forest
Portland Bill
Slimbridge
Bristol
Chew Valley
Forest of Dean
RADNOR
BRECON
CARDIGAN
Cardiff
Severn Estuary
SOMERSET
Exmoor
DEVON
Exeter
Bodmin Moor
Dartmoor
CORNWALL
Lundy
PEMBROKE
Grassholm
Skokholm
Isles of Scilly

0   100 MILES
0   100 KM

and Weir Wood, extensive heath and woodland in Ashdown Forest, St Leonard's Forest and Kingley Vale, and downland extending westwards from Beachy Head. In Kent areas to visit are the estuaries of the Thames, Medway and Swale, and such marshes as Stodmarsh (Bitterns, Bearded Tits and Savi's Warblers), Cliffe and Egypt Bay; projecting from the south coast at Romney Marsh is the shingle area of Dungeness which has breeding Common Gulls and Common Terns and a bird observatory. Black Redstarts nest there and in and near Dover, and Kent at present has the majority of the small number of Cetti's Warblers which have recently colonised England; at Northward Hill, High Halstow, is one of Britain's largest colonies of Grey Herons.

Essex has another of the few large broad-leaved woodland areas in England, in the form of Epping Forest (Hawfinches, Redpolls, Redstarts, Nightingales and a few Red-backed Shrikes); otherwise the big centres of attraction are the reservoirs of Abberton and Hanningfield (many ducks, notably Goldeneye), while the flat, low-lying coast has the important estuaries and coastal marshes of the Stour, Blackwater and Crouch, the last extending to Foulness and Maplin.

Suffolk is especially noted for its woodland, shallow lakes, estuaries and coastal marshes, the last including the important sanctuaries of Minsmere and Havergate Island, both visitable by permit from the RSPB. Havergate holds a large proportion of the British Avocets, and other nesting birds include Sandwich Terns, Black-headed Gulls, Shelducks and Short-eared Owls; it is also notable for migrant waders and winter ducks. Minsmere's combination of marsh, reed-beds, open water and adjacent shore and woodland makes it one of the few places where over 200 species are seen in a year; Avocets nest and so do Marsh Harriers, Bitterns, Bearded Tits, Gadwall, Sandwich, Common and Little Terns, and many others. Suffolk also has an interesting colony of Kittiwakes in Lowestoft on the South Pier Pavilion.

Suffolk and Norfolk share the unique heath of the Brecks where breeding birds include Crossbills, Red-backed Shrikes, Stone Curlews and inland Ringed Plovers. Beginning in Suffolk too, but mainly in Norfolk, are the famous Broads, a large area of shallow lagoons; the more interesting of these are Barton, Hickling, Horsey and Ranworth. Here Bearded Tits and Bitterns breed in the reeds, Marsh Harriers are sometimes seen, and there are feral populations of Grey-lag, Egyptian and Canada Geese; nesting ducks include Gadwall and Garganey; and many waterfowl, waders and terns occur on passage.

Other Norfolk habitats include the extensive dune areas of Scolt Head and Blakeney Point (many terns); the coastal marshes along the north coast from Holme to Cley and Salthouse (Bitterns and Bearded Tits, many migrants, winter Snow and Lapland Buntings and Shore Larks); the low cliffs near Sheringham (Fulmars); and the Breckland sanctuaries at East Wretham and Weeting. In addition, shared with Lincolnshire, there is the Wash which may be likened to a vast estuary with its extensive mudflats, sand and shingle at low tide; in autumn and winter this area attracts countless thousands of Knots, Dunlins, and other waders, as well as ducks and geese. Also shared with Lincolnshire is Wisbech sewage farm which is a few miles from the Wash and now one of the best of its kind in the country, attracting many of the less common waders on passage. Other places of interest in Lincolnshire are the bird observatory at Gibraltar Point (where there is also a considerable dune area), the coastal marshes at Tetney, and Bardney Ponds.

Coming farther inland in East Anglia, the most remarkable area is the Ouse Washes which extend for over 18 miles from Denver Sluice in Norfolk through Cambridgeshire to Earith in Huntingdon-shire. Large sections of this area are owned by the RSPB, the Cambridge and Isle of Ely Naturalists' Trust, and the Wildfowl Trust. Many marsh birds breed here, including Black-tailed Godwits, Ruffs and other waders, a variety of ducks including Garganey and Pintail, Short-eared Owls and, occasionally, Black Terns; while in winter there are huge numbers of ducks and up to 1,000 or more Bewick's Swans.

Otherwise the inland counties of central and southern England have somewhat less to offer the visiting bird-watcher, but neverthe-less there are a number of interesting localities. The numerous gravel pits provide a habitat for Little Ringed Plovers and, as they mature, many other species. The best of the reservoirs, which attract many waterfowl and waders in autumn and winter, are perhaps Blithfield and Belvide in Staffordshire, Bittell in Worcestershire, Eye Brook in Leicestershire, Grafham Water in Huntingdonshire, Pitsford in Northamptonshire, Tring and Hilfield Park in Hertfordshire, and those in the London area, such as Barn Elms, Brent, King George V, King George VI, Queen Mary, Staines and Walthamstow. One of the most important sewage farms is now Rye Meads in Hertfordshire (ringing and population studies). Other parts of interest include Alvecote Pools in Warwickshire, the Trent valley in Nottinghamshire, and the Surrey commons at Ashtead, Bookham, Epsom, Esher, Oxshott and Thursley. Even London itself has surprising numbers of birds in the squares and parks, including Kestrels, Jays, Carrion Crows and Woodpigeons; places to visit are St James's Park (captive wildfowl and many wild ones) and Regent's Park (nearly 100 species in a year).

Tolerably widespread nesting birds in England and Wales include Little and Great Crested Grebes; Shags (west and north-east coasts) and Cormorants; six ducks (among them Shelduck, Pochard and Tufted Duck); Kestrel (and Buzzard in the west); Partridge and Red-legged Partridge; Oystercatcher, Ringed Plover, Lapwing, Redshank, Curlew, Woodcock and Snipe; four gulls and two terns; doves including Collared and Turtle; Cuckoo, Nightjar and Swift; Tawny, Little, Barn and Long-eared Owls (the last two rather scarce); Great Spotted, Lesser Spotted and Green Woodpeckers; and a much wider variety of passerines than in Scotland. Among the last are Yellow, Pied and Grey Wagtails, ten warblers (Grasshopper, Sedge, Reed, Garden, Blackcap, Whitethroat, Lesser Whitethroat except in the west, Willow, Chiffchaff and, locally, Wood), Goldcrest, Whinchat, Stonechat, Wheatear, Redstart, six tits (including Long-tailed, Willow and Marsh), Nuthatch, Redpoll and Bullfinch. In winter there are divers, geese, and many ducks (including Scaup, Eider and Common and Velvet Scoters on the coasts), Hen Harriers, many waders (such as Turnstones, Purple Sandpipers, Sanderlings, Knots, Grey Plovers, Ruffs, both godwits, and Jack Snipe), many gulls and, among passerines, Fieldfares, Redwings, Snow Buntings, Bramblings and Siskins.

Ireland

Christopher Moriarty

Black Guillemots

Three older organisations, all concerned with the protection of birds, field ornithology and the protection of water birds, have now merged to form the Irish Wildbird Conservancy (c/o 19 Dawson Street, Dublin 2), which annually publishes the *Irish Bird Report*, giving a systematic survey of rare or otherwise interesting species which have been sighted. Furthermore, they are active in all aspects of the protection and study of birds. In Northern Ireland, protection is stimulated by a regional office of the (British) Royal Society for the Protection of Birds (58 High Street, Newtownards, Co Down). The standard work on Irish birds and their distribution is *Ireland's Birds* by R. F. Ruttledge (Witherby). Ireland does not have a ringing centre and so, if one finds a ringed bird, it should be reported to the country of origin.

IRELAND

Ireland is an island of about 30,000 square miles in the Atlantic Ocean. It lies close to Great Britain and the main Continental land mass but enjoys very mild winters. The bird fauna is to some extent that of an oceanic island rather than an extension of the Continent. The list of native birds is comparatively short, but the variety of scarce passage migrants is impressive and the numbers of nesting sea birds and wintering ducks and waders are spectacular. The latter are attracted especially by the fact that the lakes and coastal waters rarely become icebound.

The surface of the land is very varied. There are numerous mountain ranges close to the coast and a few inland. The slopes are gentle and peaks of more than 3,000 feet are few. Even on the highest, snow seldom lies for more than a few weeks. Much of the centre of the country is flat lowland, partly peat bog and partly rich grazing land. There are few extensive deciduous woods but coniferous plantations are plentiful and increasing: most of these are on the mountain slopes.

Rivers and lakes are abundant. In the south-eastern quarter of the country the former tend to be broad and sluggish with muddy estuaries. In the Cork-Kerry region, however, rivers are mostly rapid except where they open into lakes such as those of Killarney and Waterville. The Shannon basin occupies about a third of the country. This river and its tributaries wander slowly through the plains passing through numerous large and small lakes on their way. Towards the north the River Erne breaks up into a maze of lakelets in its upper reaches and lower down forms the broad and open Lower Lough Erne. In the north-east the large, shallow Lough Neagh occupies an area of 153 square miles. The coast is as varied as the land. There are many miles of sandy beaches, interrupted by the river estuaries and by steep cliffs with rocky islands offshore.

The birds living in the cultivated areas differ little from those found in similar regions in adjacent European countries. Blackbird, Song Thrush, Robin, Great, Blue and Coal Tits, Dunnock, Starling, Linnet, Chaffinch and House Sparrow are among the commonest residents. Compared with neighbouring countries the most striking points in the Irish land bird fauna are the missing species. For example, Barn and Long-eared Owls are virtually the only owls to be found and neither of them is common. Amongst the hawks Kestrels and Sparrowhawks are the only common species though Hen Harriers are increasing. A few other distinctive features of the fauna are worth mentioning. The Hooded Crow is the common race of crow. Choughs are common on many of the sea cliffs: Waterville and Glencolumbkille are good areas to look for them. Grey Wagtails and Dippers are found beside clear lowland rivers as well as by mountain streams.

On the poorer land, where trees and hedges are scarce, Meadow Pipits and Skylarks are abundant in summer. Red Grouse are frequently seen on the heather slopes and the bogland has a resident population of Snipe and Curlew. It must not be thought from these paragraphs that there is any shortage of birds on rich or poor land but bird-watching visitors to Ireland will undoubtedly find that the most remarkable regions are the lakes and coast and therefore these are given the fullest treatment.

During the breeding season the coast is populated by immense numbers of sea and ocean birds. Great and Lesser Black-backed Gulls, Herring Gulls, Kittiwakes, Razorbills, Guillemots, Shags and Fulmars may be seen at easily accessible cliffs in all parts of the country. Within a few miles of Dublin City is Howth Head. From there, going clockwise around the coast, the most easily reached cliff colonies are Bray Head, Helvick Head, the Cliffs of Moher, many miles of the north Mayo coast, Horn Head, Fair Head and Islandmagee. All these places are easily reached by car while the city bus service goes to within a couple of miles of the Howth cliffs. Black Guillemots, Rock Doves and Cormorants may also be seen on many of the cliffs; Eiders nest on the north and north-west coasts.

Little Terns, Ringed Plovers and Oystercatchers are well distributed residents on sandy or shingle beaches. Sandwich, Common and Arctic Terns have colonies on low-lying islands in many places and Roseate Terns in a few. Tern Island, in Wexford Harbour, is a bird sanctuary with one of the finest colonies of Roseates. Any or all of the five species may be seen in summer at seaside places and Common Terns nest on islands in the larger lakes.

On the mainland cliffs the birds tend to keep to inaccessible ledges, although a reasonably close approach is always possible. The birds of the coastal islands are very much tamer and most species will permit intruders to come within a few feet. The islands, apart from the attraction of the tameness of the birds, offer several more species. Puffins are fairly common round the coast and sometimes abundant. There are over twenty scattered colonies of Manx Shearwaters, but those on Puffin Island in Co Kerry and Rathlin in Co Antrim are two of the largest. Storm Petrels nest in enormous numbers in scree or stone walls on many uninhabited islands of the west. The Little Skellig bird sanctuary has a very large colony of Gannets and there are smaller gannetries on the Bull Rock and Great Saltee. Such islands are sometimes difficult to land on, but it is usually possible to hire a fishing-boat for transport. Permission from the owners of the islands is required in some cases.

Inland the most interesting breeding species are those inhabiting the lakes. Mute Swans are generally common as are Grey Herons. Mallard may be found by most lakes, Teal are somewhat less numerous, Tufted Ducks are widespread and Red-breasted Mergansers breed on the larger lakes. Great Crested Grebes are common on large and small lakes in the northern half of the country, especially on Lough Neagh; Little Grebes, Moorhens and Coots are very widely distributed. Common Scoters nest on Lough Erne. Common Sandpipers are probably the most abundant lakeside waders in the breeding season but Curlews, Redshanks, Dunlins, Ringed Plovers and Lapwings may frequently be found. Black-headed Gulls and Common Gulls nest on lake islands, often in very large numbers.

The mild winter climate, coupled with the abundance of marshy and muddy estuarine land with sheltered bays, explains the very large numbers of waders and ducks to be seen from September to April. The North Bull Island in Dublin Bay is a bird sanctuary with a salt marsh and a sheltered lagoon; it is accessible by road. The Duncrue Street marsh at Belfast is another excellent urban salt

IRELAND

marsh. Indeed it is safe to say that all the larger coastal towns have fine areas for winter bird-watching. Amongst the commonest ducks are Wigeon, Pintail, Teal, Mallard and Shelduck. The waders include Curlews, Oystercatchers, Bar-tailed Godwits, Knots, Dunlins, Sanderlings, Ringed Plovers and Redshanks. Scarcer ones, often confined to the passage seasons, are Whimbrels, Greenshanks and Black-tailed Godwits, though the last are now increasing and may be seen in winter and summer. Many other species, including several American waders such as the Pectoral Sandpiper, occur more or less regularly.

In winter, the coastal waters offer Great Northern and Red-throated Divers as well as Red-breasted Mergansers, Goldeneyes and Common Scoters. Brent and Barnacle Geese are widely distributed. Greenland Whitefronts are the commonest grey geese. At least half of the world population of Greenland Whitefronts winters on the Wexford Slobs. Part of the North Slob has been opened to the public and a tower has been built which allows a very close approach and superb views of this splendid flock.

Finally, as something of an offering for specialists, there are the migrants, which are regularly watched on certain headlands and islands. In the last fifteen years or so a number of observatories have been established on such islands as Great Saltee and Tory (now more or less abandoned), Cape Clear and Copeland and the promontories of St John's Point and Malin Head, the most northerly point of the mainland. Apart from the appearance of spectacular numbers of migrating birds, especially passerines, a great many species which were once considered merely as vagrants have been shown to be annual visitors. Sea-watching from these points has been very rewarding: Great, Cory's and Sooty Shearwaters among other species are frequently seen and even the occasional Black-browed Albatross has appeared.

Iceland
and the Faroes

Arni Waag

Snowy Owl

The zoological department of the Museum of Natural History is the centre of ornithological activities on Iceland. The only ornithological organisation is the Society for the Protection of Birds, which has achieved a great deal since its foundation in 1962. Articles on the birds of Iceland appear in *Náttúrufraeðingurinn*, the journal of the Icelandic Natural History Society.

The only bird reserve is Eldey, a rocky island off the coast of Reykjanesskagi, which has a very large colony of Gannets. There is a National Park at Thingvellir. Most bird species are protected by law, but in certain places eggs are still collected for human consumption. Shooting is well controlled, but on the larger bird rocks Puffins and Guillemots are still caught for the market; this is a tradition which is almost impossible to stamp out. Visitors should realise that it is strictly forbidden to photograph Gyr Falcons, White-tailed Eagles, Little Auks and Snowy Owls near their nests.

If one finds a ringed bird in Iceland, the ring should be sent to: Náttúrugripasafnið, P.O. Box 532, Reykjavík, Iceland.

If one finds a ringed bird on the Faroes, the ring should be sent to: Universitets Zoologiske Museum, Ringmaerknings Afdelingen, Universitetsparken 15, Copenhagen, Denmark.

ICELAND AND THE FAROES

Iceland is a large island in the North Atlantic. The southernmost point, Dyrhólaey, is 63° 24′ N and the northern tip 66° 32′ N. The western extremity, Bjargtangar, is 24° 32′ W and the easternmost point, Gerpir, 13° 30′ W. The area of the country is roughly 34,000 square miles. Iceland is the westernmost country in Europe, and only 180 miles from the east coast of Greenland. Except in the south, where there is extensive low-lying grassland, the coast is much indented with fjords and bays, and in the north large valleys cut deep into the highlands. The interior is a high plateau of mountains, glaciers and vast eroded areas and is devoid of human settlement. Rivers are innumerable. Most of the larger ones arise in the glaciers and have milky, turbid water: their bird life is generally poor. There are many lakes, both in the lowlands and in the central highlands, though most are quite small. The largest is Thingvallavatn in the south, with cold water, but perhaps the best known is Mývatn in the north-east. The country enjoys an oceanic type of climate, the summers being cool and the winters comparatively mild. The relative mildness of the climate is due to the influence of the Gulf Stream.

The lowlands are mostly well covered with vegetation and there are extensive areas of bog and moorland. However, there are also some large sections with post-glacial lava flows and gravel plains with only scattered vegetation. As one approaches the mountains the vegetation becomes generally sparser and on the high plateau vast areas are completely bare, although there are some sheltered oases among the mountains.

Iceland is very thinly populated compared with other European countries and extensive areas are untouched by man. As the population increases the lowland habitats are gradually changing. Nearly all the areas of marshland around the coast have been, or are about to be, drained and turned into farmland. This intense activity has caused big changes in the bird life.

About 260 species of birds have been recorded in Iceland. Of these only 80 nest or have attempted to nest, and 12 are common passage migrants or winter visitors. The rest are accidentals and casual visitors. The last category consists mainly of passerine birds of European origin, the most common of which are Chiffchaffs, Willow Warblers, Blackcaps, Garden Warblers, Chaffinches, Bramblings, Redstarts and Robins. Quite a few of the accidental visitors come from America. For example, Parula Warblers have been recorded the most, but others, such as American Robin, Hermit Thrush, Indigo Bunting, and so on, have all been identified once or twice. Species which are recorded annually, but not so often as twenty times a year, include Bar-tailed Godwit, Ruff, Grey Plover, Goldeneye and American Wigeon. Other regular visitors recorded less than twenty times a year are such seabirds as Pomarine and Long-tailed Skuas, and Sooty and Great Shearwaters.

Compared with other European countries the number of nesting species is low. On the other hand, the total number of certain species is so large that they fully compensate for the comparatively small variety. Some of these, such as Puffins, Fulmars, Kittiwakes and both Guillemots and Brünnich's Guillemots, congregate in millions around the coast where suitable cliffs are found.

In the last sixty to seventy years the number of species of nesting birds has increased considerably. The following breeding birds have colonised since the beginning of the present century: Shoveler, Tufted Duck, Pochard, Lesser Black-backed, Herring, Common and Black-headed Gulls, Short-eared Owl and Starling. Coot, Lapwing, Swallow, Fieldfare and House Sparrow have all made nesting attempts, but have not yet settled as permanent nesting birds. Owing to its isolation and to other factors Iceland is not fully settled zoologically. The climate has been becoming gradually warmer since 1920 and, if no reverse change takes place, we may expect further additions to the list of breeding birds.

Many of the more common birds such as Mallard, Golden Plover, Ringed Plover, Whimbrel, Redshank, Snipe, Great Black-backed Gull, Black-headed Gull, Arctic Tern, Meadow Pipit, Wheatear and Raven are found almost everywhere in Iceland, except in the extensive deserts of the interior.

In Reykjavík and its vicinity there are several good places for observing birds. The centre of the town has a lake where many ducks can be seen, and this is also the only capital city in the world which has a colony of Arctic Terns in its centre. The visitor will not need to stay long in the town before he hears the melodious song of the Redwing. In fact, this song will follow him in most places throughout the country. Another passerine, the Redpoll, has in recent years become a common nesting bird in Reykjavík. White Wagtails are also found in the town. In the last ten years Starlings have increased enormously in Reykjavík and the surrounding area. During the breeding season the harbour of Reykjavík is not especially good for birds, but later the number of gulls increases and then in October, when the Iceland Gulls arrive from Greenland, it is possible to see as many as eight species there. A little west of the town is a point called Seltjarnarnes, which is a very good spot for shore birds in spring and autumn. The most common shore birds are Ringed Plover, Dunlin, Purple Sandpiper and, among passage migrants, Knot, Turnstone and Sanderling. Birds of the last three species can be seen throughout the summer. Not very far from Reykjavík on the Reykjanes peninsula are two bird cliffs, Hafnaberg and Krisavíkurberg, on which all the typical cliff birds are represented, namely Shag, Herring and Glaucous Gulls, Kittiwake, Razorbill, Puffin, Guillemot and Brünnich's Guillemot. Black Guillemots are found under boulders at the bottom of most of the sea cliffs and also in crevices. On Reykjanes, Grey Phalaropes nest near the village of Sandgerði, while Purple Sandpipers and Snow Buntings also breed on the barren plain behind it. Not far away, at the lighthouse at Garðskagi, is Iceland's only bird observatory. There are many Puffins, Black Guillemots and other sea birds on the isles in the fjord north of Reykjavík.

Along the highway west from Reykjavík, Fulmars can be seen on the cliffs; indeed, these birds are found on almost every cliff around the coast. About 30 miles from Reykjavík and only a short distance from the main road, the lake of Medalfellsvatn has Whooper Swans and Great Northern Divers and, at the outlet, Harlequin Ducks. In Hvalfjörður many shore birds, Eiders and gulls can be seen. Multitudes of gulls, mainly Great Black-backed, Lesser Black-backed,

Glaucous and Black-headed, and also Fulmars, are attracted to the whaling station.

The fertile lowlands of Borgarfjörður have most of the common nesting birds of Iceland. In recent years Black-tailed Godwits have invaded the area and now nest fairly commonly. On the isles off the coast north of Borgarfjörður many species of sea birds such as Shags and Cormorants nest. From the mouth of Borgarfjörður to the Snae-fellsnes peninsula the seashore is mostly sandy, and at low tide extensive mud and sand flats emerge. These flats are inhabited by countless flocks of Knots, Turnstones, Sanderlings, Dunlins and Ringed Plovers. In the migration season, when passage migrants are mixed with summer visitors, the sand flats seem to be alive with birds.

The Oystercatcher is a typical nesting bird on the seashore in this part of the country. Grey Phalaropes nest on the island of Hjörsey, not far from the coast. Here also Brent Geese on passage can be seen in considerable numbers, mainly where eel-grass occurs; on the adjacent lowlands White-fronted Geese are common migrants in spring and autumn. Barnacle Geese are also seen on passage in this area. Short-eared Owls are found here in suitable places, but they are not common. Near the south coast of Snaefellsnes, just east of Búðir, there are several small lakes with rich bird life. From the roadside one can see Great Northern Divers, Red-throated Divers, many different ducks, Slavonian Grebes, several colonies of Black-backed Gulls, Arctic Terns, Red-necked Phalaropes and so on.

Stapi and Hellnar are good places for Kittiwakes and in any case are worth visiting for the spectacular scenery. On the tip of this peninsula are two cliffs with Kittiwakes, Fulmars, Guillemots and Brünnich's Guillemots. Near the village of Sandur, just below the glacier Snaefellsjökull, is one of the largest terneries in Iceland. On the northern side of Snaefellsnes, in the Grundarfjörður area, there are colonies of Glaucous Gulls on the cliffs, while on Melrakkaey, an island in Grundarfjörður, the Glaucous Gulls actually nest on the ground.

Breiðafjörður has many small islands with abundant bird life, particularly large populations of Shags and Cormorants, and Grey Phalaropes nest on some of the islands. The best way to get to these islands is to hire a boat from the village of Stykkishólmur. White-tailed Eagles can also be seen in the Breiðafjörður area. North of Hvammsfjörður, in the cliffs of Klofningur, there are large colonies of Glaucous Gulls.

The mountainous and indented north-western peninsula has several places of ornithological interest. Three of the largest bird cliffs in Iceland are in this region. The first is Látrabjarg at the westernmost tip of the peninsula, which is 8 miles long with an average altitude of about 490 feet. It has been estimated that as many as two million pairs of Brünnich's Guillemots and Guillemots nest there. The other two cliffs, Hornbjarg and Haelavíkurbjarg, are close to each other on the northern tip of the peninsula. Between Önundar-fjorður and Dýrafjörður, on the cliff of Bardi, is one of the largest colonies of Glaucous Gulls in Iceland, and Mýrar farm in Dýra-fjörður has the largest Eider colony with about 7,000 pairs. The permission of the landowners is required before visiting Eider colonies in Iceland. In large Eider colonies in north-western and western Iceland single male King Eiders are often seen, as a rule mated with female Eiders. King Eiders are regular winter visitors, mainly to the western part of the country, but they do not nest in Iceland. The north-western peninsula is the main region in Iceland for Gyr Falcons.

In the northern lowlands, between the villages of Hvammstangi and Blönduós, there is an area of lagoons, lakes and marshland offering a variety of waterfowl. In spring hundreds of Whooper Swans feed in the lagoons and on the flooded marshes while waiting for the ice on the highland lakes to thaw. Gyr Falcons nest on cliffs near the lagoon of Vesturhóp practically every year. The wide and fertile district of Skagafjörður also has a varied avifauna and this is the main resting place of the Barnacle Goose on its way to its nesting grounds in Greenland. On the delta of the river Héradsvötn, near the town of Sauðárkrókur, there is an extremely good area which is often overlooked by bird-watchers, but which holds almost all the duck species found in Iceland. Besides the common waders such as Dunlins and Whimbrels there are also considerable numbers of Black-tailed Godwits, which have recently moved into this area. The high rocky island of Drangey in Skagafjörður has numerous

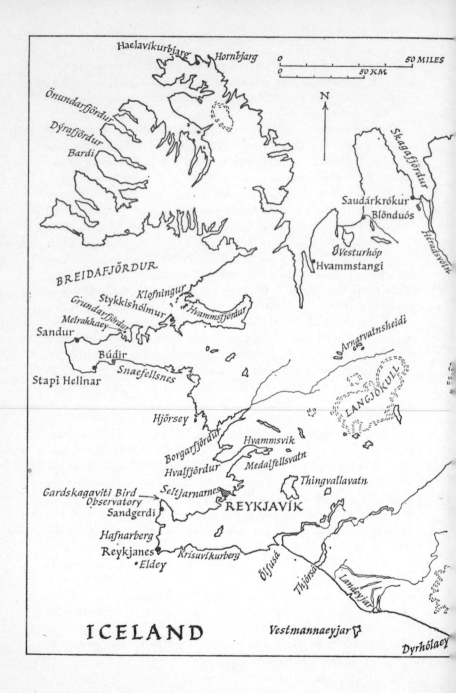

ICELAND

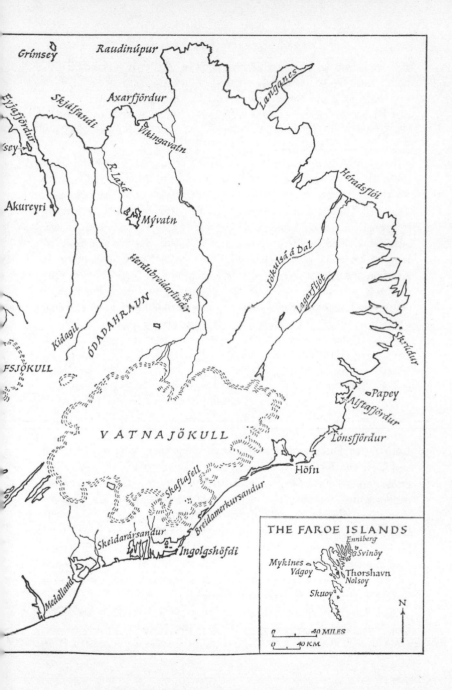

Grímsey

Raudinúpur

Langanes

Eyjafjördur

Skjálfandi

Axarfjördur

Víkingavatn

sey

R. Laxá

Héradsflói

Akureyri

Mývatn

Jökulsá á Dal

Herdubreidarlindir

Lagarfljöt

Kidagil

ÓDADAHRAUN

Skrúdur

FSJÖKULL

Papey

Alftafjördur

VATNAJÖKULL

Lónsfjördur

Höfn

Skaftafell

Breidamerkursandur

Skeidarársandur

Ingolgshöfdi

Medalland

THE FAROE ISLANDS

Enniberg

Svinöy

Mykines
Vágoy

Thorshavn
Nolsoy

Skuoy

N

0   40 MILES

0   40 KM.

cliff birds and here, as on all the cliffs in northern Iceland, Brün-nich's Guillemots outnumber the ordinary Guillemots. A pair of Gyr Falcons nests almost every year in Drangey. The Eyjafjörður district has many river deltas with much the same species as in the Skagafjörður area. Common Gulls occur here in a number of places among Black-headed Gulls.

In Akureyri, the principal town of the north, Redwings and Red-polls are very common, and this is the only place in Iceland where Fieldfares have nested several times, although not as yet regularly. The island of Hrísey has exceptionally large numbers of nesting Ptarmigans. From Akureyri a boat goes every second week to the island of Grímsey off the mouth of Eyjafjörður, and it is also possible to get there by air from Akureyri. There are still a few pairs of Little Auks on this island. Wrens are quite common in Vagla-Skógar, one of the largest birch woods in the country, about 12 miles east of Akureyri. The lowlands beyond the bay of Skjálfandi form the best Ptarmigan country in Iceland. The Mývatn area, particularly re-nowned for its waterfowl, provides the main breeding grounds of all the sixteen species of ducks which nest in Iceland. The delta of the River Laxá has a few large Eider colonies, the river itself has Harle-quins, Goosanders and Barrow's Goldeneyes, and the lake is a veritable paradise for ducks. The most common species in Mývatn are Scaup and Tufted Duck which appear in almost equal numbers. Other common species are Barrow's Goldeneye, Common Scoter, Long-tailed Duck and Red-breasted Merganser. Wigeon, Gadwall and Teal are the most numerous of the dabbling or surface-feeding ducks, and Mallard, Pintail and Shoveler are less common. Gold-eneyes and American Wigeon are recorded annually in the Mývatn area although there is no evidence of nesting. There are other birds too, including several hundred Slavonian Grebes and many land birds. Nowhere else in Iceland are Snipe and Red-necked Phalarope so abundant. Several pairs of Gyr Falcons and Merlins nest in the mountains and in the larger lava stacks in the area. Merlins are also widely distributed throughout the country.

The Axarfjörður district has another good waterfowl lake, Ví-kingavatn, sometimes called little Mývatn, because almost all the same species of duck are also found here in large numbers. The extensive sandy delta of the River Jökulsá is the nesting ground for a couple of hundred Great Skuas, the only colony in the north. On Raudinúpur, a promontory in the north-eastern corner of the mouth of the Axarfjörður bay, there is a small colony of Gannets. Off the shore of this part of the country Long-tailed and Pomarine Skuas are occasionally seen on migration. There is another large bird cliff on the peninsula of Langanes in the north-eastern corner of Iceland.

Moving southward, we come to the deltas of two great rivers, Jökulsá á Dal and Lagarfljót, where there is a small isolated colony of Great Skuas and, farther up, a large colony of Arctic Skuas; the latter are very common throughout Iceland. Up from the Heradsfloi along the River Lagarfljót is a good area for Greylag Geese. Hallormastaður, the largest area of woodland in the country, has the same species of birds as other woods in Iceland.

Two of the islands off the coast, Skruður and Papey, have enormous numbers of sea birds. Puffins are found there in tens of thousands and there is a fairly large colony of Gannets on Skruður. Álftafjörður and the lagoon of Lonsfjörður are very good for the common waders.

The extensive glacial sand plains of Breiðamerkursandur and Skeiðarársandur have the largest colonies of Great Skuas in the northern hemisphere and it is estimated that there are as many as 1,500 pairs in Breiðamerkursandur. Indeed, Great Skuas and also Arctic Skuas and Great Black-backed Gulls can be found on all the larger sandy plains along the south coast. The headland of Ingolfshöfði has yet another bird cliff and here ordinary Guillemots far outnumber Brünnich's Guillemots. The best place for vagrant species is certainly the district of Öraefi, which lies between Breiðamerkursandur and Skeiðarársandur.

West of the vast sand plains in the Medalland district there is still some uncultivated boggy land and this is the headquarters of the Water Rail in Iceland. Close to the village of Vík several large colonies of Puffins are found on grassy slopes. In this district the first Lesser Black-backed Gulls were found nesting in 1929. From here they have spread westwards and are now common nesting birds as far west as the area around Hvalfjörður. At Dyrhólaey, the southernmost tip of Iceland, there are small bird cliffs and a colony of gulls

(Great Black-backed, Lesser Black-backed and Herring Gulls), and in recent years Gannets have nested on one of the stacks in the vicinity.

The Vestmannaeyjar or Westmann Isles offer much of interest. Besides the myriads of cliff birds, this is the only place where Manx Shearwaters, Leach's Petrels and Storm Petrels breed in Iceland. In four of these islands Gannets nest in fairly large colonies.

The extensive lowlands in the south of Iceland have some interesting birds, although large areas are cultivated. Here Black-tailed Godwits are common and at migration time White-fronted and Pink-footed Geese are abundant mainly in the Landeyjar district. Greylag Geese are very common nesting birds all over the lowlands. At the mouth of the rivers Thjórsá and Ölfusá, on the south coast there are good places for gulls and shore birds.

Most of the highland plateau of Iceland is devoid of vegetation except in a few places and also around some lakes where the typical birds are Great Northern and Red-throated Divers, Whooper Swan, Pintail, Scaup and Long-tailed Duck. Land birds include Golden Plover, Purple Sandpiper, Wheatear and Snow Bunting. In the oases sheltered by the south-eastern corner of the large Hofsjökull glacier, vegetation is extremely profuse and the bird life quite varied. Besides more common birds, Pink-footed Geese breed in their thousands and Snowy Owls have also been suspected of nesting in the vicinity. Other much smaller colonies of Pink-footed Geese are found in Herðubreiðarlindir, north of the huge Vatnajökull glacier, and at Kidagil, north-east of Hofsjökull. Snowy Owls nest in a few places on the western edge of Iceland's largest lava field, Odáðahraun.

The best time of the year for bird-watching in Iceland is the latter half of May and the first three weeks in June.

As can be seen from the tables at the end of the book most of Iceland's nesting birds are summer visitors; some of these leave as early as July and some winter visitors appear in August.

In Reykjavík and in other densely populated areas a few species of passerine birds can be seen. A small proportion of the Redwing population winters in Iceland and Redpolls are conspicuous at this time of year. Wrens are frequently seen by the seashore and even in Reykjavík and other towns.

Thousands of Snow Buntings enter towns and villages during severe weather, with the odd Merlin in their wake. The Iceland Gyr Falcon is often seen during winter near the seashore and also in towns, particularly when the Ptarmigan population is at its lowest. Among the passerines, Fieldfares and Blackbirds are regular winter visitors. Ravens are also very conspicuous at this time.

The Lesser Black-backed Gull is the only gull which is a total migrant. It leaves in October–November, by which time the Iceland Gulls have arrived from their nesting grounds in west Greenland. Winter waders are confined mainly to the seashore of south-west and south-east Iceland, Purple Sandpipers being by far the commonest. They can be seen by the thousand in some areas. Turnstones are also very common on the shore in the Reykjavík area, and so are Oystercatchers and Redshanks. Rarer waders seen in winter are Snipe, Knot and Sanderling, the last being very rare at this time of the year. Regular winter visitors among the waders are Curlews, Bar-tailed Godwits (even though they do not come in the twenty-record category) and Ruffs, while Grey Plovers are seen nearly every year. Both Great Northern and Red-throated Divers can be watched on the sea, but mainly in the south.

Many of the ducks are migrants but, in recent years, more and more of them have stayed throughout the winter. A part of the Teal population, for example, is seen pretty consistently in winter where ponds and streams are frozen. Wigeon are very common in the Reykjavík area in winter. Scaup and Tufted Ducks are now seen annually on the sea around Reykjanesskagi. Barrow's Goldeneye is resident in Iceland, and prefers lakes and rivers. In winter it is quite common at the outlet of Thingvallavatn. The Long-tailed Duck is very common on the sea all round Iceland, and the Harlequin is also common, mainly in places where the sea is rough. The most abundant duck is, however, the Eider.

The Faroe Islands

This group of mountainous islands is situated between Norway and Iceland, about 220 miles north-west of the Shetland Isles. The climate is oceanic. The islands are high and rugged with perpendicular cliffs. Here the cliff birds are the same as in Iceland, except that Glaucous Gulls, Little Auks and Brünnich's Guillemots do not breed.

It is an experience to sail among these islands with their steep grass-covered mountains and to see the immense variety of bird life on the cliffs. Enniberg, the northernmost point of the Faroes, is the largest sea bird cliff in the islands. On Svinoy, one of the northern islands, both Great Skuas and Arctic Skuas nest in fairly large colonies.

Skuoy and Mykines are also of interest, the latter having the only Gannet colony in the Faroes. During migration many vagrants have been observed at Nolsoy, which is near Thorshavn, the capital of the Faroes.

Nearly all the breeding birds of the Faroes are also to be found in Iceland. Common species which nest here, but not in Iceland, are Rock Doves, Rock Pipits, House Sparrows (which invaded the islands quite recently) and Hooded Crows.

These remote islands can be reached by regular shipping routes from Reykjavík or Copenhagen. Icelandair in Reykjavík operates an air service. The Faroes airport is situated on Vágoy, which is two to three hours by boat and car from Thorshavn.

Norway

Kai Curry-Lindahl

Cranes

The Zoological Museum in Oslo (Sarsgaten 1), and the museums at Stavanger, Trondheim and Bergen are all active in the field of ornithology. Stavanger Museum maintains a migration station in Revtangen in southern Norway and, in co-operation with the Norwegian Ornithological Society, it publishes the magazine *Sterna*. Ornithological work is also carried out by the State Wildlife Station (Statens Viltundersøkelser) at Vollebekk, and by the universities.

If one finds a ringed bird in Norway, the ring should be sent to: Stavanger Museum, Zoologisk Avdeling, Stavanger, Norway.

NORWAY

Norway, with its coasts and mountains, is geographically somewhat of a paradox. Although one of the smaller European countries, it is the longest, extending from 58° N to 71° N, while its western and eastern extremes stretch from 5° E to 31° E. It has a seaboard of 1,655 miles, but if every fjord and island is taken into account, the actual shoreline runs to about 12,500 miles. As the fjords penetrate deep into the uplands and forests, sea birds often range far inland. There are numerous lakes, some as long and narrow as the sea fjords, and torrents and waterfalls add to the grandeur of the mountain scenery.

The greater part of Norway lies above or beyond the tree line and may be considered an arctic region. At lower altitudes there are woods of mountain birch, which, in turn, give place to evergreen forest. Only the extreme south-east of the country falls within the limits of the European deciduous forests, here represented chiefly by the oak. Western Norway, with its mild winters and cool, damp summers, has a special type of coastal woodland, the so-called fjord wood. As climatic conditions differ perceptibly from fjord to fjord, depending on the width of the inlet and the prevailing winds, the woodlands too show local variations. A first impression of the forest zone in the fjord districts of Rogaland, Hordaland, Sogne and Fjordane can therefore be very confusing. Deciduous trees often predominate over large stretches, but here and there pines become plentiful. The limits of forest also vary considerably, fluctuating in Rogaland between 975 and 2,275 feet above sea level. These variations are not, of course, solely attributable to climatic conditions, but are due to a number of factors, including snow conditions and such human activities as clearance and livestock grazing.

In some places the alder occurs at altitudes up to 1,625 feet, where it gives place to the mountain birch, which ascends the slopes for another 325 feet. Alder and birch also meet, though at different altitudes, on some of the mountains farther inland, far enough away from the sea, one would expect, for its influence on local conditions to be reduced. To the west of the highlands the maritime districts have a very heavy rainfall (up to 158 inches yearly), and it is possible that the influence of the fjord on the local distributuon of trees and plants may have been exaggerated. In addition to alder, the elm, hazel and rowan all grow on the slopes below the birch belt. This vegetation pattern is unique to Scandinavia and its influence on the fauna, and in particular on the vertical distribution of birds, is obvious. Blackcaps and Icterine Warblers, for example, may be found as high as deciduous trees grow around many of the fjords, and farther inland both these species spend the summer at altitudes of 3,250 feet in the last of the birch woods. Elsewhere they are lowland species. These forests, together with the bird cliffs along the coasts, offer a degree of specialist interest unequalled throughout the rest of Scandinavia.

Summer and winter alike the gulls are supreme along the coast. Herring, Great Black-backed and Common Gulls, with Kittiwakes, can be seen throughout the year, and these are reinforced in summer by Lesser Black-backed Gulls, Common and Arctic Terns, and Arctic Skuas. Cormorants and Shags are found along the whole coastline. Fulmars breed on Rundø and some smaller islands near Ålesund, and on Rost in the Lofotens. Rundø also supports a flourishing colony of Gannets, about 500 strong, and there may be another in Syltefjord in Finnmark. The most populous Kittiwake colonies lie to the north of the arctic circle. One, at Vardo on the coast of the Arctic Ocean, has more than two million birds when all the young are hatched. In some districts the Kittiwake now nests on buildings, a remarkable change of behaviour first observed at certain northern fishing villages some thirty years ago, and later at Ålesund in the south.

The pale phase of the Arctic Skua is the more common in Norway. In the north, for example, more than half the population have pale breasts, while in Spitsbergen the proportion rises to 90 per cent. Great Skuas can be seen occasionally off the coast.

Razorbills, Guillemots, Black Guillemots and Puffins inhabit the sea cliffs. The Black Guillemots lay their eggs under boulders along the shore, while the Razorbills and Guillemots share the ledges with Kittiwakes, each species keeping to its own stretch of cliff. The larger colonies include Rundø off Ålesund, Rost, Vedø and Vaerø off the Lofotens, Svaerholt-klubben at the north point of the Svaerholt Peninsula and Syltefjord at Vardø on Varanger Fjord. To reach any of these the ornithologist should hire a fishing-boat.

Compared with the rest of Europe, Norway has an imposing population of White-tailed Eagles, which breed along the coasts. In spite of persecution this eagle is strictly resident and keeps to its territory throughout the winter. At that season immature birds tend to assemble in flocks at certain places. The Golden Eagle also breeds along the coasts. The Osprey occurs occasionally in some parts of the western fjords, and the Eagle Owl lives in the islands and coastal mountains.

The most characteristic of the waders is the Oystercatcher, which can be seen along the whole of the Norwegian coastline. Ringed Plovers, Redshanks and Turnstones all nest there, and in winter Purple Sandpipers take the place of the summer visitors. The breeding ducks and geese include Greylags, Shelducks, Goosanders, Red-breasted Mergansers and Eiders, the last two being the commonest. In spring there are wonderful assemblies of ducks on the fjords. White Wagtails, Rock Pipits and Wheatears are widespread, all three penetrating to the outermost skerries. In some districts, such as the Lofotens, the Twite is very common. One of the most familiar sounds of the sea coasts is the hoarse croak of a passing Raven.

The number of species to be seen along the coasts increases in spring and autumn. Waders especially find many feeding grounds exposed by the falling tide, where they assemble in large numbers. But the movements of small birds, especially in the autumn, are also worth following, particularly at such stations as Lista on Norway's south-western extremity, at Revtangen on Jaeren south of Stavanger and on Utsira, south-west of Haugesund. Tourists who reach the Finnmark coast may encounter stragglers from the high north. The Glaucous Gull is a regular summer visitor although it has never been known to breed here. In August and September, south-bound Grey Phalaropes are on migration along the coast of Finnmark,

Pomarine Skuas appear in autumn and Steller's and King Eiders in winter.

As the tree line recedes towards the north the open wastes extend to the seashore in Finnmark. Here Shore Larks may nest on the same beach as Eiders, while Little Stints breed on the coastal tundras in the Porsanger and Varanger peninsulas.

The ornithologist visiting Norway should first of all make for the forests and uplands because, from a European standpoint, the bird life of those regions is more distinctive than that of the coasts. Here the botanist will recognise three regions; the conifer forests, the montane birch woods and the arctic (alpine) region. The last named can be divided again into two: the willow zone and the lichen zone. The former is characterised by bushes of willow and dwarf birch with various heaths, while the latter consists of moors covered with low-growing heaths, mosses and lichens; at higher altitudes this is the only type of vegetation to be found amongst the barren screes and perpetual snows of the mountain summits.

The altitudinal limit of these regions and zones decreases as one travels north. The tree line reaches 3,900 feet in south Norway, 2,600 to 3,900 feet in central Sweden, 1,950 to 2,600 in south Lapland, 1,625 to 2,437 in north Lapland, and in Finnmark descends to sea level a little short of the extreme north of Norway.

Only certain districts known to be worth a visit are here mentioned. In Setesdal, in Aust-Agder north of Kristiansand in south Norway, there are conifer and birch forests, marshes and hills. Here the breeding birds include Ring Ouzel, Willow Tit, Tengmalm's Owl, Golden Eagle, Peregrine, Merlin, Willow Grouse, Black Grouse, Capercaillie, Golden Plover, Goldeneye, Velvet Scoter and Black-throated Diver. In addition, Ortolans, Bramblings, White-backed Woodpeckers, Eagle Owls and Goshawks can be seen.

Hardanger Vidda, inland from Hardanger Fjord, is an extensive plateau varying in altitude between 3,900 and 4,550 feet. This region is interesting because of its southerly position (it lies roughly between Bergen and Oslo) and the influence of the maritime climate. As early as mid-June the greater part of the Vidda is clear of snow, and the ice has disappeared from the lakes. At the same time of year most of the Swedish uplands at similar altitudes are still under snow and ice. Characteristic birds of Hardanger Vidda are Raven, Field-fare, Bluethroat, Wheatear, Reed Bunting, Lapland Bunting, and Meadow Pipit among the passerines, Scaup and Common Scoter among the ducks, and Dotterel, Golden Plover, Dunlin and Snipe among the waders. Greenshanks, Great Snipe and Willow Warblers also breed locally, with Purple Sandpipers and Snow Buntings on the higher ground and, in lemming or vole years, there are birds of prey, owls and Long-tailed Skuas. Snowy Owls can always be expected to breed on the plateau when lemmings are abundant. Hardanger Vidda is crossed by a motorway which is open in summer. From the hotel at Dyranut the visitor can reach the breeding places of most of these birds in the course of a day.

In Hedmark, north-east of Oslo and some way along the road to Hamar and Lillehammer, there is some interesting bird country within easy reach of the capital. Lake Mjøsa is fringed with low-lying wet ground, the haunt of many ducks and waders. The valleys are cultivated—Corncrakes and Lapwings occur there, but there is dense conifer forest in, amongst other places, Romedal, Vang, Furnes and Ringsaker, where the ground rises from 1,950 to 3,250 feet above sea level. In this region of different altitudes and habitats the breeding birds include Rook, Siberian Jay, Crossbill and Parrot Crossbill, Brambling, Ortolan, Snow Bunting, Grey-headed Wagtail, Fieldfare, Redwing, Bluethroat, Black Woodpecker, Eagle Owl and Tengmalm's Owl, Merlin, Goshawk, Black-throated Diver, Green Sandpiper, Golden Plover, Dotterel, Crane, Capercaillie, Black Grouse and Hazel Grouse.

One of Norway's most interesting ornithological regions is the Dovre Fjeld, north-east of Gudbrandsdal. Both motorway and railway pass right through the best area, the sanctuary of Fokstumyra, which is about $3\frac{1}{2}$ square miles in extent. This area of marsh lies 3,087 feet above sea level, and includes birch woods and several lakes. The Rondane massif rises to the south-east of Fokstumyra and east of it there is conifer forest up to 2,925 feet and birch wood for a further 325 feet. The scenery is most varied, with forests, marsh, lakes and rivers. Here one can see Siberian Jay, Crossbill, Ring Ouzel, Three-toed Woodpecker, Eagle Owl, Golden Eagle, Rough-legged Buzzard, Great Snipe, Red-necked Phalarope, Wood Sandpiper, Greenshank,

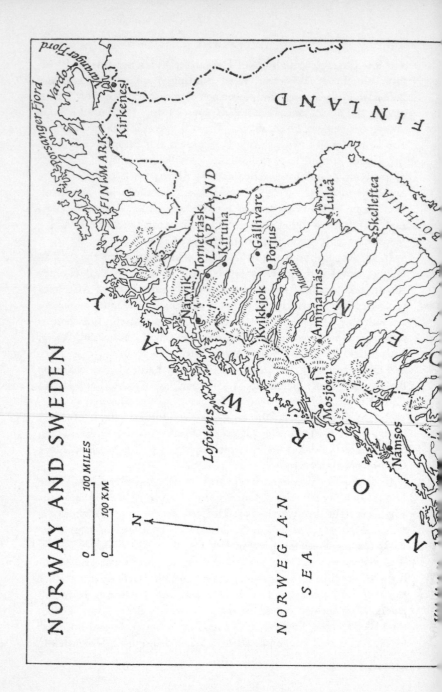

NORWAY AND SWEDEN

NORWEGIAN SEA

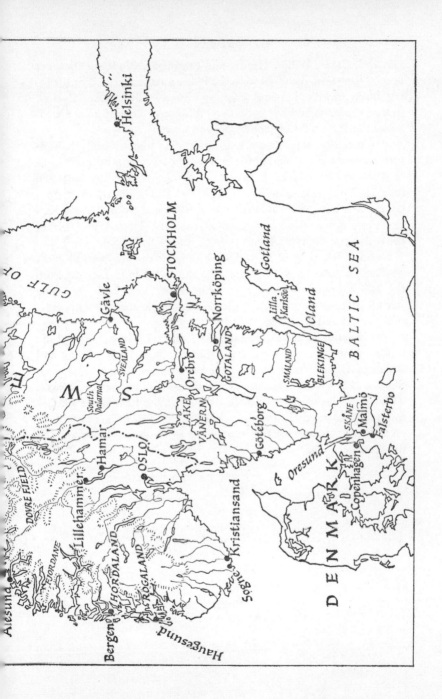

Dotterel, Crane, Willow Grouse and Ptarmigan. No fewer than 134 species have been recorded from the Fokstumyra area, and the breeding birds include Lapland Bunting, Snowy Owl, Hen Harrier, Scaup, Common and Velvet Scoters, Whimbrel, Great Snipe, Broad-billed Sandpiper, Purple Sandpiper and Crane.

The extensive boulder-strewn, tundra-like plateau land of Finnmark, crossed by a high-altitude motor road, offers no great concentrations of bird life. Amongst the species which may be noted here are Red-throated Diver, Long-tailed Duck, Ptarmigan, Long-tailed Skua and Arctic Redpoll. On the Tana river and in the Kirkenes region the visitor has a chance to see the Arctic Warbler from the end of June and into July.

Stabbursdal, west of Porsanger Fjord, claims the world's most northerly conifer forest. The motorist can travel some four miles up the valley, though only on a very bad road. This leads to a fine stretch of pine forest with Capercaillie, Three-toed Woodpecker, Siberian Jay and Waxwing.

The bird life on Spitsbergen is arctic, with lakes in and around the tundra. Along the shore are King Eiders, Pink-footed, Brent and Barnacle Geese, Grey Phalaropes, Sanderlings, Knots, Pomarine Skuas and Ivory and Glaucous Gulls. Eiders nest on the inland lakes. The commonest birds are Little Auks, Puffins, Brünnich's Guillemots, Fulmars and Kittiwakes, all of which occur in large numbers on the cliffs on and near the coast. Sabine's Gulls are found only in the extreme north.

Sweden

Kai Curry-Lindahl

Dotterel

The centre for ornithological activities is the Swedish Ornithological Society (Sveriges Ornitologiska Förening, Östermalmsgaten 65, Stockholm), which publishes the magazine *Vår Fågelvärld*, and maintains the Ottenby ornithological station in Öland and a similar station on the Italian island of Capri. An affiliated society in Skåne (Skånes Ornitologiska Förening, c/o Zoologiska Institutionen, Lund), maintains a station at Falsterbo. There are other migration stations at Torhamns Udde in Blekinge, at Ledskär in Uppland and at Kvismaren in Närke.

Ornithological research is also undertaken by the Committee for Nature Conservation of the Royal Swedish Academy of Science in Stockholm (which is responsible for ringing), and by the Nordiska Museet and Skansen, also in Stockholm. The latter institute publishes *Acta Vertebratica*, a journal which mainly contains articles on ornithology. The Natural History Museum in Göteborg and the Swedish Hunting Union (Svensk Jägareförbundet) in Stockholm are also active in the ornithological field; the latter runs its own research stations in southern and central Sweden.

The Swedish Society for the Protection of Nature (Svenska Naturskyddsföreningen, Riddargatan 9, Stockholm) concerns itself with problems of bird protection. The Swedish section of the International Council for the Protection of Birds is made up of representatives of the Society for the Protection of Nature, the Hunting Union and Swedish Ornithological Society. The address is: Nordiska Museet and Skansen, Stockholm.

If one finds a ringed bird in Sweden, the ring should be sent to: Ringmarkningscentralen, Riksmuseets Vertebratavdelningen, Stockholm, Sweden.

SWEDEN

The backbone of Sweden is an ancient mountain range of which the crest forms the border with Norway. The country is divided into three administrative divisions: Norrland, Svealand and Gotaland, but one can recognise four main physical divisions, namely the northern mountains and lake region district, covering all Norrland and the western part of Svealand; the lowlands of central Sweden; the Småland highlands, in the south and south-east; and the plains of Skåne, occupying the extreme south of the peninsula. The greatest heights are along the Norwegian border, several exceeding 6,000 feet. Kebnekaise (6,965 feet) in northern Lapland is the highest point. Sweden's 96,000 lakes cover about 9 per cent of the country, and the largest lie in the central lowlands. The lowlands resemble the coastal belt, having fertile plains of clay, with innumerable lakes including Vänern, Vättern and Hjälmaren. The Småland highlands in the heart of Gotaland are detached from the main Swedish highlands. The coast of Sweden is fringed with islands which shelter the mainland from the open sea.

Ornithologically, Sweden can be divided into five regions: the deciduous belt, the mixed or southern conifer belt, the northern conifer belt, the sub-arctic region (including the mountain-birch woods and the wastes beyond the tree line) and the coastal regions. The greater part of the country lies within a zone corresponding to the taiga farther east, and this is clearly reflected in the avifauna.

Southern Sweden and the coastal districts along the Gulf of Bothnia are for the most part under cultivation. So, too, are the valleys of the wooded and upland districts, but agriculture becomes less and less in evidence as the land rises to the west and north. Large stretches of wild country, marsh and woodland can, however, still be found in the south. Of the numerous lakes it is the more low-lying which have the richest bird life.

Sweden has sixteen national parks, and a large number of nature reserves, most of which are administered by the Royal Swedish Board of Crown Lands and Forests in Stockholm. All the national parks are open to visitors, with the exception of certain areas in Muddus in Lapland and Gotska Sandön in Gotaland. Nature conservation is the responsibility of the Swedish Board for the Conservation of Nature, established in 1963.

Several parts of the coast of Skåne are worth a visit. From the Hälsingborg motorway at Sjölunda, close to Malmö, the traveller looks out over a landscape of marshy fields, lagoons, tidal flats, huge industrial tips and large factories. Numerous swans, ducks, waders, grebes and gulls can be found here throughout the year. Shovelers and Pochards nest here, and migrating Ruffs pause to display on the meadows. The Little Tern is one of the birds which breed on the island of Gråen off Landskrona. In winter, Whooper and Mute Swans assemble by the thousand in Öresund off Malmö, Landskrona and Hälsingborg. The coasts at Foteviken, Höllviken and Vellinge all repay a visit, as well as Flommen between Skanör and Falsterbo, where the breeding birds include Shelducks, Avocets, Redshanks, Oystercatchers, Lapwings, Kentish Plovers, Dunlins and, occasionally, Sandwich Terns and Yellow Wagtails.

Falsterbo is one of the most interesting migration centres in Europe. Over it pass impressive numbers of birds, chiefly passerines and raptors, but also ducks, waders, gulls, terns and Swifts. The autumn migration at Falsterbo is unequalled in northern Europe, at least as far as birds of prey are concerned. Kestrels and Sparrowhawks leave in the first week of August and are soon joined by Ospreys and Honey Buzzards. Sparrowhawks continue to depart throughout the autumn, and on some days more than 1,000 Honey Buzzards and up to 14,000 Buzzards fly over Falsterbo. The Swallow exodus attains its maximum in September, when tens of thousands may pass over in a single day. At the end of September, Chaffinches are the commonest migrants, with flocks of up to 145,000 passing by in one day. Migration over Falsterbo really reaches its climax from mid-September to mid-October.

Observation of the autumn migration at Falsterbo can best be made from Nabben, the southern point of the peninsula. Access is by a footpath, and the motorist should leave his car when he reaches the golf links which occupy the southern half of the peninsula. Small birds can often be found resting in the bushes around the lighthouse. The best time for watching diurnal migration is from dawn to about noon. After that, movements diminish in intensity, but at times they can persist practically throughout the day.

The farmlands of Skåne are broken up in certain places by small hills, lakes, beechwoods and tree-clad ridges. Such country is found above and around the lakes in the interior of Skåne: Yddingen, Fjallfotasjön, Börringesjön, Björkeråkrasjön, Sövedsjön, Snogeholm-ssjön, Ellestadssjön, Krankesjön, Vombsjön and Ringsjön. This varied countryside is rich in bird life during every month of the year. In the autumn various birds of prey collect for the winter. Young Golden and White-tailed Eagles spend the cold months in the Sövde area, as do Buzzards, Rough-legged Buzzards, Hen Harriers and Great Grey Shrikes, and both Spotted and Lesser Spotted Eagles have been reported. The Red Kite has also recently taken to wintering in the neighbourhood. Geese by the thousand—chiefly Bean Geese with some White-fronted—graze near the lake, flying up each night in long skeins to roost on the open water. Some of these geese leave after a short time, while others settle there for months, and in the milder winters may remain until the following spring.

Fine ornithological countryside can be found in Bökeberga, Häckeberga and Sövde—districts west and east of Romeleåsen in south Skåne. The Wood Warbler is one of the characteristic birds of this region, and Grey Herons, Kestrels, Hobbies, Red Kites, Sparrowhawks and Goshawks nest there. Thrushes, warblers, fly-catchers and tits sing amongst the foliage, with Thrush Nightingales in the thickets below. Tree Sparrows are found near the farms and other human habitations.

Among the lakes of Skåne, Yddingen ranks as one of the finest, with such birds as Great Reed Warblers, Red-necked and Little Grebes, and sometimes a Golden Oriole nearby at Torup. The Black-necked Grebe nests at Snogeholmssjön. Krankesjön, about 19 miles east of Lund, is another fine bird lake, where most of the species which frequent the lakes of central and southern Sweden can be found. Reed Buntings and Sedge, Reed and Great Reed Warblers sing amongst the reeds. Out on the open water there are Great

Crested Grebes and Garganey and many other ducks. In some years the Black-necked Grebe breeds amongst the Black-headed Gulls. Common and Black Terns, Coots, Moorhens and Water Rails are plentiful, and the larger reed beds hold Bitterns and Marsh Harriers.

From a road on Karups Marsh, one or two miles north of Sovdesjön, Black-tailed Godwits will be seen or heard through April, May and June, together with many other species, including Corncrakes and Spotted Crakes. The same species can be noted at Hammarsjön near Kristianstad in north-east Skåne, where one can drive on to Håslöv or Visby meadows on the north side of the lake and watch the displaying Ruffs at close range from the car. Hammarsjön also has the birds listed for Krankesjön and, in addition, Oystercatchers and sometimes Avocets. The lake is visited by gulls and terns from the neighbouring sea coast. Sövdesjön is particularly interesting in the autumn, when the Kingfishers come to the stream between there and Snogeholmsjön.

Farther to the north, along the west coast of the province of Halland, lie two of Sweden's more interesting bird resorts, Morups Tånge at Glommen, north-west of Falkenberg, and Getterön at Varberg. Tawny Pipits breed at Morups Tånge, as they do on the south coast of Halland, and from June to October gulls, terns, waders, ducks and small birds pass by in large numbers. Much the same may be said of Getterön, but it also has breeding Ruffs, Black-tailed Godwits and Avocets, and in winter Short-eared Owls. Collared Doves are numerous in Varberg. Ospreys and a number of shore birds nest still farther north at Tjolöholm and inland of Kungsbackafjord, where Bean Geese and northern waders alight on migration, and White-tailed Eagles sometimes spend the winter.

Blekinge is the most south-easterly Swedish province, and has several ornithological attractions, particularly the skerries with their colonies of Caspian Terns. At Torhamns Udde, the Swedish mainland's south-eastern extremity, it is possible to drive right out to the point (foreigners require a permit from the military authorities) and watch the passage of migrants, mostly ducks, geese, waders, terns and small birds, with some birds of prey. Several shore birds also breed there.

Småland has only a few good bird lakes, but the province has one quite special lake, Kävsjön. This is a very shallow piece of water surrounded by extensive swamps which are in turn almost entirely encircled by an area of moorland, known as Store Mosse, where there are Golden Plovers. In several places Store Mosse is broken up into swamps and tarns. The area of marsh at Kävsjön (about 24,700 acres in extent) really represents a fragment of Lapland in southern Sweden. While climate and latitude enable some southern animals to live at Kävsjön, the district's similarity to Norrland attracts several birds from higher latitudes to breed there, and at the time of the spring migration birds from the high north also alight there. On a spring evening the overhead cantering sound of a Jack Snipe might persuade the listener that he is on a Lapland marsh.

This blending of south and north, both in plant and animal life, makes Kävsjön an exciting place to explore, particularly in April, May or June. None of the birds breeding in this great area seem very plentiful, yet the list of species seen during an excursion of a few days is quite astonishing. Whooper Swans, Bean Geese and sometimes a White-tailed Eagle appear here after the ice breaks up at the end of March or the beginning of April.

From the tower on the west side of the lake the visitor can watch several pairs of Cranes on their breeding ground in April or May. These birds breed at several other places in this great swamp region, which is one of their favourite haunts in southern Sweden. Ducks and waders nesting there include Pintail, Wigeon, Curlews, Wood Sandpipers, Snipe and Ruffs. The slightly drier moorland has many other birds, among them Redshanks and Dunlins. Out on the lake itself Mute Swans, Garganey, Shovelers, Tufted Ducks, Pochards, and Goldeneyes swim among the weeds. In spring, the entire bird life of the swamp by night and day produces a multitone chorus with hundreds of Snipe, Water Rails, Spotted Crakes and so on, while in the nearby forests one can hear the sharp note of the Green Sandpiper, the deep bass of the Eagle Owl, the churring of the Nightjar, the little song of the Redstart and the fine trill of the Woodlark.

Off the east coast of southern Sweden lies the island of Öland (87½ miles long) with Ottenby Bird Station on its southern point. The shores, meadows and woods there have migrants almost all the year round, and especially in April and May and from June to October. The waders and passerines predominate, but geese, ducks, gulls and terns are all common. The breeding birds include Scaup, Linnets, Red-backed Shrikes, Barred Warblers, Icterine Warblers, and, within recent years, Red-breasted Flycatchers, while Golden Orioles sometimes nest there.

At Beijershamn on south-west Öland one can walk comfortably along a pier just over a mile long which runs out into Kalmarsund to form a boundary between the open sound and the brackish lagoons and swamps. After catching a glimpse of a Barred Warbler among the bushes, one could walk on to the pier and glance out to the left, to look at the various sea birds. Or one might turn to the right to watch the birds of the freshwater habitats. The same glance could take in Common Terns fishing over the waves and Black Terns hawking above the lagoons. The pier is also a good place from which to watch the great spring and autumn movements of sea birds through Kalmarsund.

Stora Alvaret in south Öland is a limestone outcrop of great interest to the botanist, and unique in Europe. Such birds as Skylarks, Meadow Pipits, Wheatears, Lapwings, Redshanks, Ringed Plovers and Golden Plovers breed there, while Cranes alight for a while in September. Southern Öland also has fine deciduous woods at Borga, south of Borgholm, at Halltorps farther south and at Österskog. Icterine Warblers and Thrush Nightingales can be heard everywhere, as well as other passerines.

Södviken on the north-east coast of Öland offers many attractions, among them breeding Shelducks, Avocets and Little Terns. Little Gulls and Black Terns fly over from the nearby marshes and Red-necked Phalaropes often pass the summer in or near the bay.

Öland also has a number of shallow fens rich in bird life, most of them towards the north of the island, Gillsby Mosse, Petgarde Fräsk and Knisa Mosse being the most important. As little rain falls in Öland, it needs little decrease in precipitation to change the water level and the appearance of these fens. Birds therefore shift from fen to fen in different years. The Öland marsh birds include Montagu's and Marsh Harriers, Black-tailed Godwits, Ruffs, Dunlins, Garganey, Teal, Shovelers, Tufted Ducks, Pochards and Black-necked

Grebes. Öland's bird haunts can all be visited without any trouble, as they lie within easy reach of the motor roads.

In the Baltic, cliffs with interesting birds are found on the limestone islands of Stora and Lilla Karlsö. Guillemots and Razorbills occupy ledges on cliffs that are 130–200 feet high, and both islands have Herring Gulls, Black Guillemots, Eiders, Common Scoters, Ringed Plovers and Arctic Terns. Lilla Karlsö has a large colony of Great Black-backed Gulls. House Martins build under the overhanging ledges only a few feet above the breakers, Rock Pipits enliven the shore, and Thrush Nightingales, with Icterine and other warblers, sing among the trees at Hien on Stora Karlsö. There is a regular service from Klintehamn to these two islands, which are now reserves.

The woods of Gotland still harbour many birds, of which the Collared Flycatcher is the most interesting. This bird is also to be found in the island's parks, mixed woods and among conifers. Other birds of the deciduous woods are Icterine Warblers, Red-backed Shrikes, Fieldfares, Thrush Nightingales, Wrynecks, Nuthatches, Cuckoos, Sparrowhawks and Tawny Owls.

The visitor to Visby is sure to see the Collared Flycatcher, as it breeds in the Botanical Gardens, where the Greenish Warbler has also nested. The shores near Visby have numerous birds which also occur along almost the entire coastline of Gotland: Oystercatchers, Redshanks, Ringed Plovers, Eiders, Velvet Scoters, Common and Little Terns and several gulls.

Four of Gotland's fens, marshes and lakes should be mentioned, namely Lina Myr in east Gotland east of Visby, Storsund farther to the east, and Tingstäde Fräsk and Fardume Fräsk in north Gotland. Lina Myr has been drained several times but it still has Little Gulls, Black Terns, Black-tailed Godwits, Pintail, Corncrakes, Marsh Warblers, Grasshopper Warblers and, occasionally, River Warblers, while Storsund has Black Terns and Greylag Geese. Little Gulls breed at Tingstäde, and Pintail at Fardume.

The ornithologist will find north Gotland, with Fårö, one of the most interesting areas in the province. Near Marpis, Lansnäsa and Ödehoburga on south Fårö there are open pine forests. Stock Doves lay their eggs in abandoned Black Woodpecker holes. The calls of

Red-backed Shrikes, Sparrowhawks, Merlins, Hobbies and, at dusk, Nightjars can be heard in this splendid forest; but its pride is the Roller. This brilliantly coloured species keeps to the sunny, pine heaths near the sea, which abound in insect life.

From Lake Vänern in the west to the Baltic in the east the central part of Sweden has low-lying country with lakes and cultivated areas. Remnants of Cambro-Silurian sediments are widespread, and there are mountain faults and valleys as well as the deep depression occupied by Lake Vättern. The lakes are easily accessible and many are rich in vegetation and birds. The ornithologist will find much to interest him in certain bays of the four largest lakes, namely Vänern, Vättern, Mälaren and Hjälmaren.

In the northern part of Lake Vänern, there is an interesting archipelago of islands and rocks with such maritime birds as Great Black-backed Gulls, Oystercatchers and Turnstones. The best place for birds along the shores of Vänern is Kilsviken, south of Kristinehamn and west of Road 64. Side roads run to Hygn and Säby and one can then continue on foot or hire a boat. Here sea birds meet those of the fen and marsh, and Kilsviken, with its reed beds lying between the more open Vänern and Stormossen, is a marshy wilderness with Black Grouse, Cranes, Golden Plovers and Red-throated Divers. Great Black-backed Gulls from Vänern circle over Kilsviken, which is the home of Bitterns and innumerable ducks—chiefly Pintail and Wigeon—while Red-throated Divers from the tarns on Stormossen pass overhead to fish in Vänern. Capercaillies and Goshawks haunt the conifers near the east shore of Kilsviken, where Little Ringed Plovers pipe during the spring nights. The other side of the bay is fringed with deciduous woods with their characteristic fauna.

Just outside Karlstad, the capital of Värmland, lies Hammarön, a delta region of easily accessible swamps and half-overgrown bays, through which the river Klar flows into Vänern. Northern ducks and waders, such as the Smew and Grey Plover, stop here on migration. About one hundred bird species breed on Hammarön, and seven species of ducks nest in large numbers—among them Garganey and Wigeon. The conifer forests on the southern part of the island have Capercaillies, Black Grouse and Hazel Grouse.

In the triangle between the towns of Skara, Kalköping and Skövde in Västergötland lies Hornborgasjön. Once Sweden's finest bird lake, this has been spoiled by various attempts at drainage, and is an outstanding example of useless destruction, and of what can happen when elementary ecological rules are ignored. Despite this, the region still attracts birds, although only a fraction of their former abundance and variety, and the lake is now a marsh about $15\frac{1}{2}$ miles square. It becomes most interesting to the ornithologist in the last three weeks of April, when northbound Cranes assemble on the fields between Dagsnäs and Stora Bjurum, south-west of Hornborgasjön. In some years as many as 3,000 Cranes can be seen together. They can be watched at quite close quarters from the roads, provided one does not leave the car. They pass the whole day on the meadows, rising at dusk in great flocks to spend the night on the lake, and returning at dawn in long straggling bands. Hen Harriers nest in Hornborgasjön, while at Stenum, in the north-west of the swamp, Grasshopper Warblers and Corncrakes can be heard. There is a colony of Black-necked and Slavonian Grebes on the east side of the swamp. The marshy region around the lake is, however, almost totally overgrown and difficult to explore.

Billingen, a mountain to the east of Hornborgasjön, is worth a visit at any time of the year. Deciduous and conifer woods alternate on its slopes, but hazels grow everywhere. The bird life is most interesting in spring, when the slopes are white with cherry blossom. Billingen must hold the largest Swedish population of Hawfinches, which occur in only a few places in the country. While the Black Woodpecker keeps largely to the conifers, it may wander into the deciduous woods and even chisel out its oval nest hole there. Great Spotted, Lesser Spotted and Green Woodpeckers and Honey Buzzards are also found in the woodlands. Sixty different species in all have nested on these wooded slopes. At higher levels the deciduous woods are replaced by spruce forest. Here Nutcrackers nest in greater numbers than in any other place in Sweden. Their abundance on Billingen is doubtless related to the widespread hazel thickets found here. In September and October it is easy to watch a stream of Nutcrackers laden with nuts passing between the hazels at the foot of the mountain and the spruces. Crested Tits and other passerines of the spruce forests are also found at Billingen.

East of Vättern and directly north of Highway 4 lies what is probably internationally the best-known of Sweden's bird lakes. This is Tåkern, where nearly one hundred species have been recorded at one time or another, the number of species and individuals varying from year to year. Visitors to Tåkern are recommended to make first for Holmen, in the south-west part of the lake. From Väversunda on Road 50 between Vättern and Tåkern, a minor motor road runs to Tåkern and Holmen. This passes swamps rich in bird life, where water meadows and large reed beds stretch between the farmlands and the open water. At Holmen a wooded point runs out into the marsh where at night one can hear most of the marsh bird calls. As the point does not extend beyond the reeds, one must hire a boat to reach the open water. A second tongue of land runs into Tåkern at Svanshals. Here the reed belt is less extensive, and the point reaches the open water. The habitats west and east of the point differ, and more species are to be seen than at Holmen. At Glänås, directly east of Svanshals, there is an observation tower on the shore. Amongst the birds breeding on or near Tåkern are Marsh Harriers, Ospreys, Bitterns, Mute Swans, Pochards, Tufted Ducks, Great Crested, Red-necked, Black-necked and Slavonian Grebes, Curlews, Snipe, Dunlins, Ringed Plovers, Little Ringed Plovers and Spotted Crakes. During the spring and autumn passage the number of species is considerably increased. Practically all the waders and water birds breeding in Sweden occur at Tåkern.

Many bird species can be studied from the observation tower at Oset, at the mouth of Svartån in the extreme west of Hjälmaren and close to the town of Örebro. The surrounding district has a mixture of industry, agriculture and wild country. Crows and gulls forage, and Little Ringed Plovers nest around the yard of the town's cleansing department. At Oset itself deciduous woods, marshy meadows and reed beds hold all the birds to be expected at this latitude. From the observation tower one can watch ducks and Great Crested Grebes displaying, Ospreys fishing, and Honey Buzzards on their pairing flights. At the time of the autumn passage many waders alight at Oset on their way from the Arctic, while ducks and swans abound on the reserve in Hjälmaren Bay. Over two hundred species have been recorded there.

The best known bird lake in the Stockholm area is Ågestasjön, quite near the suburb of Farsta. The lake holds its greatest variety of species during the spring and autumn migrations. Mute Swans, Mallards and Coots alight as the ice breaks up. Reed Buntings sing among the withered sedges in March, when the Black-headed Gulls scream over their old breeding places. Then several other species arrive: Pochards, Goosanders, Great Crested Grebes, Water Rails and Moorhens in early April, followed by Teal, Wigeon, Shovelers, Tufted Ducks, Snipe, Reed Warblers and Ospreys. The surrounding fields, oak woods and spruce forests have long since—often in March —welcomed their resident or passing Siskins, Skylarks, Snow Buntings, Starlings, Woodlarks, Chaffinches, Meadow Pipits, Stock Doves, Buzzards, Mistle Thrushes, Song Thrushes, Robins and Woodpigeons, in that order. Bramblings, Sparrowhawks, Woodcocks, Yellow Wagtails, Whinchats, Redwings, and Willow Warblers return to their haunts in April; Cuckoos, Blackcaps, Redstarts, Whitethroats, Lesser Whitethroats, Wood Warblers, Pied Flycatchers, Tree Pipits, Nightingales and Wrynecks arrive in May. Curlews, Snipe, and Common and Green Sandpipers spend time by the lake, many of the Snipe remaining to breed. Bean Geese, Gadwall, Pintail, and Garganey also visit the lake on passage in the spring. Reed Buntings, Yellow Wagtails, Red-backed Shrikes, Reed and Sedge Warblers, Lesser Spotted Woodpeckers, Tawny Owls, Mute Swans, Mallard, Teal, and Tufted Ducks all nest by the lake, and Ospreys and Common Terns are to be seen there daily throughout the summer. At midsummer the northern part of the lake is practically overgrown with reeds and sedges, and everything is then quiet. From August onwards one can sometimes hear the Caspian Tern's heron-like call. By then the passage of southbound waders has been in full swing for some time, with Wood Sandpipers, Ruffs, Greenshanks, and, in some years at least, Spotted Redshanks. Later in the autumn come the packs of Wigeon, Mallard and Teal. Jays collect acorns, while Nutcrackers rifle the hazel thickets. Shore Larks, Red-throated Pipits, Bluethroats and Chiffchaffs are all to be seen in September. In October and November Great Grey Shrikes are usually in evidence, and there are Whooper Swans, Scaup and Goldeneyes on the water. Snow Buntings pass in November and

December when the Rough-legged Buzzards take up their quarters, some of them for the winter. In short, there is no dead season at Ågestasjön. There is often enough open water for the Mute Swans all through the winter, and Dippers haunt the stream which flows from a smaller lake, Magelungen.

With its wooded islands Mälaren recalls the Baltic coast archipelago. The shoreline of this lake is enormous, the wide bays gradually dwindling to creeks overgrown with water weeds and swarming with Black-headed Gulls. No two bays are alike, deciduous woodland alternating with conifer forests, steep cliffs and low-lying fields. Ospreys are almost as typical of the lake as Common and Herring Gulls. About one hundred pairs breed in the central area, and they seem to be on the increase.

Some of Mälaren's bays are celebrated for their bird life. Söderfjärden, on the south side of the lake, lies between Strängnäs and Eskilstuna near Highway 3. The finest part of this bay is commanded by a ridge. With its dense, extensive reed beds, this is the Bittern's headquarters in Sweden. In some years up to six females nest there, and as many as eleven males have been heard booming at the same time. On June nights, which are never wholly dark in central Sweden, the Bitterns call from dusk to dawn.

Hjälstaviken has become the best known of Mälaren's bird-haunted swamps. This is the part of Mälaren to the north of the bridge which carries Highway 18 over Ekolsundsviken. The Gadwall is the great rarity to be seen at Hjälstaviken, but Bitterns have been heard, and occasionally Grasshopper Warblers, and Little and Baillon's Crakes. In addition, Hjälstaviken has the Meadow Pipit, which winters here in mild seasons, and the Black-necked Grebe, a rare bird in Södermanland but common in Uppland. The lake is also visited by many migrants. A fine view over Hjälstaviken and its birds can be obtained from Kvarnberget on the eastern shore of the bay, which is now a reserve.

The most interesting birds of Asköviken, some miles from Västerås, are the Little Gull and Black Tern. Both nest there regularly, which is unusual in central Sweden.

South Dalarna is a part of Sweden frequently visited by tourists. The province has one outstanding bird lake, Hovran, at Hedemora.

Besides many of the typical lake birds, the breeding species include Short-eared and Long-eared Owls, Hobbies, Peregrines, Merlins, Red-backed Shrikes, Icterine Warblers, Ortolans, Scarlet Grosbeaks, Corncrakes, and Goldeneyes, with Tengmalm's and Pygmy Owls, Three-toed Woodpeckers and Hazel Grouse in the forests beyond. Grasshopper Warblers have been heard singing, and all the usual birds of passage have been reported.

Of great importance to those interested in the distribution of animal life are certain lakes and bays in the coastal district of Norrbotten, far to the north along the coast of the Gulf of Bothnia. Gammelstadsviken close to Luleå, Presöfjärden farther north, and Sladan north of Råneå are centres of a bird life which, in Sweden, is otherwise only to be found in the south. Here Wigeon, Little Gulls, and Great Crested and Red-necked Grebes breed, the last being fairly common in Norrbotten. These species, like many others, have colonised Sweden from the north or east, and settled on the lakes in Norrbotten which, with their luxuriant growth of water weeds and reeds, so closely resemble those of the southern provinces. Despite its northerly situation Gammelstadsviken has one of the most varied populations of marsh and water birds in Sweden. Here in spring and autumn hosts of migrants pass by on their way to and from the Norrland forests and mountain lakes.

Every spring, from March to May, a stream of northbound ducks and divers passes through Kalmarsund. The flights can best be watched from Skägeenäs, the peninsula north of Kalmar, where the Swedish Ornithological Society has one of its observatories, Revsudden. Goldeneyes, Eiders, Long-tailed Ducks, Common Scoters, Scaup, Goosanders, and Black-throated and Red-throated Divers are seen on passage. A remarkable feature of the Eider's migration is that some males have already begun to move south by 1st May, while others are still travelling north. The southward passage goes on continuously until mid-November. In the autumn the migrants visiting Kalmarsund include Brent and Barnacle Geese and Velvet Scoters.

The archipelago outside Stockholm and along the coasts of Södermanland and Uppland is surpassed in extent and complexity only by the Greek archipelago. This coastal realm is one of the distinctive natural features of Scandinavia. From Stockholm some 62 miles of island-studded waters extend to the outermost skerries and shoals at Svenska Björn. Spruce and mixed forest clothe the islands in the innermost zone; then comes a belt of birch and other deciduous species; nearer again to the sea trees give place to bushes and other low-growing plants; and last of all lichen-covered and bare skerries face the open sea. The fauna of this varied region also changes from zone to zone. Mute Swans, Mallard, and Great Crested Grebes swim among the innermost islands, just as they do on some mainland lakes. Beyond this Common Scoters, Tufted Ducks, Goosanders and Red-breasted Mergansers breed, and a few pairs of White-tailed Eagles build in the taller pines. Still further out to sea lie the domains of Eider, Razorbill and Black Guillemot. Common, Herring and Lesser Black-backed Gulls and Common Terns are to be seen throughout the whole region. Black-headed Gulls keep mostly to the inner islands; Great Black-backed Gulls, Arctic and Caspian Terns and Arctic Skuas to the outer. Greylag Geese breed on a few islands off Uppland.

The conifer forests, one of the predominant natural features of Sweden, represent the western outpost of the great Eurasian taiga. In southern Sweden these woods are scattered here and there, as a rule on the higher ground, while in the centre and north they form an almost continuous belt of forest, where cultivation does little more than follow the river valleys. True forest birds can be met with in southern Sweden, but their numbers become much greater the farther north one travels. Taiga birds are therefore most likely to be seen in the conifer forests of northern Lapland. In Sweden marshes and bogs are both numerous and large. Some, especially those in Lapland, are vast, and to explore them one would need a proper expedition. The winter fauna in central and northern Sweden is comparatively poor in number of species. Here it is possible to give an account of only a few of the interesting forests and marshes.

Travellers going by car on Highway 4 from Norrköping to Stockholm cross right through Kolmården. This is a forest complex, much of it still unspoilt, with Cranes on the bogs, Peregrines and Eagle Owls on the cliffs, Hobbies in the woods and Ospreys on the lakes, which also have Black-throated Divers. The area between

Stavsjö, close to the Highway, and Lake Virlången can be recommended. Many small paths make it easy to move about, although it is best to leave the beaten track entirely.

In Kilsbergen, on both sides of Highway 18 between the towns of Örebro and Karlskoga, the forests have some of the characteristics of those of northern Sweden. By night one can hear Tengmalm's Owls, Pygmy Owls, and sometimes an Eagle Owl. Besides Black Grouse and Hazel Grouse, a whole series of birds nest here: Mistle and Song Thrushes, Redwings, Siskins, Bullfinches, Willow Tits, Goldcrests, Jays, Stock Doves, woodpeckers, Woodcocks, Golden Plovers, Green Sandpipers, Cranes, Black-throated Divers, Goldeneyes, Goshawks and Peregrines.

Right across Jämtland and on into Norway, Highway 75 and the railway run through mountain country. The best locality for birds in this region is Lake Ånnsjön with its surrounding bogs, and both the motor road and the railway run to Enafors and Handol, not very far from the lake, where lodgings can be easily obtained. This district is not so easily explored at the time of the spring thaw, and care is required in the deeper bogs.

With forest, mountain and marsh all so close at hand, Ånnsjön has a very varied avifauna. Thirty-two waders and water birds have nested here at one and the same time. A selection from the list of birds breeding at Ånnsjön will show, more than any description, the importance of the district: Grey-headed Wagtails, Hen Harriers, Wigeon, Pintail, Scaup, Velvet and Common Scoters, Goldeneyes, Goosanders, Red-breasted Mergansers, Black-throated and Red-throated Divers, Curlews, Whimbrels, Golden Plovers, Red-necked Phalaropes, Temminck's Stints, Ruffs, Broad-billed Sandpipers, Greenshanks, Wood Sandpipers, Cranes and Arctic Terns. Lesser White-fronted Geese have been known to breed on the lake. Eagle and Tengmalm's Owls, as well as Siberian Jays and Three-toed Woodpeckers, nest in the conifer woods while the mountains around the lake—Snasjögarna (4,702 feet) and Bunnerfjällen (5,050 feet)—have birds of the open country such as Dotterels, Purple Sandpipers, Lapland Buntings and Snow Buntings.

In spring and early summer the traveller in Västerbotten and south Lapland can stop his car almost anywhere along the roads in the forests and alongside the bogs, and have every chance of seeing or hearing such birds as Red-throated Divers, Hen Harriers, Black Grouse, Capercaillies, Hazel Grouse, Cranes, Wood Sandpipers, Greenshanks, Ural Owls, Short-eared Owls, Tengmalm's Owls, Pygmy Owls, Three-toed Woodpeckers, Black Woodpeckers, Siberian Jays, Willow Tits, Chiffchaffs, Siskins, Mealy Redpolls, Crossbills and Parrot Crossbills, Rustic Buntings and Bramblings. Several species of thrush are also found. The nights are light in June, and the small hours of the day the most rewarding to the ornithologist. By July the forests have become almost silent, and the birds are difficult to locate.

The bird life at Ammarnäs in Övre Gautsträsk in Vindeldalen, at the end of a motor road, is typical of the upper conifer region of southern Lapland. Any marsh here will be a resort for ducks and waders during the spring and summer. In addition to several of the species mentioned above, this district has Golden Eagles, Goshawks, Temminck's Stints, Red-necked Phalaropes, Hawk Owls, Ring Ouzels, Dippers, Dunnocks, Great Grey Shrikes and Ortolans.

In Norrbotten and northern Lapland one is more likely to find such birds as Velvet Scoters, Jack Snipe, Spotted Redshanks, Eagle Owls, Great Grey Owls, Siberian Tits and Pine Grosbeaks.

From Luleå and Boden the broad valley of the Lule runs northeast into the deep forests. The valley is a migration route, both in spring and autumn, and many birds may be seen there on passage. The conifers on both sides of the valley hold interesting north Lapland birds, among them Great Grey and Ural Owls.

Farther to the north, motor roads and the railway run to Jokkmokk, Gällivare and Porjus. Excursions in the forests and bogs around these centres can be very rewarding. The secluded forest bogs hold Bean Geese; Siberian Jays and Siberian Tits are quite common; Pine Grosbeaks breed in the forests; Cranes, Spotted Redshanks, Greenshanks, and Jack Snipe frequent some bogs; and Eagle Owls, Golden Eagles and Peregrines each have a few eyries. In addition, Muddus National Park has Whooper Swans, Red-necked Phalaropes, Broad-billed Sandpipers, Waxwings, and Rustic Buntings. About 155 species have been recorded from Muddus National Park, a high figure for Lapland.

The motor road between Gällivare and Porjus twice runs into the northern part of Muddus National Park, and it is easy to make short trips into the reserve. For a longer stay in the north and central parts of the district the visitor must make preparations for an expedition. More accessible and also more striking areas can, however, be found in the southern half of the park. Here several excursion routes have been marked out. The most interesting of these is best reached by taking the motor road from Porjus to Ligga and Skaite near Mudduksjokk in the south-west part of the park. There one leaves the car and takes the four-mile track to the Muddus falls, where there is a bothy with sleeping accommodation for eight people. Or one can continue a further five miles to Muddus Luobbal, where there is a second bothy. The country hereabouts is rich in birds, and an observation tower commands a wide stretch of marsh and bog. Quite close to this and within the national park lies a reserve which is closed to visitors between 15th March and 31st July. Permission to enter the reserve may, however, be granted for scientific research purposes. The keys of the two huts in Muddus National Park can be obtained on application to the Swedish Turistforeningen's offices in Porjus, or at the Hotel Gästis in Jokkmokk.

To the north of Muddus National Park and Stora Lulevatten lies the largest bog in north-west Europe, Sjaunja, a reserve 780 square miles in extent. For mile after mile enormous swamps stretch between marshy conifer forest, moors, heaths, lakes and tarns. Many birds breed in Sjaunja, among them the Broad-billed Sandpiper and the Whooper Swan. As there are no roads, a visit to this bog necessitates either a time-consuming expedition or the use of a seaplane or helicopter.

The motor road from Jokkmokk to Kvikkjokk cuts across the north Lapland conifer forests, and runs on as far as the foot of the high mountains. Everywhere along this route one comes across interesting forest birds and, in the delta at Kvikkjokk, many ducks and waders.

Many areas of the northern Swedish conifer forests remain unexplored, so the visiting ornithologist can still make new discoveries. Bird species vary greatly in status, however, from district to district. They are often scarce in planted or 'improved' woodlands, and many bogs and lakes are equally disappointing. It is the damper, more primeval forests, and especially those on southern slopes, which hold the greatest numbers of birds.

The Swedish mountains stretch in a chain 625 miles long from northern Dalarna in the south to the extreme north of Lapland. In Dalarna the mountains are mostly low, Fulufjäll being the first to rise above the 3,250-foot contour, but farther north they become higher. In Dalarna the mountain birds include Ravens, Snow Buntings, Ring Ouzels, Bluethroats, Golden Eagles, Rough-legged Buzzards, Whimbrels, Wood Sandpipers, Golden Plovers, and Dotterels. The next province to the north, Härjedalen, has what may be termed true high 'fjall'. Here a number of birds reach their southern limits on the Swedish uplands, namely Tufted Ducks, Scaup, Long-tailed Ducks, Common and Velvet Scoters, Great Snipe, Redshanks, Greenshanks, Temminck's Stints, Purple Sandpipers, Broad-billed Sandpipers, Red-necked Phalaropes, Long-tailed Skuas and Ptarmigan. Härjedalen's fell country is traversed by two main motorways which divide into several branch roads. One of them crosses the summit of Flatruet, a high plateau above the tree line, a resort of the Great Snipe.

The Jämtland fells are the most southerly of the Swedish uplands to harbour Gyr Falcons, Hen Harriers, Ringed Plovers and Ruffs. Storlien, in the birch belt near the Norwegian frontier, is reached either by railway or by Highway 75. There one is surrounded by the birds of the birch woods. The Great Snipe occurs at Storvallen near Storlien.

Tärnafjäll, near the Ume river in southern Lapland, is interesting ornithologically, especially on its lower slopes and around its lakes and valleys. A motor road runs the length of the Ume valley and on into Norway. The tourist centres for the district are Tärnaby and Hemavan. A good road system also enables the motorist to cover more ground than elsewhere on the Swedish uplands. The best district for birds is the southern part of Tärnasjön, north of Tärnaby, but there is no road there. Rasjejaure, west of Tärnasjön, is the most southerly breeding place of the Lesser White-fronted Goose in Sweden. Birds are very numerous on the delta in Lake Laisan between Tärnaby and Hemavan, and also on the swamps farther upstream. Laisan lies on the boundary between the conifer and birch woods.

Farther north, at Ammarnäs in the valley of the Vindel, the ornithologist has a unique opportunity to study bird life above the conifer belt, but he must do so on foot. Lilla Tjulträsk, north-west of Stora Tjulträsk, Marsivagge, a bog north of the last named lake, and the valley of the Vindel river with the surrounding mountains, can all be recommended as places to see most of the arctic and sub-arctic montane birds. Among others, Marsivagge has Great Snipe, Broadbilled Sandpipers, Dunlins, Ruffs, Red-necked Phalaropes, Temminck's Stints, Greenshanks, Lesser White-fronted Geese and Hen Harriers.

In the heart of the wild country beyond the roads lies Svaipa Sanctuary which has an area of about 195 square miles. The nearest place is Adolfström, on Lake Yraf in the valley of the Lais river, about 15 miles as the crow flies from the centre of the reserve. To reach and visit the district one has to take a boat up the Lais and bring provisions and equipment for an expedition. This is one of the finest regions in Scandinavia for arctic and sub-arctic birds. The Red-throated Pipit has its most southerly breeding-station in the Scandinavian uplands, and both Great Snipe and Lesser White-fronted Geese are relatively common, as well as many northern and sub-arctic ducks, waders and passerines.

Europe's three largest national parks—Sarek, Stora Sjöfallet and Padjelanta—together have an area of about 2,150 square miles. The bases for these extensive wildernesses are Kvikkjokk in the south and a new road from Porjus, north of Lake Langas. This region is one of the most difficult of access in Sweden, and requires proper experience of mountain country. An excursion can be very fruitful, but the best localities lie several days' walk apart, and at least a fortnight should be allowed for a tour of the district. There are tourist centres near the Stora Sjöfallet National Park, but none in Sarek and Padjelanta. In Padjelanta, however, shelter for the night is provided at huts on the tracks marked out for ramblers. The Arctic Warbler and the Little Bunting have nested in Sarek.

Abisko National Park in Torneträsk is the next most northerly, but at the same time the most accessible, of the seven national parks in

Lapland. It is situated on the railway, and there is a comfortable tourist hotel in the birch belt at 1,300 feet above sea level. Just beyond the National Park, Låktatjåkko tourist hut stands on the barren fell, 3,900 feet above sea level.

The Arctic Warbler breeds on the slopes of Juolja. The Gyr Falcon has a breeding site in the national park where, of course, numerous mountain birds occur at different altitudes.

In north-east Lapland, close to the Finnish frontier, the two roads which unite at Karesuando give the motorist access to an interesting region with large marshes and imposing birch-clad moors. Here and there off the roads can be found such birds as Greenshanks, Ruffs, Jack Snipe, Pine Grosbeaks, and Siberian Tits. The more promising district, where Gyr Falcons, Whooper Swans, Jack Snipe, Bar-tailed Godwits, Arctic Redpolls and Red-throated Pipits breed, can be reached only by an organised expedition following, for example, the Lainio river from Soppero.

The Swedish uplands have yet to be thoroughly explored, and many of their birds vary in status and distribution from year to year, so visiting ornithologists can still make further discoveries.

Finland

Kai Curry-Lindahl

Caspian Tern

The centre for ornithological activities is the Zoological Institute of Helsinki University, in close co-operation with the Zoological Museum. These two establishments form the headquarters of the Ornitologiska Förening, which publishes the magazine *Ornis Fennica*. Other societies, such as Societas pro Flora et Fauna Fennica and Societas Zoologicae et Botanicae Fennicae 'Vanamo' in Helsinki, occasionally carry articles on birds in their publications.

There are ornithological stations on Signilsskär and Lågskär in the Åland archipelago, on Ronnskår near Porkala district in the Gulf of Finland, at Yteri, near Pori, and on Valsörarna, both on the Gulf of Bothnia.

If one finds a ringed bird in Finland, the ring should be sent to: Museum Zoologicum Universitatis, P. Rautatiekatu 13, Helsinki, Finland.

FINLAND

Finland lies almost entirely within the conifer zone with pine, spruce and birch as the predominant trees. In the extreme north wide stretches are covered with a sparse growth of stunted birches typical of the sub-arctic region. Nearly a third of the total land area consists of marshes and bogs, which are scattered everywhere through the forests, and there are about 55,000 lakes, all with very irregular shorelines.

With their marshes and lakes, the seemingly monotonous Finnish woodlands offer in fact an ever-changing variety of environment both to birds and ornithologists. Next in importance comes the coast with its archipelagos. The south-western districts of the country are the richest in bird life. They are also the most highly cultivated, and deciduous trees are comparatively common.

The varied fauna of the Åland archipelago, a complex of over 6,000 islands and rocks between Finland and Sweden, includes such widely differing species as the Great Black-backed Gull and the Nutcracker. On the wooded islands, tits, flycatchers, warblers—among them the Icterine—and thrushes are all well represented, and the Ortolan may be looked for about the clearings and fields. The Barred Warbler nests among the more southerly islands, as well as on those of the Åbosund archipelago, and White-tailed Eagles and Eagle Owls still survive here. The lakes on the larger islands have Shovelers, Tufted Ducks, Pochards and Black-necked Grebes. Signilsskär on Åland is very favourably situated for the study of migration.

The marine bird life of the Åbo archipelago, between Åland and the Finnish mainland, does not differ from that of the Åland complex, and the same species also breed on the islands in the Gulf of Finland. Between Hangö and Helsinki there are large sea bird colonies on Tvärminne (with a zoological station), in the Jussarö district and Hättö reserve in Barösund archipelago, and also on the islands around Porkala, Esbo and Krykslätt. The Aspskär reserve off

Lovisa, farther to the east, has colonies of Razorbills, Black Guillemots and some Guillemots. On the Finnish side of the Gulf of Bothnia, Yteri at Pori, Valsörarna in the Vasa archipelago, and Hailuoto, west of Oulu, are all of particular interest to the ornithologist. Yteri is remarkable for the number of waders that alight there on migration. The Valsörarna group holds the same sea birds as the southern archipelago, but they are also visited by imposing flights of migrants which breed in northern Europe, and there is a large population of Scaup.

Limingoviken, about 9½ miles south of Oulu, is one of the regions richest in species on the Finnish coast. The shoreline is fringed with wide grassy dunes, which, farther inland, give place to willow scrub. Here are to be seen Red-necked Grebes, Wigeon, Pintail, Scaup, Marsh Harriers, Spotted Crakes, Curlews, Jack Snipe, Ruffs, Red-necked Phalaropes, Scarlet Rosefinches and Yellow-breasted Buntings. The last species, which is the great ornithological attraction of Limingoviken, lives in the willow scrub and, in smaller numbers, in the birch woods beyond. With all the birds of passage that alight there, the mixture of northern and southern species at Limingoviken is particularly interesting.

Terek Sandpipers have nested off Oulu, and Little Gulls at Haukipudas to the north of the town. Here, too, can be found such breeding birds as Hen Harrier, Willow Grouse, Golden Plover, Whimbrel, Temminck's Stint and Short-eared Owl.

The majority of Finland's numerous lakes are disappointing to the ornithologist. Vegetation is scanty, and the only characteristic birds are Black-throated Diver, Goosander, Red-breasted Merganser, Common and Lesser Black-backed Gulls and Common Tern, with Common Sandpipers along the water's edge. Goldeneyes are plentiful in the Finnish forests. Mallard and Teal resort to lakes of all types, and on some northern waters, which offer an abundance of food, Wigeon and Pintail are to be seen. In southern Finland, shallow, partly overgrown lakes may have Marsh Harriers, Pochards, Garganey, Shovelers, Little Gulls, and three species of grebes: Great Crested, Black-necked and Red-necked. Ospreys, of course, fish in all suitable waters.

Among the lakes of southern Finland, Ruski reserve at Borgå,

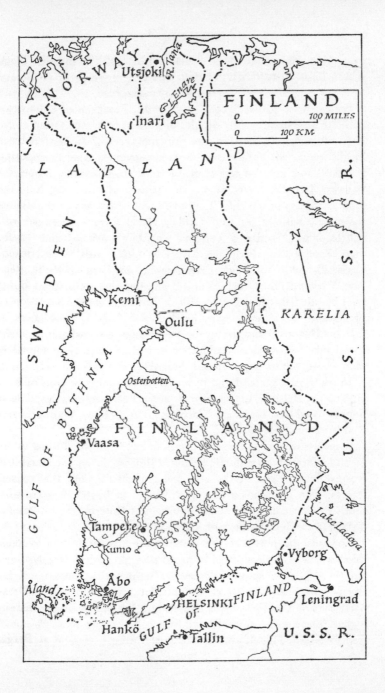

FINLAND

0 ——————— 100 MILES

0 ——————— 100 KM.

east of Helsinki, is one of the richest in bird life. The majority of the marsh birds characteristic of that part of Europe occur there, and they can easily be seen from the nearby motor road.

Smew, Bean Geese, Spotted Redshanks, Broad-billed Sandpipers and Ruffs all breed in the district of Kuusamo in east Österbotten.

In Finland, as in Sweden, two principal types of conifer forest can be distinguished: spruce on the wetter ground, pine on the drier ridges. There are also stretches intermediate in character between the two. It is the mixed woods of spruce and birch that hold the greatest variety of bird life. There will be found many of the species associated with taiga: Capercaillie, Hazel Grouse, various owls (Eagle, Hawk, Ural and Tengmalm's), White-backed and Three-toed Woodpeckers, Fieldfare, Mealy Redpoll, Crossbill and Parrot Crossbill, and Rustic Bunting. In the more northern woods, Siberian Jay, Waxwing, Pine Grosbeak and Brambling also occur. The marsh-land has Red-throated Divers, Black Grouse, Cranes, Wood Sand-pipers and Short-eared Owls. Farther to the north, there are such marsh birds as Whooper Swan, Jack Snipe, Greenshank, Spotted Redshank, Broad-billed Sandpiper and Ruff. The Bean Goose is scarce here, but its population is flourishing in the south of Finland.

In south-east Finland and in a small area along the Gulf of Finland east of Helsinki, the visitor may see or hear Nightingales, Grass-hopper Warblers, Greenish Warblers, Blyth's Reed Warblers, and Red-breasted Flycatchers.

A species which has recently begun to appear in the Finnish coni-fer and mixed woods is the Red-flanked Bluetail. It has been recorded from different parts of the country, but chiefly from the eastern forests. The most favoured region seems to be the western and southern slopes of Jauhovaara Mountain at Katerma, in the Kumo district of east Karelia near the Russian frontier.

Towards the north of the country the conifer forests become thinner and give place to widespread straggling birch woods. Here and there hills rise above the tree line. In the north-west, around the River Könkämä, Kilpisjärvi and Haltiatunturi, and again in the north-east on the Tana River and around Utsjoki, the hills become higher. The country around Lake Inari is broken up by cliffs and is thinly wooded. This enormous lake is, as it were, an inland arctic sea with an archipelago of about 3,000 islands. North of Inari, there is a wilderness of marsh and lake where one can see Ruff, Jack Snipe, Broad-billed Sandpiper, Red-necked Phalarope, and Temminck's Stint, with Lapland and Rustic Buntings and Yellow Wagtails in some places.

A motor road runs from Ivalo by Inari northwards towards Utsjokim and another westwards by the low Peltotunturi mountains to Karigasniemi and onwards into Norway. Both roads pass through a dreary barren wilderness. Any birds there are concentrated around the marshes. Besides the species mentioned above, the country around Karigasniemi holds Long-tailed Duck, Dotterel, Whimbrel, Spotted Redshank, Long-tailed Skua, Red-throated Pipit, Great Grey Shrike, Waxwing, Bluethroat, Siberian Tit, Pine Grosbeak and Snow Bunting. North of Karigasniemi there is a chance of finding Bar-tailed Godwits on the upland marshes. Meadow Pipits and Wheatears abound everywhere. The last named also range on to the low mountains around Enontekiö, east of the river Könkämä. The Gyr Falcon breeds in the mountain gorges around this river, and can be seen flying over the valley. A motor road follows the river to Lake Kilpisjärvi, where there is a tourist station. The birds of the high mountains above the lake include Scaup, Long-tailed Duck, Velvet Scoter, Rough-legged Buzzard, Dotterel, Dunlin, Shore Lark, Ring Ouzel, Bluethroat, Twite, and Lapland and Snow Buntings.

Denmark

Kai Curry-Lindahl

Little Gull

Many organisations, centred on the Zoological Museum of Copenhagen University, carry out ornithological research, and the Danish Ornithological Society (Dansk Ornithologisk Forening) is housed in this museum (Universitetsparken 15, Copenhagen). The society publishes two periodicals: *Dansk Ornithologisk Forenings Tidsskrift* and *Feltornithologen*. The Vildbiologisk Station, Kalø Rønde, and the Museum of Natural History in Aarhus also do ornithological work.

There are several nature reserves in Denmark, some of which cannot be visited without special permission. Information on this can be obtained from: Naturfredningsrådet, Sortedam Dossering 23, Copenhagen. There are four biological field stations in operation, on Amager near Copenhagen, at Blåvandshuk on the west coast of Jutland near Esbjerg, and at Tipperne and Jordsand, also in Jutland.

If one finds a ringed bird in Denmark, the ring should be sent to: Universitets Zoologiske Museum, Ringmaerknings Afdelingen, Universitetsparken 15, Copenhagen, Denmark.

DENMARK

The highest ground in Denmark is no more than 563 feet above sea level, and the rest of the country lies below the 325-foot contour. Although predominantly an agricultural country with at least three-quarters of its area under cultivation, the landscape is varied, partly because so much of Denmark consists of islands. There are, in fact, 483 islands with a total area approaching that of the long mainland peninsula of Jutland. This gives Denmark a total shoreline of 4,625 miles, and the beaches, lagoons and bays, with their rich avifauna, are easily accessible. The scenery in many parts of Denmark is also diversified by woods of varying extent, and these account for almost a tenth of the whole. The country lies within the European deciduous belt, with oak and beech as the characteristic trees, although conifer plantations are now very widespread. Other biotopes include dunes, heaths and moorland.

Jutland is the area promising the greatest interest to the ornithologist. The best localities for breeding birds, migrants or winter visitors mostly lie along the coast, where in many places broad flats provide good feeding grounds at low tide.

Three of the best places to see bird life in Denmark are on the west coast of Jutland: at Tipperne on Ringkøbingfjord, and at Nisumfjord and Vejlerne between the sea and Limfjord. The Danish fjords are quite different from those of Norway, being often shallow and broad, and surrounded by low-lying beaches. These coastal districts support abundant bird life at all times of the year. In the autumn vast numbers of waders and ducks migrating down the coasts of Jutland alight for a while at Tipperne, Nisum and Vejlerne. Many winter here, together with geese and gulls, and the spring brings great flights of water and shore birds to Jutland's coasts, where many species remain to breed.

Now a reserve, Tipperne and Klaegbanken consist of extensive grassy flats with freshwater pools in the southern and eastern parts of Ringkøbingfjord. A tongue of land almost cuts the fjord off from the open sea, with the result that the water of the inlet is mostly brackish. Among these varied surroundings of grassy flats and dunes, salt, brackish and fresh water, birds with differing requirements can find suitable feeding and breeding grounds.

Among the birds breeding at Tipperne there are several that are rare in northern Europe, including the Black-tailed Godwit, here outnumbered only by the Lapwing. Redshanks, Ruffs, Dunlins, Curlews and Snipe are other waders that make nests among the grass. The Avocet is common at Tipperne, one of its many resorts in Jutland. Shelducks and Oystercatchers can be seen along the tideline and Kentish Plovers on the sand, while the bright colours of the Yellow Wagtail stand out among the grasses. But the commonest birds at Tipperne are the gulls: Common, Herring and Black-headed. The last-named are the most plentiful, the numbers in some years rising to over 10,000 pairs on the islands in Nymindestrommen and to over 6,000 on Klaegbanken. Two of the rarer terns nest at Tipperne, namely the Sandwich and Gull-billed, and the reserve also attracts Common and Arctic Terns. Other breeding birds include Montagu's Harriers and Skylarks.

During the breeding season Tipperne may seem alive with birds, yet the spring and early summer are relatively quiet compared with the late summer and autumn when the migrants arrive in enormous numbers. There are sometimes up to 7,000 Pink-footed Geese, as many as 4,000 Brent Geese, more than 1,000 Greylags (this in September), 500 Shelducks and up to 45,000 Teal and Wigeon; in the winter thousands of swans assemble there, chiefly Whooper and Bewick's. Waders also alight at Tipperne in vast numbers. The Bar-tailed Godwit has sometimes been represented by 8,000 birds at once, the Dunlin by about 6,000 and the Curlew and Whimbrel by up to 1,000 each. About 1,000 Avocets have been counted there on a single August day. The Great Black-backed and Herring Gulls appear at this time in flocks more than 2,000 strong.

Tipperne is a reserve so it cannot be completely explored without the permission of the Naturfredningsrådet (see p. 92).

The Ringkøbing area has several other good localities for birds,

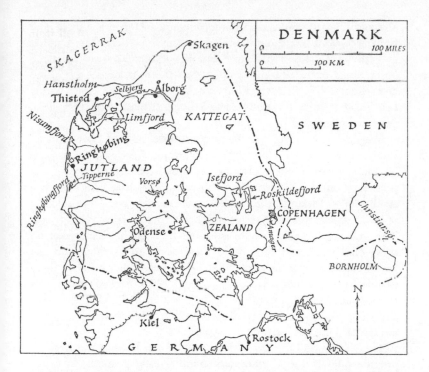

such as Stadil Fjord and Husby Sø, where the Little Gull has sometimes bred. In both Denmark and Sweden this bird is capricious in
its choice of breeding sites and moves from one lake to another.
Other birds frequenting these localities include Marsh Harriers,
Bitterns and Black Terns, and one can also see these birds as well as
Montagu's Harriers and Spoonbills farther north at Nisumfjord.
Over the greater part of this region the visitor cannot leave the roads,
but in fact he can often watch the migrating waders at close quarters
without leaving the car. Bøvling Klit is the best viewing point.

Both Vejlerne, near Selbjerg, and Bygholm, in northern Jutland
east of Hanstholm and between the sea and Limfjord, have numerous
marsh birds; these include the Spoonbill, which has nested at
Vejlerne, its most northerly breeding station in the world. The Greylag Goose is very common at Vejlerne, which is its headquarters in
northern Europe. At the right time of year the Bittern can nearly

always be heard, and Marsh and Montagu's Harriers, Pintail and Shovelers, Gull-billed and Black Terns also breed here. The marshes at Vejlerne are closed to visitors, but a good view of the district can be obtained from Tommerby church on the road between Thisted and Ålborg. The Tawny Pipit can be seen on the drier, sandy beaches and dunes at various places in north Jutland, such as Skagen, and also in Zealand.

Skagen, the long point at the northern extremity of Jutland, is an excellent vantage point for watching migration. In spring the passage of ducks, birds of prey, pigeons and small passerines is very impressive. South of Skagen and north-east of Fredrikshavn there is a small group of islands, the Hirsholmene reserve, with large colonies of birds, chiefly gulls and terns, which vary in size from year to year. The most remarkable species breeding here is the Kittiwake: on these cliffless islands they build their nests on boulders, on the ground close to rocks or even on the driftwood. Other birds on these islands are Common, Herring, Lesser Black-backed and Great Black-backed Gulls, Sandwich Terns, Black Guillemots, Turnstones and Rock Pipits. Unauthorised landing is forbidden at this reserve, but the bird life can easily be studied from a boat.

The seas around the Danish islands between Jutland and Zealand provide one of the Cormorant's main fishing grounds in north Europe, with Vorsø in Horsensfjord as its favourite haunt. Here there is also a colony of Grey Herons, and Cormorants often appropriate their nests. Large numbers of ducks winter at Vorsø, which is now a reserve with a biological laboratory.

The Danish heaths are gradually disappearing owing to the invasion of agriculture and forestry. The most extensive survive in Jutland, but these are poor in the higher forms of animal life. Yet several species can be found closely associated with such an environment, even though not confined to it, and Montagu's Harrier is one of them. At the beginning of the present century this bird was rare in Jutland, whereas the Golden Plover was common. The latter has now all but vanished, clearly disliking the encroachment of the forests on to the open country. The Kestrel is another heathland bird, although it is by no means restricted to the more open, sparsely wooded areas. The Black Grouse can still be seen on open heathland, such as Borris

Hede in Jutland, but it gives place to Partridge and Pheasant as these areas come under the plough. The only passerine bird of particular interest on the Danish heaths is the Great Grey Shrike, which breeds sparingly in southern and central Jutland. This bird has a discontinuous distribution in western Europe, the nearest breeding places to the north of Jutland being in the Norwegian uplands. The Skylark is generally scarce on the Danish heaths, although on some, including the Hansted reserve, it has become surprisingly common. This reserve, which lies to the west of Thisted between Hanstholm and Klitmöllen, is one of the few places in Denmark where there is still a small population of Golden Plovers. A few Cranes breed here and, on the small lakes, Wood Sandpipers.

The commonest habitat in Denmark is farmland, with Rooks, Pheasants and Partridges. There is still a scattering of White Storks, although the numbers of occupied nests are gradually but steadily decreasing, as is the case elsewhere in northern Europe. Kestrels, Buzzards and Long-eared Owls are all birds of the vole-infested farmlands. Barn Owls are common on the farms themselves and Little Owls in the woods. A newcomer to northern agriculture is the Collared Dove, which reached Denmark in 1948, and by 1953 had spread over the greater part of the country from Jutland to Bornholm.

Breeding birds in the deciduous and mixed woods include Grey Heron, Golden Oriole, Hoopoe, Icterine Warbler, Nightingale, Buzzard, Hobby, Honey Buzzard, Goshawk, Sparrowhawk and Tawny Owl.

One can wander at will in the great national forests of Silkeborg, Sønderskov and Østerskov in Jutland, which contain all the common birds to be expected in this part of Europe, including the Kingfisher.

The rarest of the ducks breeding in northern Europe, the Red-crested Pochard, nests at Nakskov Indrefjord in western Lolland. Here there are also Mute Swans, Garganey, Pochards, Black Terns, Marsh Harriers and Great Reed Warblers, with Arctic Terns, Ringed Plovers and Avocets on the outer islands. Brent Geese assemble on passage, as well as large numbers of ducks, birds of prey and small passerines.

Two places in the neighbourhood of Copenhagen, Dyrehaven at Jaegersborg and Kongelunden on Amager, seldom disappoint the ornithologist. Both are open to visitors, and their deciduous woods hold most of the Danish woodland birds. The Barred Warbler nests in Kongelunden. In several places in Denmark and southern Sweden this warbler and the Red-backed Shrike are neighbours, an interesting association which is also known in other parts of Europe.

A good variety of birds can be seen in the agricultural districts of Denmark's eastern province, Zealand. One of the finest forests in Zealand, and also one of the richest in bird life, is Jaegerspris between Isefjord and Roskildefjord, with a varied selection of woodland, islands, meadows and lakes. Many birds of prey winter here, among them Golden and White-tailed Eagles and Rough-legged Buzzards.

Several of the lakes in Zealand have a number of waterfowl. Although most of these lakes are private, there are two exceptions, namely Søborg and Utterslev Mose at Brømshøj near Copenhagen, where Black-necked Grebes and Greylag Geese breed.

The northern point of Zealand, Gilbjerhoved Klint near Gilleleje, is a good locality to watch migration, where large numbers of birds of prey and small passerines pass through in spring.

Bornholm, with its precipitous cliffs, is Denmark's only rocky island. Geologically it is more closely related to Sweden than to Denmark. This is particularly noticeable in the extensive areas of granite in the north-eastern part of the island. In the south-west the sea washes on to sandy flats, above which Sandwich Terns flit, while Lesser Black-backed, Herring and Common Gulls search for carrion. The Eider breeds on Bornholm, and so does the Black Redstart. The Christiansø group of islands, lying about 12½ miles to the north-east of Bornholm, are really the first outposts of the Baltic archipelago, if only on a small scale. This is very noticeable in the fauna, since one of the islands, Graesholm, holds the only Danish colonies of Guillemots and Razorbills, both species that are found in several other places in the Baltic. There are also large colonies of gulls (Herring, Lesser Black-backed and Common) as well as of Eiders. In fact, the Eider population of about 900 pairs is the largest in the Baltic.

Graesholm, which is strictly protected, is important as a locality in which migrants assemble under conditions favourable to the observer. As a result, several species on the Danish list were first reported from this island.

Poland

Derwent May

Great Bustard

The main organisations concerned with ornithology are the Zoological Institute of the Polish Academy of Sciences, which publishes *Acta Ornithologica* (with good English summaries); and the Ornithological Section of the Polish Zoological Society, which publishes *Ornithological Notes* (in English). There are also ornithological laboratories at Warsaw and Kraków Universities, an Institute of Ecology in the Polish Academy of Sciences, and field stations in woodland near Warsaw (under the Institute of Ecology), at Milicz, Lower Silesia, and outside Gdánsk on the north coast (both under the Zoological Institute). At all these places excellent ornithological work is proceeding.

If one finds a ringed bird in Poland, the ring should be sent to Stacja Ornitologiczna IZ PAN, Ringing Office, p-ta Sobieszewo k. Gdanska, Gorki Wschodnie, Poland.

POLAND

Poland is a country with a great wealth of birds, and its people are taking a growing interest in bird-watching. The visitor from western Europe will find its avifauna often unexpected, yet not so different as to be wholly bewildering.

Across the centre of Poland swings the eastern end of the great, undulating north European plain, in most places cultivated and mainly sown with rye. Spring, and the first green shoots, do not come till late in April; but by July the rye is cut, and there follows a long gentle autumn, with October always warm and pleasant. In the south of the country are the high mountains—to the west the Sudeten mountains, to the east the Carpathians with the High Tatra rising above them. The northernmost part of the country is by contrast very low, and dotted everywhere with lakes, especially in the former East Prussia, a land of broad lakes frequently formed at the points where the Ice Age glaciers melted. The Baltic Sea coast is a succession of sandspits and lagoons; the sea is sometimes frozen in January and February.

The ornithologist setting out into the countryside from any of the big cities of the central Polish plains—Warsaw, Łódz, Poznań or Bydgoszcz—will quickly find himself in open, cultivated country, giving way in places to wilder scrub, and criss-crossed everywhere by fine deciduous or coniferous woodland. Most of the common passerines of western Europe are to be found in their familiar habitats in this countryside, though many, such as Chaffinches, Skylarks and Robins, are mainly summer visitors. Some of the less familiar species that will quickly draw attention to themselves are Golden Orioles, Serins and Icterine Warblers in many bigger suburban gardens and parks. The Short-toed Treecreeper is also a bird of the town parks, where it is more common, particularly in western areas, than the Treecreeper, which in Poland is more strictly a woodland bird. The Collared Dove is now common in parks and tree-lined streets.

Out in the open fields, or on their woodland edges, the thin song of the Ortolan Bunting is a universal sound; Blue-headed Wagtails are everywhere; the Hooded Crow is a common scavenger; four shrikes are all fairly common, the Great Grey and Red-backed all over Poland, the Woodchat more abundant in the centre and the Lesser Grey more in the east and south. Hoopoes and Rollers are common on the roadside, the latter especially east of the Vistula. The White Stork is often seen in the fields, and it nests on farmhouse chimneys or trees, usually where a platform has been specially built for it. In the more deserted scrubland and rough pasture throughout Poland, various exciting species may be found: Tawny Pipits and, in the damper places, Bluethroats; Buzzards and Black Kites, provided there are trees for nesting; and Quail. Of more restricted distribution in the open lands are Red-footed Falcons and probably Lesser Kestrels, around Lublin in the south-east; and Great Bustards, in the broad, rolling lands in the north-western quarter of Poland, from Szczecin to Zielona Góra. The Scarlet Rosefinch, a bird of the scrub, has spread from the eastern lands along the north coast.

Turning to birds of the woodland—as opposed to mountain forests and the deep forests of the eastern border, which we shall consider later—many interesting species are tolerably common. In conifer woods there are Crested Tits and, especially in spruce woods in the west of the country, colonies of nesting Fieldfares (including one in the park in Torún). Firecrests are common in spruce woods, especially in Silesia. The Bullfinch, it might be noted, is a bird of the conifer woods in Poland. The Goshawk is not rare in Polish forests. In mixed and deciduous woodland, six species of woodpeckers, besides the Wryneck, may be come across (two others, more common in the deep forests, will be mentioned later): the Green, the Great Spotted and the Lesser Spotted are found in all kinds of woodland, the Grey-headed fairly widely in mixed woods, while in the deciduous woods of the eastern and southern parts of the country are White-backed and Middle Spotted Woodpeckers. Apart from the Chiffchaffs, Willow Warblers and Wood Warblers, and the Blackcaps and Garden Warblers, some of the more decidedly eastern European species of warblers are familiar birds—the Icterine, already mentioned, the Barred Warbler and the River Warbler, and rather more rarely, in the north of the country, the Greenish Warbler. Red-breasted Fly-catchers are also quite common, except in the south-west. Peregrines, as well as Sparrowhawks and Hobbies, are woodland birds in Poland. The Hazel Grouse is another unusual and attractive species scattered throughout the woodlands.

A third habitat of the plains is the water meadows and willows and rushes of the many wide river valleys—the Vistula, making a great S-bend across the country from north to south, passing through Kraków, Warsaw and Torún and flowing into the Baltic near Gdánsk; the Odra, coming down from the Sudeten mountains and shortly afterwards forming the western boundary of Poland; and the many tributaries of both these great rivers.

Besides Redshanks, Snipe and Curlews, there are Black-tailed Godwits and Ruffs breeding widely in the water meadows of these rivers, and in the north-east of the country Great Snipe are also present. In waterside willows, the Penduline Tit's fascinating nest is not difficult to find, and the Thrush Nightingale haunts the willows and reed beds—though it should be added that in woods and even in town parks the Thrush Nightingale is commoner than the Nightingale on the east side of the Vistula, though hard to distinguish except at very close range. Other inhabitants of the marshy edges of rivers are Little and Common Terns, often in mixed colonies, Little Bitterns, Spotted Crakes and Water Rails.

The extensive peat-bogs along the River Biebrza have an extremely interesting avifauna. The breeding birds include Great Snipe, Ruff, Aquatic Warbler, Montagu's Harrier, Golden, Spotted, Lesser Spotted and White-tailed Eagles, Pintail and Shoveler.

Most of the birds so far mentioned are to be found in suitable habitats throughout the lowlands of the country. (In passing I might mention that there are three national parks in the middle of Poland where the wild life is especially carefully protected; the Kampinoska forest just west of Warsaw, a large area just south of Poznań, and another north-west of Kraków.) But the lakes of the northern provinces add another wealth of species to Poland's avifauna. The two biggest lakes in what used to be East Prussia and is now Olsztyn province, are Mamry and Śniardwy, with the pleasant town of Gizycko on the neck of land joining them. Farther east, over by the

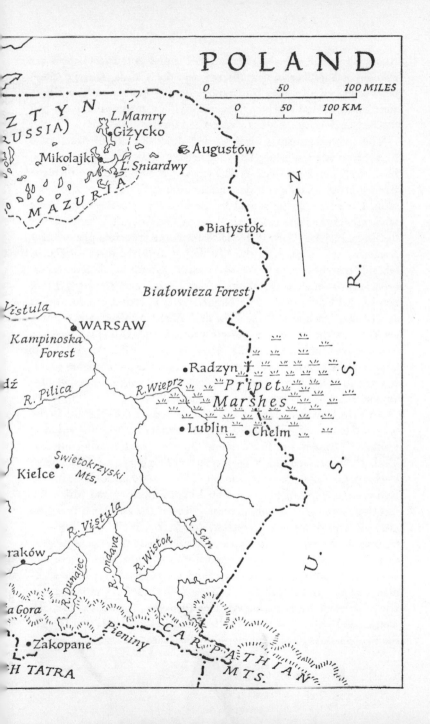

Russian frontier, are the remote lakes round Augustów; there are also important lakes west of Olsztyn near the Vistula estuaries, small lakes scattered all across Pomerania, and a group round Wrocław in south-west Poland of which those near Milicz, north of Wrocław, on the Barycz river, are especially renowned for their bird life.

The riverside nesting birds already described are of course also found around these lakes; but they are only a beginning to the rich bird life. The Great Reed Warbler is common but less so than the Reed Warbler; Savi's Warbler and the Marsh Warbler are also common, the latter having spread to the cornfields in the south-west; while round the lakes east of the Vistula, the Aquatic Warbler is not uncommon. The Bearded Tit is to be found in a few places: near Saczecin, near Elblag and the Vistula bay and in Lower Silesia. In lakeside marshes are to be found Marsh Harriers; in lakeside woods, especially in the north, White-tailed Eagles and Ospreys, Black Storks and Cormorants. The Night Heron is found in two places: at Bielsko Biala and at Przeciszów near Zator in Silesia, where there are colonies that have been closely studied. In lakeside marshes are Black Terns and Little Gulls (a colony near Elblag); also Little Crakes and Cranes. In one particular district, the marshy lakes round Radzyn and Chelm on the western edge of the Pripet marshes, White-winged Black Terns have bred and may still be found.

To turn to water birds in the stricter sense: the Mallard is the only resident duck, but there is a great variety of breeding summer visitors. Garganey and Ferruginous Duck are particularly common, Teal, Shoveler, Gadwall, Wigeon, Tufted Duck, Pintail, Goldeneye, Pochard, Goosander and Red-breasted Merganser are all to be found. Red-crested Pochard have bred on Lakes Śniardwy and Mikolajki. Greylag Geese are the only breeding geese—the two main breeding grounds are Milicz near Wrocław, and Lake Goplo near Torún—though all the other regular European geese pass through on migration. Mute Swans are found especially in the north and there is a large and famous colony of them (and Cormorants) on Lake Lukniany. Little Grebes and Great Crested Grebes are common, there are colonies of Black-necked Grebes through Mazuria (as the lake district of Olsztyn province is called) and in Pomerania and Silesia; the Red-necked Grebe is found on smaller lakes.

In Mazuria begin also the deep forests of north-eastern Poland, of which the greatest is the Bialowieza forest on the frontier south-east of Bialystok, the only remaining home of European Bison and now a national park. There are a number of species virtually confined to these forests and to the mountain forests in the south. Such are Crossbills and Collared Flycatchers (though the latter are sometimes found in more open woodland); Three-toed Wood-peckers; Tengmalm's Eagle, Ural and Pygmy Owls; Short-toed Eagles and, in the north-eastern forests but not in the mountains, Spotted Eagles and more commonly Lesser Spotted Eagles; and Black Grouse and Capercaillie—though these also occur in some parts of the Carpathians.

Strictly mountain birds are comparatively few. In the small range between Kraków and Warsaw, the Swietokrzyski mountains, the Honey Buzzard is particularly frequent. Passerines breeding along the southern mountains in small numbers are Alpine Accentors, and in the summer Water Pipits, Wallcreepers (especially in the Pieniny range), Ring Ouzels, and Redwings in the Carpathians and Tatra. (Redwings have been found in small numbers in north-east Poland.) Snow Finches and Rock Sparrows have nested, but it is uncertain whether they do now, and Scops Owls may be found. Golden Eagles are sometimes seen and may possibly nest here and there. Some of the finest national parks are in these mountains: the one in the Sudeten mountains has already been mentioned; there is another in the High Tatra above the winter sports centre of Zako-pane, a third just to the west round the mountain Babia Góra, and a fourth farther east in the beautiful Pieniny district. The Swietokrzy-ski mountains also have a national park on them, east of Kielce.

To come finally to the Baltic coast: this part of Poland is more interesting for migratory birds than breeders. Arctic and Sandwich Terns have bred near Gdánsk; Shelduck, Ringed Plover, Dunlin and Oystercatcher breed along the coast. But in the autumn there is a great wader migration all along the coast—the Hel peninsula offers particularly good watching, while the island of Wolin forms a national park. Grey Plovers, Little Stints, Broad-billed Sandpipers and Bar-tailed Godwits are perhaps especially interesting, but most of the European waders are to be observed. Several interesting species of passerines are also occasionally noted along the coast in autumn, notably Arctic Redpolls, Red-throated Pipits and Yellow-browed Warblers.

The visiting ornithologist is less likely to be in Poland during the severe winters, but in conclusion some of the birds that are to be seen only at that season should be mentioned. Twites are fairly widespread. In the woods and forests of the north and north-east appear Snowy Owls, and Hawk Owls; the Rough-legged Buzzard, sometimes called the 'winter buzzard' in Poland, spreads over the country and Waxwings are common for a while in Warsaw and other city parks. Snow Buntings are seen especially on the northern lake shores, Shore Larks on the coast, and out at sea, while it is not frozen, Whooper Swans, Long-tailed Ducks, Velvet Scoters, Slavonian Grebes and Red-throated Divers.

Czechoslovakia

F. J. Turček

Black-necked Grebe

There is considerable interest in ornithology, among both amateurs and professionals. The Czechoslovakian Ornithological Society has its headquarters in Prague, and its own ringing station; it publishes the periodical *Sylvia*, which appears annually. Almost all the universities, and even some secondary schools, carry out ornithological work and have several ornithological and biological field centres. The Czechoslovak Academy of Sciences has a zoological research department in Brno, where special attention is paid to ornithology.

If one finds a ringed bird in Czechoslovakia, the ring should be sent to: Krouzzkovaci stanice, Narodni Museum, Vaclavské Nam., Prague I, Czechoslovakia.

CZECHOSLOVAKIA

Czechoslovakia is a long narrow country, some 470 miles from north-west to south-east and only about 170 miles at its widest. The total area is rather more than 82,000 square miles, of which one third is forest and woodland. Bohemia and Moravia, which together form the western part, have both plains and hills. Moravia is open to the south-east, making it easier for animal and plant life to spread from the Hungarian plain. Slovakia, forming the eastern wing of the republic, is narrow and tapering, and can indeed be called a land of geographical contrasts. An extension of the Hungarian plain cuts into it from south to north to a depth of some 80 miles forming an extensive lowland area about 300 feet above sea level; this gives way to hilly and finally mountainous country rising to almost 8,000 feet. In general, western Czechoslovakia is more industrialised and geographically uniform, whereas the east is more varied with wooded mountains to the north and a predominantly agricultural south. The western part of the country is open to the biotic and climatic influences of the Atlantic system, whereas Slovakia enjoys a predominantly Continental climate.

Since the end of the Second World War more and more of the land has been taken over for industry or agriculture, with far-reaching effects on the fauna and flora. In partial compensation the government has established a number of reserves and national parks. Some of the reserves are intended to cover all forms of fauna whilst others are purely bird sanctuaries, including special sanctuaries for Great Bustards, Cormorants, White-tailed Eagles and Grey Herons.

The shooting and trapping of birds, including netting, is in general illegal, and egg-collecting is likewise banned. There is, however, an open season for a few species such as Hooded Crows, Magpies, Jays, Goshawks and Sparrowhawks. In some of the sanctuaries even photography and access are prohibited.

About 300 species occur regularly in Czechoslovakia and approximately 210 of these breed. The last twenty years has seen a number of new invaders, among them Bee-eaters, Syrian Woodpeckers, Collared Doves and Imperial Eagles from the south and south-east and Scarlet Rosefinches and Redwings from the east and north-east.

In the north-western corner of Czechoslovakia there is a large bird sanctuary, the Novozámecký lakes, in the undulating country near the cliffs of Děčín. This is occupied by up to two hundred species throughout the year and is the farthest point north and west at which two of them—Savi's Warbler and Bearded Tit—are encountered in the country. Greylag Geese breed there, and Carrion Crows can also be seen at what is the easternmost limit of their distribution. In fact, western Bohemia is the transition zone between the western Carrion Crow and the eastern Hooded Crow, and both races and also hybrids can be seen.

At Plana, on the eastern limit of the Bohemian spa country, not far from Marienbad, there is a lake of considerable ornithological interest where nesting Black-winged Stilts and other waterfowl can be observed. The surrounding region with its mainly coniferous woods and wide tracts of farmland affords the observer a wide choice of species native to such habitats.

The Šumava range forms the watershed of the Vltava or Moldau River and not far from the source of this river is the country's largest dam, the Lipenská. The country is well wooded with almost virgin coniferous forest, mainly spruce, interspersed with mountain meadows and occasional boggy tracts. This area is one of the best preserved in Czechoslovakia and, apart from the more usual and widespread mountain and forest birds, the main attractions are nesting Redpolls at comparatively low altitudes and the presence of Capercaillies, Tengmalm's Owls, Ring Ouzels and others in the dense forests.

The romantic mediaeval castle of Hluboká on the Vltava contains a museum of shooting and hunting trophies. The surrounding district is well supplied with lakes and ponds, the largest being Lake Bezdrev, which has numerous ducks, grebes, gulls, herons, waders and so on. Nearby at Vodňany there is a hydrobiological station and the country's only fisheries school.

The south Bohemian or Lake Třebon district is a lacustrine zone of considerable significance. The stretches of water are surrounded by marshes, meadows and woodland with pines dominant. Whilst every lake and pond has its quota of waterfowl it is the three largest lakes, Velký Tisý, Malý Tisý and Rožmberk, which have most to offer the ornithologist. At the first there is an ornithological field station which offers accommodation and facilities for field work. Avocets, Black-winged Stilts, Grey Herons, Purple Herons, Curlews and other birds nest there. Vagrant flocks of Great White Egrets have appeared there at the end of the summer. These lakes are particularly interesting during the spring (March–April) and autumn migrations, but wintering birds are also to be seen there.

Krkonoše, better known as the Riesengebirge, is a well-known winter sports area, but it still contains large tracts of unspoilt country, mostly mountain spruce forest but with a fair amount of bog and sub-alpine meadows interspersed with rocky outcrops. This is the only place in Czechoslovakia where Dotterels nest regularly. On the rocky slopes of this mountainous region there are Alpine Accentors, while Tengmalm's Owls call on the fringes of dense woods which are also the home of Three-toed Woodpeckers, Goldcrests and various tits; the mountain meadows have Ring Ouzels, Tree Pipits, Water Pipits and various other species. The greater part of this alpine region is preserved as a national park and wildlife sanctuary.

The Jeseníky mountains, in which the highest peak, Praděd, reaches nearly 4,000 feet, have been called 'the zoo' because of the wide spectrum of wildlife to be found there, especially birds and mammals. These mountains show clearly defined timber belts ranging from beech in the foothills and valleys through a mixed deciduous and conifer belt on the lower slopes to an imposing forest of spruce gradually thinning out to scattered stands near the tree line and finally giving way to sub-alpine meadows. The lower timber belts have Red-breasted Flycatchers, White-backed Woodpeckers and Stock Doves, as well as tits, Nuthatches, Wood Warblers, Willow Warblers, Black Woodpeckers and others. Higher up in the spruce forests there are Capercaillies and Black Grouse. The transition zone from forest to meadow has a rather park-like aspect and this is the home of Ring Ouzels, Three-toed Woodpeckers, Coal Tits, Gold-crests, Firecrests and Crested Tits. A little higher up, in the alpine meadows with their cliffs and rocky slopes, there are Meadow Pipits and Water Pipits, as well as a flourishing population of Skylarks. The area is easily accessible and it is possible to drive almost to the top of Praděd. There are a number of hotels, spas and other tourist facilities at and near the foot of the Jeseníky mountains.

The karst region of southern Moravia has a warm dry climate. The countryside is prairie-like with limestone cliff formations and numerous caves, amongst them a celebrated one at Macocha. The fauna is in general warmth-loving and includes Peregrines, Rock Thrushes and Ortolan Buntings.

The Pavlovské hills are on the southern frontier of Moravia. Here the country is undulating with low hills, fields, orchards and vine-yards interspersed with oakwoods and contains two interesting intro-ductions: Ibex and Rock Partridge. On rocky ridges of the hills, and in some cases on the slopes, there are Rock Thrushes, Ortolan Buntings and Wheatears, while Tree Pipits, Skylarks, Woodlarks, Hoopoes and various others are found on the fringes of the woods. Peregrines and Kestrels are occasionally seen. Rollers, Golden Orioles, various warblers, Nightingales and many deciduous forest birds nest in the woods and orchards on the lower slopes.

The Lednické lakes form a string of shallow lakes and ponds which have been in existence since the fourteenth century. They are heavily fringed with reeds and surrounded by marshes and swampy meadow land. Enormous numbers of birds pass through in spring and autumn; many also nest and there is always a good variety of species to be seen. A biological station at Lednické is devoted primarily to ornithological field work. Mallard, Pochard and Ferruginous Ducks nest here and Spotted Crakes, Little Crakes, Purple Herons, Grey Herons and Spoonbills are by no means rare visitors. Cormorants nest in the old trees of the park surrounding Lednica castle. Red-shanks, Black-tailed Godwits, Curlews, Avocets, Black-headed Gulls, Black Terns and Common Terns nest on the shores of the lake, in the marshes and meadows; Bearded Tits can be found in the reed beds and Penduline Tits on the islets and in the willows fringing the shore. The whole of this area is easily accessible by car from Austria.

The lower reaches of the River Morava and its basin are rich in bird life. Ferruginous Ducks and Greylag Geese can be seen there in season and in most places Black Kites, Marsh Harriers, Montagu's Harriers, Curlews, Black Terns and Common Terns nest. Great Bustards and Stone Curlews can be seen in the fields and meadows along the valleys of the Morava basin, and Short-eared Owls are to be found in the marshes. The damp oakwoods bordering the river abound in Rollers, Savi's Warblers, Grasshopper Warblers, Dunnocks, Woodchat and other shrikes, Penduline Tits, Golden Orioles and a host more.

The highly industrialised area around Ostrava and Bohumín includes a fairly extensive system of shallow man-made lakes, very much overgrown, which are the haunt of Black-headed Gulls, Coots, Tufted Ducks, Ferruginous Ducks and various other water and marshland species. The bird population has been increased by the arrival of several colonies of Rooks and by Pheasants which live mostly in the reeds around the ponds.

The Little Carpathians extend to within the frontiers of Slovakia. Their southern and eastern slopes are mainly covered with vineyards, orchards and oak and beech woods. They have a richly variegated fauna which includes nesting Sakers, Red-footed Falcons and Imperial Eagles. Scops Owls are mainly confined to the vineyards and the edges of the woods. The western slopes of these mountains fall away into the great Zahoria plain which extends westwards to the River Morava. The plain is in parts wet and marshy with nesting Greylag Geese, in parts dry and sandy with extensive pine woods and nesting Stone Curlews.

Jurský Šúr is a reserve covering an area of marshes, bog and woodland with fantastically shaped old trees. It covers rather more than 1,200 acres not far from Bratislava, the capital of Slovakia. There is a biological station whose work is mainly ornithological. The more interesting birds include Hen Harriers, Honey Buzzards, Black Kites, Purple Herons, Bitterns, Black Storks, various grebes and ducks, Bearded and Penduline Tits, Syrian and Middle Spotted Woodpeckers and many others.

The Trnava region is flat, predominantly agricultural country with a number of recently made artificial lakes. There are several stretches

of woodland where Red-footed Falcons, Scops Owls and Rollers
nest, while Marsh Harriers, Coots, Moorhens, Spotted Crakes,
Water Rails and many shore birds frequent the ponds and marshes.
This area is a popular gathering place for migrants. The town of
Trnava has an interesting museum, which specialises mainly in
ornithological exhibits.

Biskupice is a sanctuary on the Danube with two contrasting
features: on one side, high banks of gravel covered with savanna-
like vegetation and on the other low-lying marshland with willows

CZECHOSLOVAKIA

0   50   100 MILES

0   50   100 KM

and poplars intersected by a maze of small channels. This sanctuary
is mainly for Cormorants, of which there are now more than one
hundred pairs, but Grey Herons and Bearded and Penduline Tits are
found there and in October and November it is an assembly area for
hordes of migrating geese.

The Gabčíkovo area forms the central part of Žitny Island which
lies at the confluence of the Danube and Little Danube. The whole
area is low-lying, criss-crossed with small channels and ditches and
densely wooded with willow and poplar. This jungle-like archipelago

gives way in turn to salt marshes, low-lying meadows and finally to agricultural land, the whole teeming with a wide variety of bird life: Pochard, Gadwall, Teal, Mallard, Cormorant, Curlew, Black-tailed Godwit, Reed Bunting, Purple Heron, Grey Heron, Night Heron, Bittern, Little Bittern, Snipe, Stone Curlew, Bluethroat, Bearded Tit, Penduline Tit, White-tailed Eagle (nesting), Marsh Harrier, Montagu's Harrier, Nightingale, Dunnock, Collared Dove, several warblers, Lesser Grey Shrike, Black Stork and others. Moustached Warblers have also been observed, their occurrence being confined to this one region. In late summer, wandering flocks of Great White Egrets and Spoonbills are commonly seen.

Near Zlatná there is a special sanctuary of about 2,400 acres for Great Bustards.

The lower reaches of the River Hron, with its low wooded banks, house a large colony of Grey Herons and smaller ones of Night Herons and Little Egrets. Kingfishers and Sand Martins nest where the banks are high, whilst Stone Curlews frequent the gravel beds and dry stretches along the river.

In the country between Šahy, Modrý Kameň and Lučenec there are cliffs and hills, with loess deposits, which house a flourishing population of Bee-eaters. The small wooded areas in this locality are well stocked with Rollers, Hoopoes, Woodchat Shrikes and Lesser Grey Shrikes.

Lesser Spotted Eagles, Hazel Grouse, Red Kites, Red-breasted Flycatchers and White-backed Woodpeckers nest in the xerophilous oak woods on the steep banks of the River Hron, whilst Eagle Owls are found in the cliffs and rocky outcrops and Sand Martins are common lower down on the river banks.

The best preserved natural forests in Slovakia are those in the Polana Mountains, the highest peak of which is about 4,000 feet above sea level. These forests have beech, fir and maple on the southern slopes and spruce on the northern. Nesting birds include Spotted Eagles, Three-toed Woodpeckers, Red-breasted Flycatchers, Capercaillies, Hazel Grouse, Water Pipits, Crossbills (almost all the year round) and Black Woodpeckers.

Slovakia's largest stretch of water is the Oravská dam. This is the scene of intense activity during the spring and autumn migrations, but nesting is still comparatively limited since the dam is as yet too new to offer adequate shoreline vegetation. However, fair numbers of ducks and other aquatic birds already nest there and White-tailed Eagles are regular visitors. Scarlet Rosefinches have started to nest in the willows and Ural Owls live in the surrounding conifer forest. The museum in the ancient castle of Oravský Podzámok contains a fine collection of local birds.

The lovely upper reaches of the River Váh are bordered by clumps of low willow where Scarlet Rosefinch, Fieldfare and Magpie nest. Siskins are frequent visitors and Dippers and Kingfishers can often be seen.

Czechoslovakia's largest national park, covering more than 90 square miles, is situated in the High Tatras, the country's highest mountains, which rise to some 8,000 feet. The region is a popular holiday resort, well provided with hotels, camps and sports centres and served by a funicular railway. Some parts of the Tatras National Park are the strict preserve of wild life and may be entered only by special permission of the park authorities. Birds include Hazel Grouse, Capercaillie, Black Grouse, Black Stork, Golden Eagle (nesting), Raven, Nutcracker, Three-toed Woodpecker, Wall-creeper, Rock Thrush (up to 5,000 feet), Ring Ouzel, Redpoll, Peregrine, Water Pipit and Alpine Accentor. Serins, Collared Doves and numerous Magpies nest in the gardens at altitudes of about 3,000 feet.

The Slovenský Kras area is typical karst country with the usual limestone topography—sink-holes, caves, abrupt ridges and irregular rocky outcrops. It has been deforested for many centuries and has suffered considerable erosion, but measures are in hand for its gradual reafforestation. The climate is very warm and dry and the generally poor soil supports Mahaleb cherry, manna ash, barberry, privet and stands of Hungarian oak. This is the only area in Czechoslovakia where Rock Buntings nest. Rock Partridges have recently been introduced and other birds include Rock Thrushes and Nightingales, the latter being very common. Black Kites and Short-toed Eagles are found in the fields, whilst Peregrines, Sakers, Kestrels, Ravens and Jackdaws nest among the rocks and on the cliffs.

In the south-east corner of Czechoslovakia there is an area largely formed by the valley of the River Tisa, which rises in the Carpathians and normally floods its banks in the spring. This is a region of creeks, pools and marshes housing a multitude of ducks, crakes, Black-headed Gulls and Black Terns; Bluethroats nest in the bushes and Red-footed Falcons in the trees.

The Senné basin is the most important migratory area in Slovakia, particularly for waterfowl, and it has its own ornithological station. Cranes, Ruffs and other waders, ducks, geese, Caspian Terns and so on can be seen in vast numbers, especially during the spring migration. Nesting birds include Black-headed Gull, Black Tern, White-winged Black Tern, Whiskered Tern, Pintail, Pochard, Water Rail, Spotted Crake and Little Crake. Drainage schemes, here and elsewhere, are of course bound to have some effect on the bird life.

Germany

Herbert Bruns

White Stork

In spite of the existence of two Germanies, German ornithologists are united in one organisation, the Deutsche Ornithologische Gesellschaft, which has members in both countries. This society publishes two periodicals, the *Journal für Ornithologie* (quarterly), and *Die Vogelwarte* (twice yearly). Other publications include *Ornithologische Mitteilungen* (Wiesbaden), *Beiträge zur Vogelkunde* (Leipzig), and *Der Falke* (Leipzig and Jena). The *Deutsche Bund für Vogelschutz* (Steinauer Strasse 33, Frankfurt am Main, Fechenheim) has a branch in each of the federal states of West Germany, and in most of the large towns, and does much to popularise the protection and study of birds. The Rossitten bird migration station was moved to Schloss Möggingen, near Radolfzell on Lake Constance, after the second world war. Heligoland observatory, now housed in Wilhelmshaven, still has a field station on the island.

If one finds a ringed bird in West Germany, the ring should be sent to Vogelwarte Radolfzell, Schloss Möggingen, 7761 Möggingen; or to Vogelwarte Helgoland, Umfangstrasse, 2940 Wilhelmshaven-Rüstersiel.

If a ringed bird is found in East Germany, the ring should be sent to: Vogelwarte Hiddensee, Kloster am Hiddensee, Bahnstation Stralsund.

GERMANY

Germany extends from the North and Baltic Seas southwards to the Alps, a distance of almost 620 miles. Altitudes vary from almost 10,000 feet down to sea level, and the terrain is itself very diverse—seashore, plains, meadows, forest, heathland, moorland, bog, lakes and mountains—so it is not surprising that the avifauna is also very variable. Forests (deciduous, conifer or mixed) cover about 27 per cent of the total area.

W. Makatsch has given a total of 421 bird species for Germany, which may be compared with the 602 species listed for Europe by R. T. Peterson, G. Mountfort and P. A. D. Hollom in *A Field Guide to the Birds of Britain and Europe* (1974 edition). Even the individual provinces of Germany have totals of 300-350 bird species, of which half breed.

Germany may be conveniently divided into four natural areas:

    a) the sea coasts and islands
    b) the northern plain between the coast and the central
       mountains
    c) the central mountains
    d) the Alps

Within the whole area the literature on the avifauna has, however, been based on the provinces, or Landen. Thus, in recent times avifaunas have been published for Mecklenburg, Saxony, Hesse, the Rhineland, Bavaria and so on. These are convenient geographical divisions for local naturalists and so they will be used here, although the frontiers of the Landen are, of course, artificial and not natural boundaries. It would not be possible, owing to lack of space, to provide a complete list of all the localities of ornithological interest, and anyone wishing to study a particular region in detail must refer to the specialist literature.

Heligoland

This island occupies a rather special position for it was formerly the site of Vogelwarte Helgoland (Heligoland Bird Observatory), and an outstation is still maintained there. The island became well-known ornithologically during the last century owing to the work of H. Gätke. Many rarities and vagrants can be seen there, particularly during migration periods. Among those nesting there, special mention should be made of the Guillemots, Kittiwakes and Razorbills.

Schleswig-Holstein

The province of Schleswig-Holstein forms a natural unit, situated between the North Sea and the Baltic Sea. It has a variety of terrains (low hills and numerous lakes in the east, dry hilly terrain or Geest in the centre, marshland in the west) and it surpasses most other German provinces in its wealth of bird species and individuals. The number of species which have been recorded there is 316, of which 182 breed.

Good areas for birds on the North Sea coast include Rantumbecken on Sylt, Amrum, the low-lying islets of Norderoog and Suderoog and the island of Trischen. Breeding birds include Herring Gulls, Arctic, Common, Little and Sandwich Terns, occasionally Gull-billed Terns and Avocets and Ringed and Kentish Plover. Autumn visitors include various waders, and in winter there are numerous species of ducks, Barnacle and Brent Geese, Shore Lark, Twite and Snow Bunting. Characteristic birds in the marshy areas are Lapwing, Redshank, Ruff, Black Tern, White Stork, Grey Heron, and in autumn large flocks of Golden Plovers. The Haseldorfer and Wedeler marshes near Hamburg are particularly rich in species, including Bluethroat, Aquatic Warbler, Corncrake, and in autumn, winter and spring large numbers of waterfowl.

In the central part of the Geest area most of the heath and moorland areas have disappeared and with them the Golden Plover as a breeding bird, but the following species still breed in some parts: Wood Sandpiper, Curlew, Snipe, Teal, Montagu's Harrier, Short-eared Owl, Black Grouse (rare), Black-tailed Godwit, Ruff, Dunlin, Black-headed and Common Gulls, Raven, Great Grey

Shrike and Barred Warbler. The conifer forests have Nightjars and Turtle Doves, and some woods Black Woodpeckers.

The hilly country in the east is rich in birds, particularly in song birds, e.g. Thrush Nightingales. Some species, such as Savi's Warbler and River Warbler, have come in recently, but they are still rare.

The lakes of eastern Holstein have Black-headed and Common Gulls, Great Crested, Black-necked and Red-necked Grebes, Mallard, Teal, Gadwall, Shoveler, Pochard, Tufted Duck and Goldeneye, Greylag Geese and, in winter, White-fronted Geese, Whooper and Bewick's Swans. The Red-crested Pochard breeds on Fehmarn, the Red-breasted Merganser and Goosander on the Baltic Sea coast and on some lakes, and the Crane in the Lauenburg area. Among birds of prey the Marsh Harrier, White-tailed Eagle, Red Kite, Black Kite and Honey Buzzard still breed, and the passage migrants include Osprey and Steppe Buzzard.

The Baltic Sea coast of Schleswig-Holstein has fewer birds than the North Sea coast, but there are good places to observe migration as, for example, in Fehmarn Sound and, in autumn, Gelting Birk, Schwansener See and the mouth of the Schlei. At some places, such as Botsand, the breeding birds include both Ringed and Kentish Plovers, Avocet, Redshank, Broad-billed Sandpiper, Snipe, Dunlin and Shelduck. From late summer onwards numerous marsh and shore birds arrive as visitors, among them some rarities. The waterfowl and waders are particularly striking and can be seen, especially in April and May, in the western part of Fehmarn.

Hamburg

In a city state such as Hamburg the changes in habitat brought about by human encroachment are very considerable. Nevertheless, White Storks still breed in the marshes and in the Vierlande area, Bluethroats in a few places (e.g. Steinbeler Moor), and the Black Woodpecker in the Wohldorfer Wald.

Over the course of a number of years the impressive total of 140 bird species has been recorded for the Ohlsdorfer Friedhof, Europe's largest area of parkland, and the city's park has over 100 species recorded. During winter, sawbills, numerous other ducks, divers and gulls appear regularly on the Aussenalster Lake (450 acres) in the centre of Hamburg, where a noteworthy total of 77 species has been recorded.

Lower Saxony and Bremen

The North Sea islands have numerous sea and shore birds: Herring and Black-headed Gulls, Common, Arctic, Little and Sandwich Terns, Kentish and Ringed Plovers, Redshanks, Lapwings, Oystercatchers and, in some places, Eiders. Knechtsand in the Weser estuary is known for the tens of thousands of moulting Shelducks. Another excellent place for an ornithological trip is to Jadebusen at migration time and also in the winter. Avocets breed on the coast of East Friesland and the marshes have numerous Black-tailed Godwits, Redshanks and Lapwings. Farther north, the high moors have the last Golden Plovers in Germany, as well as Curlews and Snipe. In East Friesland the Cormorant colony at Lütetsburg is also worth seeing.

For a long time one of the best places for birds in north-west Germany has been the Dümmer See, an area for which about 250 different species have been recorded, 145 of them breeding. Unfortunately, numbers have decreased.

Between the Weser estuary and the lower Elbe there are good bird areas at Teufelsmoor and on the lakes and moors of the Hadeln area, where the Black-winged Stilt breeds and in places the Barred Warbler is not rare. The Crane still breeds in the north-eastern part of Lower Saxony, which is relatively sparsely populated.

There are several good bird lakes not far from Hanover, including the Steinhuder Meer, and even in the city itself. This is an area that has been well covered by ornithologists, but it is still possible to come across rarities and as an example, over a period of ten years, ornithologists at Hildesheim have made twenty-four sight records of the rare Little Crake and Baillon's Crake, in addition to Water Rails and Spotted Crakes. Waders and various waterfowl can be seen in the Brunswick area at Riddagshauser.

The bird life changes in the hill country of the southern part of Lower Saxony. In particular, the conifer forests of the Harz mountains are relatively poor in species and individuals. The Grey-headed Woodpecker can be seen in the hills and possibly also Tengmalm's Owl (Salling, Harz and Luneburg Heath) and Nutcracker (Harz). In some places the Red Kite is now the commonest bird of prey, and the Black Kite is not rare. On the other hand, the Peregrine has unfortunately decreased considerably in numbers. For some years the Citril Finch has been seen at Torfhaus in the Harz mountains.

Mecklenburg, Brandenburg and Sachsen-Anhalt

The Baltic coast of Mecklenburg provides numerous ornithological treats. For instance, the following breed on Rügen: Shelduck, Red-breasted Merganser, Caspian, Common, Arctic, Little and Sandwich Terns, Ringed Plover, Dunlin, Ruff, Redshank and Avocet. Also, the lakes of the interior of Mecklenburg still have numerous marsh birds, waterfowl and birds of prey. This is due partly to the relatively sparse human population and partly to efficient nature conservation, especially of birds of prey. Here the breeding populations of the White-tailed Eagle and Osprey have actually increased. Other species of note include Lesser Spotted Eagle, Red Kite, Black Kite, Black Stork, Raven, Black-throated and Red-throated Divers, Bittern, Little Bittern, Crane, Greylag Goose, Goosander, Red-crested Pochard, and Red-breasted Flycatcher. Good localities for birdwatching include: Tollense See, Müritz, Lewitz, Galenbecker See, Anklawer Stadtbruch and Krakower See.

In the Mark of Brandenburg, mention may be made of the Schorfheide, north of Berlin (Goosander, Roller, Red-breasted Flycatcher), Gülper See at Rathenow (Black-headed Gull and Black Tern colonies, Great Bustard, Black Grouse, Ruff), Rietzer See in the Brandenburg area (waterfowl and marsh birds, Great Bustard, Crane, Aquatic Warbler), Peitzer See near Cottbus (a good place for waders and ducks on passage), and Golmar Luch west of Potsdam. Other species worthy of special mention include Black-throated and Red-throated Divers, Shelduck, Tufted Duck, Pochard, Ferruginous Duck, Teal, Garganey, Gadwall, Shoveler, Greylag Goose, Water Rail, Corncrake, Little Crake, Great Bustard, Crane, Bittern, Little Bittern, Black Stork, Black Kite and Red Kite.

In the Drömling area Lapwings, Curlews, Snipe, Black-tailed

Godwits, Teal and Garganey are still numerous. The Haldensleben area has Red and Black Kites, Goshawks, Hobbies and Honey
Buzzards, in addition to Buzzards, Kestrels and Sparrowhawks
which are common throughout Germany. Ravens and Black Storks
have been recorded in the Klötze area and at Haldensleben. In
contrast to West Germany, the Pheasant is very rare.

North Rhine-Westphalia

Notable species in this region include Tawny Pipit, Ortolan
Bunting and Middle Spotted Woodpecker; these also occur in Lower
Saxony and Schleswig-Holstein. There is a large colony of Black-
headed Gulls in the nature reserve at Zwillbrocker Venn and the
Soest area has Quail, Great Grey Shrike and Montagu's Harrier.
Tengmalm's Owls and Nutcrackers are very rare in the Sauerland.
The Möhne Dam is particularly good for observing waterfowl
(especially during migration and in the winter when there are nu-
merous ducks, mergansers and divers); other good places for water-
fowl are Halterner Stausee, Baldeney See, Hengstey See and the
Dülmen and Rietberg fishponds.

It is remarkable that the densely populated industrial area of the
Ruhr is relatively rich in species, with nesting records for Little
Ringed Plover, Shoveler and Pochard and numerous ducks and
waders at migration time.

In the lower Rhine area special mention must be made of Bis-
licher Island near Xanten, where the breeding birds include Herring,
Common and Black-headed Gulls, Common, Little and Black Terns,
Oystercatcher, Black-tailed Godwit and Lapwing. The Kricken-
becker See has breeding Bittern, Little Bittern, Savi's Warbler,
Hoopoe, Kingfisher, Curlew, Marsh Harrier, Honey Buzzard and
Grey Heron, with occasional sightings of Night and Squacco
Herons. Cormorants and Ospreys are there throughout the year and
numerous ducks and waders appear as winter visitors and passage
migrants.

Rhineland-Pfalz and Saarland

The Rhine, Nahe and Mosel valleys have the warmest climate in
Germany. Several northern birds winter here and some Mediter-

ranean birds also occur, e.g. Cirl and Rock Buntings. The Pfalz is Germany's largest continuous area of forest. Here the Capercaillie and Hazel Grouse still occur locally, as do several woodpeckers, and both Peregrine and Eagle Owl. The Wallcreeper is a rare winter visitor. The upper Rhine plains are particularly rich in bird life (e.g. at Boxheim, Berghausen, Neuhofen and Eich-Gimbsheim). Here the breeding birds include Heron, Little Ringed Plover, Curlew, Shoveler, Little Crake, Grey Bittern and Little Bittern, Marsh and Montagu's Harriers, Black Kite, Kingfisher, Bluethroat and Grasshopper Warbler. The passage migrants include nearly all the European ducks.

The stretch of the Rhine between Ingelheim and Bingen-Gaulsheim is also good for seeing ducks and mergansers. Waterfowl are abundant on the Laacher See and the Ulmener Weiher in the Eifel, and near the Krombach Dam.

Apart from the Rhine region and a few places with particularly active resident bird-watchers there are still extensive areas in this province which have been little investigated: for example, the isolated parts of the Pfalz forest, Soon Idar and Hochwald, and the western Eifel. New sightings for Tengmalm's Owl and Pygmy Owl are needed from the Pfalz forest, northern Pfalz and the Donnersberg region. Several species are extending their range and therefore deserve special attention; these include Penduline Tit, Fieldfare, Nutcracker, Purple Heron, Savi's Warbler and Bonelli's Warbler.

Hesse, Thuringia and Saxony

Some 330 bird species have been recorded for Hesse, and the number is roughly the same for Thuringia and Saxony. In the central mountainous area the occurrence of Nutcrackers and rare owls is of special interest. The Eagle Owl has almost disappeared from the central mountains of Lower Saxony, but is still present in Thuringia and Saxony. Tengmalm's Owl is not so rare as was originally thought. The Peregrine has unfortunately much decreased in numbers, and so has the Woodcock.

Localities for waterfowl and marsh birds include the backwaters of the Main, Lahn and Fulda, the Eder and Diemel Dams, the lakes of the Westerwald and Vogelsberg, Enkheimer Marsh near Frankfurt,

Breitunger See in southern Thuringia and Alperspetter Marsh at Erfurt. The Nieder Lausitz area is particularly rich in species. Of the 175 species breeding in Saxony some 140 breed here, including Greylag Geese, Crane, Bittern, Redshank, Curlew, Black-tailed Godwit, Black Tern, Goldeneye, Pochard and other ducks and grebes. In the Kieferwald area the breeding birds include Tawny Pipit, Nightjar, Stone Curlew, Hoopoe and Roller.

Baden-Württemberg

Unfortunately, there is no recent avifauna for Baden-Württemberg. The Rhine between Karlsruhe and Mannheim is a good area for Curlews, Bluethroats and Nightingales, and for many marsh and water birds during the migration period. Stonechats, Wheatears and Ortolan Buntings can be seen at Tauberbischofsheim. The Swabian Alb at Heidenheim has Wheatear, Tawny Pipit, Little Bittern, Nightingale and many waders during migration.

In the deep valley of the Wutach in southern Schwarzwald there are Dippers, Nutcrackers, Kingfishers, Peregrines and also Goosanders.

Other birds in this region include Collard Flycatcher, Wallcreeper, Bonelli's Warbler, Fieldfare, Eagle Owl (unfortunately dying out), White Stork, Red Kite and Black Kite, Honey Buzzard, Quail, Black and Middle Spotted Woodpeckers (increasing) and Hoopoe (increasing).

Bavaria

Some 352 species have been recorded for Bavaria. The following may be mentioned as being particularly good localities for observing birds: the area between Wurzburg, Schweinfurt and Gerolzhofen for Woodchat and Lesser Grey Shrikes, Ortolan Bunting and Hoopoe; Hornauer See at Gerolzhofen for waterfowl; ponds between Erlangen and Hochstadt for breeding Bitterns and Black-tailed Godwits.

At Chiem See near the mouth of the Achen the regular breeders include Little Ringed Plover, Redshank, Common Tern and Bluethroat, and among the visitors are Cormorant, Whooper Swan, Red-footed Falcon, Dunlin, Little Stint, Ruff and Raven.

At Innstausee between Braunau and Passau the regular breeding birds include Tufted Duck, Kingfisher and Penduline Tit, and numerous waterfowl and the White-tailed Eagle appear as visitors.

On the Isar between Moosburg and Landshut numerous gulls, ducks and waders occur on passage. The Crag Martin breeds near Falkenstein east of Regensburg and the Wallcreeper occasionally occurs there. Goosanders breed on Walchen See and White-backed Woodpeckers at Jachenau, and other species occurring in this area include Tengmalm's Owl, Pygmy Owl, Three-toed Woodpecker, Alpine Accentor and Citril Finch.

Other breeding birds (with localities) include Night Heron (lower Bavaria), White and Black Storks (Oberpfalz, Oberfranken), Red Kite (north-west Bavaria), Black Kite, Honey Buzzard, Marsh, Montagu's and Hen Harriers, Short-toed Eagle, Peregrine and Red-footed Falcon (Schwaben and Oberpfalz), Ptarmigan (Alps above the tree limit), Rock Partridge, Capercaillie and Hazel Grouse, Corncrake, Water Rail, Spotted, Little and Baillon's Crakes, Lapwing, Little Ringed Plover, Woodcock, Black-tailed Godwit, Scops and Ural Owls (all in the Bayerischer Wald), Chough, Alpine Chough, Wallcreeper, Dipper, Fieldfare, Bluethroat, Grasshopper, River, Savi's and Barred Warblers (Danube region).

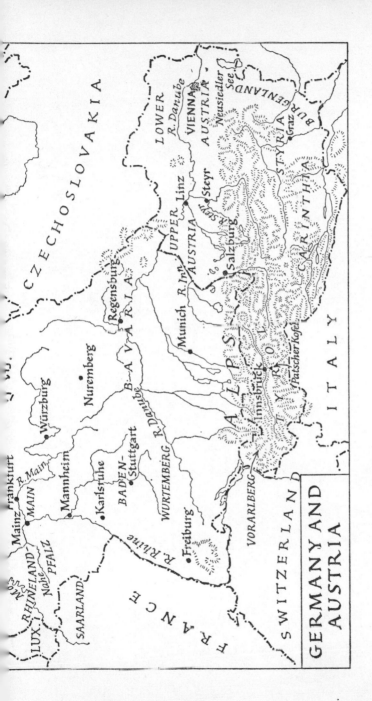

GERMANY AND
AUSTRIA

Austria

Herbert Bruns

Wallcreeper

Ornithology is less advanced in Austria than, for instance, in Germany. Nevertheless there are several bird stations including the Österreichische Vogelwarte (Wien 1, Burgring 7) in the capital, the Tiroler Vogelwarte (Beobachtungsstation Ahrnberg bei Innsbruck), the Steyrische Vogelwarte (Frojach/Mur), and the Vogelschutzstation in Linz.

There is no ringing centre in Austria, so if one finds a ringed bird the ring should be sent to the ringing centre in the country of origin.

AUSTRIA

Austria is a federal republic with the provinces of Upper Austria, Lower Austria and Vienna in the north. The others in the south are Vorarlberg, Tyrol, Salzburg, Styria, Carinthia and Burgenland.

Vorarlberg and Tyrol

In the extreme west the relatively small province of Vorarlberg is bounded on the west by stretches of the Rhine just before it flows into Lake Constance and on the south by the eastern parts of Switzerland. The breeding birds include Garganey, Gadwall, Shoveler, Red-crested Pochard, Pochard and Tufted Duck, Purple Heron, Bittern, Lapwing, Curlew, Black-tailed Godwit, Black-headed and Common Gulls, and Corncrake.

The Tyrol is, of course, a far more mountainous region with outlying spurs of the Alps in the south. The characteristic birds include Ptarmigan, Rock Partridge, Wallcreeper, Chough, Alpine Chough, Alpine Accentor, Citril Finch and Snow Finch.

To the south-east of Innsbruck, the provincial capital, the area of the Patscher Kofel (altitude 7,375 feet), has Eagle and Pygmy Owls, Alpine Swift, Three-toed Woodpecker and Crag Martin. Several of these montane birds can also be seen in the area north of Innsbruck.

Salzburg

The southern part of this province is also mountainous and here there are Alpine Swifts and Alpine Choughs, as well as Citril and Snow Finches.

In the quiet valley of Rauristal between Taxenbach and Salzach there is a chance to see a Lammergeier, while Pygmy Owls, Snow Finches and Golden Eagles occur more regularly in the Rauris area.

Upper and Lower Austria

The Staminger Stausee to the north of Steyr is a good place for waterfowl and so is the mouth of the Traun as it enters Traunsee.

In general, the northern part of Upper Austria is not much visited by tourists, and because of this it is a good area for undisturbed bird-watching. This applies both to the area between Salzburg and the Danube and to the woody Muhlviertel area to the north of this river. In the latter area there is a chance of a Hazel Grouse or a Ural Owl, and probably one or more of the rarer woodpeckers and possibly also a Red-breasted Flycatcher.

Lower Austria is also rich in woodlands, particularly in the Waldviertel, in the north-west. East of this area and north of the Danube the flatter and more productive Weinviertel has Ortolan Buntings.

Farther east and south of the Danube one comes to the Wiener-wald (Vienna Woods) on the western outskirts of Vienna where there are Red-breasted Flycatchers, Honey Buzzards, Eagle Owls and Woodchat Shrikes. On the Danube between Vienna and Hainburg the breeding birds include Cormorant, Black Kite, Saker, Penduline Tit and River Warbler. In this north-eastern part of Lower Austria there is a good chance of seeing Great Bustards. These also occur in the Moosbrunn area, south of the Danube.

Styria and Carinthia

In the Murau area of Styria birds likely to be seen include Wall-creeper and Crag Martin, and in Upper Styria, Capercaillie, Black Grouse and Three-toed Woodpecker. The hilly country in the south-east has Lesser Kestrels, Rollers, and Hoopoes.

Carinthia also has the Lesser Kestrel, as well as the Black Kite, Red-footed Falcon, Hazel Grouse, Rock Partridge, Ural, Pygmy and Scops Owls, and Alpine Swift.

Burgenland

This is the flattest part of Austria, although in the north there are the Leitha mountains where the Lesser Spotted Eagle and Black Stork have been recorded, and Goshawks and Rollers are known to breed.

However, the greatest attraction in this area is the Neusiedler See, an area of water twenty-two miles long, and in many places up to eight miles broad, but on average scarcely more than three feet deep.

The flat country between the lake and the Hungarian border is the main breeding area in Austria for the Great Bustard.

The reed beds along the Neusiedler See are in places more than three miles wide and breeding birds include Great White and Little Egrets, Spoonbill, Purple Heron, Bittern, Little Bittern, Greylag Goose, many ducks and rails, as well as Bearded and Penduline Tits, Aquatic and Moustached Warblers, and Hoopoes.

Just over the border, to the north of Kapavar in Hungary, there are extensive alder woods with Black Stork, Imperial, Spotted and Lesser Spotted Eagles, Marsh, Montagu's and Hen Harriers, Red-footed Falcon, Lesser Kestrel, Hobby, Honey Buzzard and Goshawk.

The Netherlands

Ko Zweeres

H.J.S.

Spoonbill

Dutch professional and amateur ornithologists are united in the Nederlandse Ornithologische Unie (Dovenetallaan 231, Arnhem) which publishes two periodicals, *Ardea* and *Limosa*, both of which usually appear twice yearly. Bird protection is run by the Nederlandse Vereniging tot Bescherming van Vogels (Nachtegaalstraat 60 bis, Utrecht) which was established in 1899. This society owns or maintains a number of reserves, and publishes the magazine *Lepelaar* (six times a year). The periodical *Vogeljaar* (six times a year) is published by the Stichting het Vogeljaar (Prins Bernhardlaan 2, Ede/Gelderland). Friesland has a very active Bond van Friese Vogelbeschermingswachten, which publishes *Vanellus* (ten times a year).

The Royal Netherlands Natural History Society (Koninklijke Nederlandse Natuurhistorische Vereniging, Bureau KNNV, Hoogwoud, Noord-Holland) has a special section (Contactorgaan voor Vogelstudie) for those of its members interested in ornithology, including work on the population numbers of certain species.

Work on bird migration including ringing is controlled by the Vogeltrekstation Arnhem, a section of the Institute for Ecological Research (Kemperbergerweg 11, Arnhem). Anyone finding a ringed bird is urgently requested to inform the Vogeltrekstation, even if the ring (or wing tag) gives a different address.

THE NETHERLANDS

Although the Netherlands is one of the most densely populated countries in the world it is surprisingly rich in bird life, both in the number of species and the total number of birds. More than 370 species have been admitted to the Dutch list, of which more than 150 breed regularly, some 80 are regular visitors and 140 are vagrants.

Although the country as a whole is extremely flat there is a great variety of scenery, brought about by the intensive land use necessitated by the density of the human population.

Of the total acreage of nearly 14,000 square miles, considerably more than half is devoted to agriculture: 5,100 square miles are grasslands (of which one-tenth is very wet) and 4,700 square miles are arable. Marshes and wetlands, of which one would expect to find plenty in a country where large parts lie below sea level, take up nearly one-fifth of the total area, whereas less than one-tenth is woodland, only slightly more than the 1,200 square miles that are taken up by roads, railways and built-up areas (including gardens, parks, and so on).

A large proportion of Dutch agriculture is devoted to grassland for grazing. These meadows are to be found in the low-lying polders in the west (provinces of Noord-Holland, Zuid-Holland and Utrecht) and in Friesland in the north-east. Most are below sea level and would be flooded without the assistance of the many picturesque wind-driven mills, though their task is gradually being taken over by more efficient but less attractive motorised pumps.

The 1,000 square miles of the Waddenzee in the north are exceptionally rich in bird life. However, these tidal sandbanks and mud-flats are under perpetual threat of enclosure. Such enclosures immediately reduce the bird population, because it is the tides that make the astounding wealth of marine life possible, and this in turn provides the birds with a seemingly inexhaustible amount of food. The dunes along the North Sea are another special feature of the

Low Countries. Much of this part of the country is still unspoilt, particularly the islands in the south-west, the area between the Hook of Holland and Den Helder, and the Friesian islands in the north. In some places this belt is up to five miles wide. Between the Hague and Alkmaar there are large catchment areas from which drinking water for the towns is drained. This has resulted in a considerable lowering of the water table, which has adversely influenced the vegetation and has also been responsible for a marked decrease in the bird population. However, water from the Rhine is now transported to the dunes through pipelines, and irrigation schemes have created some fine lakes which immediately attracted numerous birds. Species that had all but disappeared have returned in surprising numbers. These lakes have also proved to be very attractive for wintering ducks, and it is here that in autumn and spring Ospreys from Scandinavia may linger for weeks.

Marshlands and shallow lakes are mainly to be found in the provinces of Noord-Holland, Zuid-Holland and Utrecht, though some of the most attractive are situated in the north-western part of Overijssel and in Friesland. Quite a few of these lakes originated in former times when the Dutch farmers gave the wind a chance to enlarge the pits they made when digging for peat.

The eastern and south-eastern parts of the Netherlands are slightly hilly, and there are some woodlands, mostly coniferous. Here, too, are to be found the last remnants of the once endless heathlands. In the eastern parts of the province of Gelderland there are some very fine deciduous woods, though none is extensive.

The extreme south-east of the Netherlands, the province of Limburg, has fine rolling country and even boasts a real mountain of about 1,000 feet, though this is shared with Germany and Belgium.

Some of the finest meadows are to be found just outside Amsterdam. Numerous Black-tailed Godwits nest all round the city and some even within its own boundaries. People living in some of the new blocks of flats on the outskirts can watch the godwits in the meadows just across the road.

Expansion of the city, together with the construction of new roads, more harbours and more factories, threatens these birds of the meadows especially, the most numerous of them being Lapwings, Black-tailed Godwits, Oystercatchers, Redshanks, Ruffs and Snipe. A visit to the Zaanstreek or Waterland, both to the north of Amsterdam, gives a good idea of the numbers that nest in the low-lying meadows, some of which scarcely rise above the level of the surrounding ditches and are often flooded in winter.

In the Zaanstreek the Netherlands Society for the Protection of Birds (De Ruyterkade 100, Amsterdam) owns a reserve near the picturesque village of Westzaan. Visitors are not allowed to enter the reserve itself, but from the towpath along the dyke to the west, that starts near the tall water tower of Westzaan, they will be able to see godwits and their young on the meadows and watch Black Terns nesting among the vegetation. They will hear Snipe drumming and Bitterns booming, and see Ruffs displaying.

Other localities with numerous godwits are Vlaardingen (the Vlietland), to the west of Rotterdam; the Eempolders, north of the motorway from Baarn to Hoevelaken; the meadows north and south of Nijkerk; the Mastenbroek polder east of the old town of Kampen; and most of the low-lying parts of Friesland. A recent estimate of the number of Black-tailed Godwits nesting in the Netherlands gave a figure of 80,000 pairs.

As already mentioned some of the finest dunes are to be found on the Friesian Islands. One of the dominating species there is the Herring Gull, which has large colonies on most of the islands. One of the finest is in the Boschplaat Reserve, where conducted tours are possible, though these will not bring one near the small colony of Spoonbills. The latter settled there quite recently and are heavily guarded. Common Gulls are to be found in relatively small but steadily growing colonies. On the Boschplaat some Lesser Black-backed Gulls normally nest among the Herring Gulls, and the two often interbreed. On a few of the islands there are large colonies of Black-headed Gulls, but terns have become scarce. The small uninhabited island of Griend in the Waddenzee is the last stronghold of the Sandwich Tern. Until recently the Netherlands had more than 40,000 pairs of these birds but their numbers have now come down to less than a thousand. Common Terns too have decreased quite considerably, though small colonies of this species are still to be found on most of the islands. Little Terns, never numerous, have now become extremely scarce. Arctic Terns can be found nesting among the Common Terns.

The Curlew has become rather scarce on the dunes, but there are many Oystercatchers, both on the dunes and in the polders. Quite a few pairs of Kentish Plovers nest on the island of Texel. In early summer parts of this state reserve are closed to visitors.

To the south of this area are the fine lakes of the Muyen, another state reserve, where there is a small Spoonbill colony which is sadly declining in numbers. Here again admittance is restricted, but one can join a conducted tour and, from a safe distance, observe these beautiful birds and Montagu's Harriers. On some of the Friesian Islands the Hen Harrier also nests but none of the three harriers is numerous any more.

Although their numbers vary considerably from year to year, normally a few Short-eared Owls can usually be found nesting on the Friesian Islands, and there is a chance to see one when visiting the Bollekamer Reserve on Texel.

Near the dunes there are small woods in which numerous thrushes, tits, warblers (among them the Icterine) and finches nest. Bullfinches, however, will not be found as they are comparatively scarce in the Netherlands. Lesser Redpolls have nested recently on Texel, Vlieland and Terschelling, and elsewhere on the dunes Wheatears nest in rabbit holes and there may be an odd Grasshopper Warbler. Savi's Warbler can be heard singing near the Muyen.

Between the Hook of Holland and Den Helder there are fine areas of dune country open to visitors, e.g. just north of the Hague near Wassenaar, west of Haarlem and between Wijk aan Zee and Petten. For most of these a permit is required and this can be bought at the entrances; visitors have to keep to the paths.

In the Zwanenwater near Callantsoog there is another colony of Spoonbills and these can be observed at their nests from the dunes nearby. This privately owned reserve also has a few pairs of Marsh Warblers.

The De Kennemerduinen National Park to the west of Haarlem has a fine bird lake, which is one of the few places in the Netherlands where Black-necked Grebes nest. There is also a colony of Black-headed and Common Gulls, among which a pair of Mediterranean Gulls occasionally nests.

The Tufted Duck, a rare breeder until the second world war, has recently colonised some of these dunes and also other parts of the country. In these mainland dunes harriers have become scarce, but there are still fair numbers of Hobbies and Kestrels. Red-backed Shrikes are rare breeding birds.

On the landward side of these dunes the Willow Warbler is the dominant species, together with numerous Nightingales, Tree Pipits, Woodlarks and many other song birds. Nightjars, however, have become scarce and Stone Curlews have completely vanished. The well-wooded grounds of some of the fine houses along these dunes are very rich in bird life, mainly the small song birds. The Short-toed Treecreeper may be seen here—it is the only treecreeper to be found in the Netherlands.

On the islands in the south-west there are some very fine dunes, most of them rich in bird life. Goeree is, at present, the least spoilt of these islands and, together with Overflakkee, it offers a wide variety of scenery that makes a visit very rewarding. The best time to visit the dunes is in the breeding season, though in autumn they offer a good opportunity for watching migration.

Another unique part of the Netherlands is the Waddenzee, where literally hundreds of thousands of birds, mainly waders, gulls and ducks, are to be found at all times of the year. The visitor should go in July, August or September to see the waders on the mudflats and sandbanks. Some of the best sites for observation are on the landward side of the Friesian Islands and along the coast of Friesland and Groningen. Along the Dutch side of the Dollart in the extreme north-east hundreds of pairs of Avocets nest, often forming small colonies, and up to 18,000 have been counted in autumn.

Between Den Helder and the former island of Wieringen there are also some good places for watching waders. In late summer up to a hundred Spoonbills can often be seen here, and shortly before sunset dozens of Gull-billed Terns cross the dyke between Noord-Holland and Wieringen on their way to a communal roost near Den Helder or on Texel. There they spend the night together with large numbers of other terns and gulls, including hundreds or even thousands of

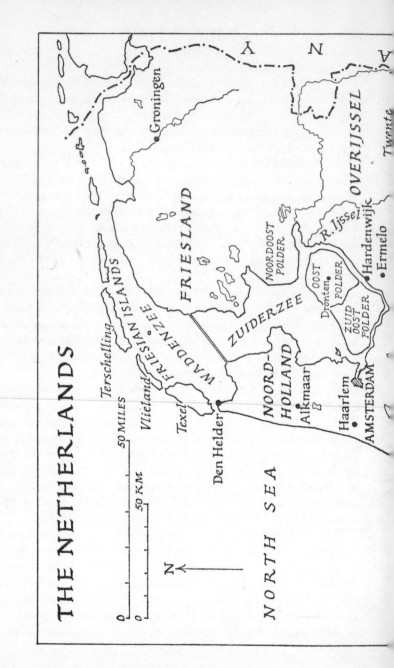

THE NETHERLANDS

50 MILES
0

50 KM
0

N

NORTH SEA

Terschelling

Vlieland

Texel

FRIESIAN ISLANDS

WADDENZEE

FRIESE ZEE

Den Helder

NOORD-
HOLLAND

Alkmaar

Haarlem

AMSTERDAM

ZUIDERZEE

FRIESLAND

Groningen

NOORDOOST
POLDER

OOST
POLDER

Dronten

ZUID
OOST
POLDER

R. Ijssel

OVERIJSSEL

Hardenwijk

Ermelo

Twente

Y

N

A

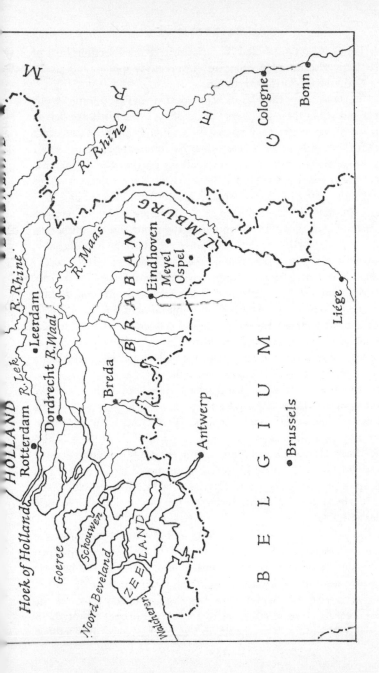

Black Terns. The Gull-billed Tern is an irregular breeding bird of the Netherlands, but a few dozen of them seem to spend a few weeks in the Netherlands during migration.

The inlets between the islands in the south-west harbour numerous waders and when the sea covers the mudflats these birds are driven on to the shore where they spend their time sleeping or preening. Tens of thousands of birds may then be found together on a few acres, as for instance in the Kroonspolders on the isle of Vlieland.

Many of these species can also be found on the artificial mudflats around some of the big cities, such as Amsterdam, Utrecht and Rotterdam. It may be dangerous to enter these areas, but if one sits quietly on one of the dykes surrounding them one can see numerous waders, particularly in late summer, including Greenshank, Redshank and Spotted Redshank, Wood Sandpiper, Ruff, Black-tailed Godwit, Little Ringed, Ringed, Kentish and Grey Plovers, and many different ducks. Little and Temminck's Stints and Broad-billed Sandpipers mix here with Knots, Dunlins and Snipe.

In their early stages the new artificial polders of the Zuiderzee, or IJsselmeer, also offer much the same kind of habitat and, though a long way from the coast, may attract the same species, including a few rarities such as the Black-winged Stilt.

Immediately after the water has been pumped out of these polders reed is sown which quickly covers the area, though there will still be very many shallow lagoons. Common Terns and even Sandwich Terns may nest there and hundreds of pairs of Avocets will also settle. Marsh Harriers build their nests in the reed beds and even the odd pair of Greylag Geese has been found breeding. Bearded Tits build up large populations and Spotted Crakes, Water Rails, Coots and Moorhens are abundant. Bitterns may appear and also several species of ducks.

In spring and autumn Greenshanks and Spotted Redshanks are numerous, as well as the commoner waders. Black Terns can be seen here by the thousands and in August one or other of the lagoons may have hundreds of Little Gulls, which interrupt their migration for weeks on end. In August many Greylag Geese arrive to stay for several weeks before moving on to southern Europe, although in mild winters quite a few remain in the Netherlands. In October their place is taken by White-fronted and Barnacle Geese. At this time a few Caspian Terns also pass through the Netherlands, along the beaches of the Veluwemeer. Ospreys may linger for a while and in winter, when quite a few Bewick's Swans are to be found on this stretch of water, a White-tailed Eagle can sometimes be seen.

Both Teal and Garganey collect on the lagoons in the new polders in astonishing numbers, together with smaller gatherings of Pintail, Wigeon and Gadwall.

A few pairs of Hen Harriers also nest in the new polders as do Short-eared Owls, whose nests have been found here even in March. Nest boxes put up for Kestrels attract astonishing numbers of these predators and some may even house a pair of Long-eared Owls, all drawn by the great numbers of voles that immediately start to colonise a new polder.

Round Dronten, a new town in the Oostelijk Flevoland polder, Dotterels have most surprisingly been found nesting on farmland, below sea level.

As the polders are brought under cultivation they become less attractive to most species of birds, though grasslands may still have numerous Lapwings, Black-tailed Godwits, Redshanks, Oyster-catchers and so on. In the meantime another polder will be under construction and will soon attract more birds. The best way to watch the birds on these polders is from the dykes or from a car, as the birds are used to traffic and will allow a car to approach quite close.

The best areas of marshland are found mainly in the west and north. The Naardermeer Nature Reserve is a fine example of this type of habitat, but Botshol, just north of Vinkeveen, is almost as good and, although it has no Spoonbills, it can offer Little Bitterns and Red-crested Pochards, which do not normally nest in the Naar-dermeer. Apart, however, from Spoonbills, the Naardermeer has colonies of Purple Herons, tree-nesting Cormorants, Marsh Harriers, Bitterns, Black Terns and many kinds of warblers, including Grass-hopper, Savi's, Great Reed and Marsh. In the duck decoy of this reserve (which can be entered only for scientific purposes) it is possible to hear and probably see Golden Orioles, of which three or four pairs normally nest in the fine old trees.

In the Nieuwkoopse Plassen, some miles south-west of the Naar-dermeer, there are a few dozen pairs of Little Bitterns. In a privately owned reserve (visitors not admitted) in the eastern part of the Plassen, near the small village of Noorden, there is what may well be the largest colony of Purple Herons in western Europe; glimpses of these may be seen from the road. Black Terns also nest here, but the Marsh Harriers have unfortunately disappeared.

East of Gouda the Reeuwijkse Plassen provides another favourite breeding area for the Little Bittern and also for Black Terns, and Great Reed and Savi's Warblers.

North of Utrecht there is another fine marshy area with numerous Black Terns and most of the other species already mentioned. Icter-ine Warblers can be heard singing in coppices and orchards near to farmhouses.

Near Twente, in the eastern part of the province of Overijssel, there is a different type of marshland. Here, with luck, one may find the Bluethroat nesting, probably at Bergvennen, near Lattrop. Sometimes Great Grey Shrikes also nest here and in autumn Cranes alight to spend the night on the farmlands. The same type of heath-land marsh occurs in the eastern part of the province of Brabant and in the adjoining part of the province of Limburg. The state reserve of Grote Peel, near the villages of Ospel and Meyel, offers the best chances in the Netherlands to see Bluethroats, though one has to go rather early in the season (late April or early May) to find them in full display. This reserve also harbours a few pairs of Bitterns, Little Bitterns and Marsh and Montagu's Harriers and sometimes Short-eared Owls. A Night Heron may be seen fishing in one of the lakes or ditches, for there is a jealously guarded small colony some-where near this reserve. Here, too, there is a large and noisy colony of Black-headed Gulls, and Black Terns nest in some of the more remote lagoons.

Both in the Grote Peel and on the Strabrechtse Heide, another state reserve just east of Geldrop near Eindhoven, Cranes alight in autumn and sometimes spend a few days in the reserves or on farm-land in the vicinity.

In this part of the country, too, one might hear and see Yellow-hammers and Corn Buntings, sometimes Reed Buntings and occasionally an Ortolan Bunting. The last can also be found else-where, but only in the east along the German border, e.g. near Ter Apel in the province of Groningen and in eastern Gelderland, near Ratum, but it is nowhere common.

Though there are canals and ditches almost everywhere in the Netherlands, natural streams have become very rare and most of the few remaining ones are badly polluted. A few clear streams are still to be found along the German border, e.g. at Twente, in eastern Gelder-land, Limburg and Brabant. Here the number of Kingfishers is extremely small, especially after severe winters, but the Grey Wag-tails seem to maintain themselves satisfactorily. Dippers no longer nest in the Netherlands, though the odd vagrant is seen.

Also in the Veluwe, near Harderwijk, there are a few streams where a Grey Wagtail can sometimes be seen, and this area is one of the strongholds of the Black Woodpecker, which has shown some increase in numbers due, probably, to the disappearance of the Goshawk from the region. To the east of Ermelo and near Hulshorst there are some fine inland sand dunes where one may find Tawny Pipits and hear Tree Pipits and Woodlarks.

The Biesbosch, south-east of Dordrecht, has extensive areas of willow, the nearest thing to virgin woodland to be found in the Netherlands. Here there is a small colony of nesting Night Herons, as well as Bitterns, Little Bitterns and Grey Herons. Bluethroats can be heard, Golden Orioles nest in the willows that are flooded twice a day, and many kinds of small song birds may be seen. Be-cause of the tricky tides visitors will need a local guide to visit the Biesbosch, but in summer small pleasure boats run sightseeing tours from Drimmelen; at that time of year, however, one misses the skeins of geese that arrive in the autumn. Greylags come in August, followed by the hundreds of White-fronted Geese that winter in the area. The closing of the inlets in the south-western delta will, in a few years, stop the tidal movements in the Biesbosch and cause considerable changes in the whole character of the area, so many bird species may leave.

No mention has been made so far of the few pairs of White Storks still to be found nesting in the Netherlands. Unfortunately their numbers are decreasing so fast that within a few years none may be left. One of their last strongholds is to be found just east of the Bies-bosch, where villages such as Hank, Dussen, Meeuwen and Dronge-len, as well as Almerk, still have White Storks nesting. To the north, Leerdam has storks nesting on its town hall, and at Molenaarsgraaf, to the west, they nest on the church.

In autumn the Netherlands offer marvellous opportunities for watching migration, because many migrants tend to travel along the coast. On some days in October literally hundreds of thousands of migrants, mainly Chaffinches, Bramblings, Greenfinches, Starlings, crows, Meadow Pipits and Skylarks can be seen, hurrying to their winter quarters in the south of England, or southern Europe, or Africa. It is difficult to advise on the best time for observation, though it will normally be in the latter half of October, and especially after some days of rain, storm or fog, when most migration is halted. When such a period is followed by a sunny day with a gentle breeze from the south-west, there is almost certain to be a steady stream of migrants pouring along the coast. But any day with mild southerly winds will bring at least some migration.

Most migrants tend to fly over the outer sand dunes, nearest the sea, so the best observation points will be on these dunes, preferably north of one of the coastal villages or towns. One has to rise early, because the largest numbers pass at or immediately after sunrise.

In winter the Netherlands harbour tens of thousands of geese, whose numbers have been growing steadily in recent years, perhaps because many of their former wintering grounds in north-western Germany have been drained and have thus lost their attraction for the birds. The first geese to arrive in autumn are the Greylags, some even in August. In recent years gaggles of more than a hundred have spent the summer in south-western Friesland, where they also spend their moulting period when they are unable to fly. In September there are hundreds of Greylag Geese in the Biesbosch and often also in the area between Willemstad and Moerdijk, along the Hollandsch Diep. Normally the White-fronted Geese do not start to arrive until well into October and most of them come even later, sometimes not until January.

If one stays at Heerenveen, there is a good chance of seeing geese along the road between this town and Groningen. There may be thousands of Whitefronts, mixed with smaller numbers of Barnacle and Pink-footed Geese. These can also be seen near the lakes north of Joure, and to the east of Lemmer. Pink-footed Geese also collect around Workum and Piaam and in other parts of Friesland. Barnacle Geese, in gaggles of up to ten thousand or more, may be seen near the village of Anjum in the north-east of Friesland.

Brent Geese have become scarce in the Netherlands since the eel grass on which they like to feed has all but disappeared. But a few hundred still winter in the Waddenzee, mainly near the Boschplaat on Terschelling, the Posthuiswad (Vlieland) and the saltings of the Eendracht (Texel). Some stay there well into April or even May. A favourite haunt of theirs at that time of year is the bird reserve at De Bol on Texel, where hundreds can be observed from the dyke when the tide is in.

Large numbers of Whitefronts can also be seen in western Brabant, in the triangle between Moerdijk, Willemstad and Breda, often together with Barnacle Geese. The same holds for the area south of Goes and for Puttinge, south-west of the ferry harbour of Perkpolder. The numbers of Barnacle Geese are smaller there, but there is a better chance to see Bean Geese.

Belgium

Ko Zweeres

Goshawk

In the Flemish-speaking part of the country the active organisation is the Ornithological Society De Wielewaal (Graatakker 13, Turnhout) which publishes the monthly *De Wielewaal* and has several local branches which organise excursions and lectures. In the French-speaking part the corresponding body is the Aves Society (De Brocquevillelaan 250/5M, Brussels), whose periodical *Aves* appears six times a year.

Scientific research is co-ordinated by the Ecology and Nature Conservation section of the Koninklijk Instituut voor Natuurwetenschappen (Vautierstraat 31, Brussels), in close co-operation with the Society of Belgian Nature and Bird Reserves (same address). The Ministry of Agriculture has published a booklet with the title *De Natuurreservaten van Belgie*. The main ornithological periodical is *De Giervalk/Le Gerfaut* (quarterly).

If one finds a ringed bird in Belgium, the ring should be sent to Koninklijk Belgisch Instituut van Natuurwetenschappen, Vautierstraat 31, Brussels IV, Belgium.

BELGIUM

In its relatively small area of 12,000 square miles, Belgium has a surprising variety of scenery. Lower Belgium (Flanders and the province of Antwerp) is nearly as flat as the Netherlands, Middle Belgium has fine, undulating country with hills of up to nearly a thousand feet, and the Ardennes in Upper Belgium rise in some parts to more than 2,000 feet.

Along the coast there is a narrow belt of sand dunes that has lost most of its attraction for birds, partly because of its narrowness but mainly because of the numerous villas, bungalows, hotels and all the other ugly paraphernalia of seaside resorts. Another and far more attractive part of Lower Belgium is the Kempenland region, along the Dutch border, where shallow lakes and heathlands are still to be found. The Hautes Fagnes in the north-east of Upper Belgium are characterised by marshland. The extreme south-east of Upper Belgium, in the southernmost part of the province of Luxembourg, known as Belgian Lorraine, differs distinctly from the Ardennes on account of its different geological origin.

In comparison with most other countries in western Europe, Belgium is well wooded, the woodlands covering nearly 20 per cent of the total area of the country. Most of these are in the Ardennes in Upper Belgium, though Middle Belgium has some very fine woods.

In 1967, Belgian ornithologists compiled their first check-list, intentionally modelling it on the Dutch check-list of 1962 to facilitate comparison. The total numbers of species are almost the same, but quite surprisingly there are considerable differences in the composition of the avifaunas of the two countries.

Thus, Belgium has considerably less than a hundred pairs of Great Crested Grebes whereas there are at least 3,300 pairs in the Netherlands. The Purple Heron has nested only once in Belgium (1943) but there are several heronries in the Netherlands with a total of at least 1,000 pairs. In the case of the Black-tailed Godwit less than 250 pairs nest in Belgium, but some 80,000 pairs in the Netherlands. On the other hand Belgium still has a thousand pairs of Buzzards and probably 150 pairs of Honey Buzzards, whereas the populations of these two species in the Netherlands are at the most one-tenth of these totals.

Lower Belgium includes the coast, with its fine sandy beaches and narrow belt of sand dunes. Partly because of the shortness of the coastline, but primarily on account of the intensive use made of the dunes for recreational purposes, waders, gulls and terns are scarce in Belgium. However, the Zwin reserve near the Dutch border has tidal sands and mudflats, where waders will linger for days or even weeks during spring and autumn migration. Kentish Plovers and Avocets nest there and the bird sanctuary administered by Count L. Lippens has a great number of waders, and also some semi-domesticated White Storks and a gaggle of Greylag Geese. This sanctuary is open to visitors.

Further down the coast, near Nieuwpoort, the mouth of the river Yser also attracts a lot of waders, mainly in spring and autumn, as well as gulls and terns. In early autumn quite a few Little Gulls can often be seen here.

About the only other area in Belgium where waders and gulls can be seen is the lower Scheldt region, where plovers and Avocets nest and non-breeding waders are present nearly all the year round, quite a few on the mudflats near Antwerp.

A special attraction of Lower Belgium in winter is the reserve for geese at Damme, near Bruges. Here there may be thousands of White-fronted Geese, often intermingled with hundreds of Barnacle Geese, and a few Bean Geese. Small groups of these species, and also of Brent Geese, may be seen in winter on the lower Scheldt.

In Flanders there was, until recently, a small colony of tree-nesting Cormorants near Meetkerke. West Flanders is also the only part of Belgium with nesting Grey Herons, but the numbers are declining.

Land birds of the coastal area include the Crested Lark (in the docks at Ostend and all along the coast), a few pairs of Hoopoes (around Knokke), and Icterine Warblers. In winter small flocks of Shore Larks and lapland and Snow Buntings can be found on the coastal dunes and in the lower Scheldt region. Kempenland in the northern part of Lower Belgium deserves special mention. Here the Hoopoe can be seen, although it is very rare as a breeding bird. Green, Great and Lesser Spotted Woodpeckers may be expected and sometimes even the Black Woodpecker and Wryneck. The Tawny Pipit is a rare breeding bird of the area, greatly outnumbered by the Tree Pipit and, in suitable habitats, by the Meadow Pipit. White and Blue-headed Wagtails are fairly numerous in the Kempenland region, but the Great Grey Shrike is much less common. Wheatears and Stonechats breed freely and so does the Black Redstart. Bluethroats and Grasshopper Warblers can occasionally be seen. Other warblers in this area are the Reed, Great Reed, Marsh and Icterine, and the Crested Tit is fairly common.

Yellowhammers and Corn Buntings are common in the Kempenland area, where the Ortolan Bunting has its last stronghold, and the marshy parts have Reed Buntings. Here there is also a good chance of hearing the mellow call of the Golden Oriole.

Of the more conspicuous species the Great Crested Grebe is scarce and the Kempenland is about the only place where one might have some chance of finding the Black-necked Grebe breeding. Teals nest in the same habitat and there may be an odd pair of Tufted Ducks, though this is still an irregular breeding bird in Belgium. The Pochard is also a scarce breeding bird, and it is only near Kalmthout that one will have a reasonable chance of finding Shelducks nesting. The Mute Swans seen in the Kempenland (or elsewhere in Belgium) will be in collections of waterfowl or will have escaped from them.

Sparrowhawks nest in the eastern part of the Kempenland, where there are also a few pairs of Goshawks and Marsh Harriers. The Hen Harrier has become very scarce, but perhaps a dozen pairs of Montagu's Harriers nest in the Kempenland. Hobby and Kestrel are the most numerous of the birds of prey, though even their numbers seem to be decreasing.

There is a chance to see the Black Grouse in the Kempenland though this species is nowhere common. In autumn Cranes linger for a day or two on farmland near one of the shallow lakes, where earlier in the season Water Rails and even Spotted Crakes may have nested. The Corncrake has decreased considerably but may still be heard calling in the cornfields of the eastern part of the Kempenland.

Waders are nowhere common in this part of Belgium, though this is one of the few regions where Curlews and Black-tailed Godwits nest, and possibly an odd pair of Redshanks.

The Black-headed Gull is a common breeding bird here, and there are a few scattered small colonies of Black Terns. The White-winged and Whiskered Terns have both been recorded in the Kempenland.

Stock Doves, Woodpigeons, and Turtle and Collared Doves are all quite numerous, the last having been first recorded at Molenbeersel in the province of Limburg in 1952.

Barn, Little, Tawny (rarely) and Long-eared Owls may be found nesting and it is the Kempenland again that can claim three of the four breeding records for the Short-eared Owl in Belgium. The Kempenland is, however, only part of Lower Belgium, though probably the most rewarding from the bird-watcher's point of view.

In Middle Belgium the provinces of Brabant and Hainaut offer some attractions, among them the fine area of marshland near Harchies on the French border. Hainaut has a fair number of Buzzards nesting in its woods and Brabant is still supposed to have some ten pairs of Sparrowhawks, though Goshawks have all but disappeared. In Hainaut one might be lucky to see one of the few remaining Marsh Harriers and in August and September Ospreys on passage may linger for some days near the well-stocked fish ponds of Middle Belgium.

Waders are scarce in Middle Belgium, though some migrating Spotted Redshanks might be seen here and perhaps a Greenshank or a Little Stint.

Upper Belgium comprises the provinces of Liège, Namur and Luxembourg. Here there are extensive woods with hundreds of pairs of Buzzards and Honey Buzzards. There are also a few Goshawks. In the province of Luxembourg isolated pairs of Red Kites may sometimes succeed in raising young, and the Black Kite has been found nesting. The province of Luxembourg also has a few pairs of Montagu's Harriers breeding there, but the last of the Peregrines that nested until recently in Liège and Namur have all but disappeared. Kestrels and Hobbies seem to succeed in keeping their footing, some of the former nesting on cliff faces along the shallow rivers.

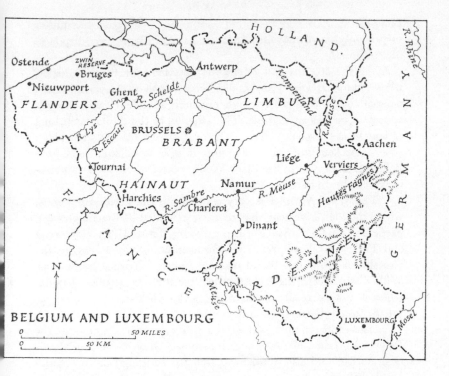

BELGIUM AND LUXEMBOURG

0 ———————— 50 MILES

0 ———————— 50 KM

Baraque Michel in the Hautes Fagnes is the only area where Red
Grouse may possibly be seen, as efforts to introduce them elsewhere
seem to have failed. Hazel Grouse are scarce breeding birds in the
province of Luxembourg and in the southern parts of Liège and
Namur; their numbers seldom exceed 250 pairs. The Woodcock
may occasionally be heard in these woodlands.

Woodpigeons and Turtle Doves are numerous in Upper Belgium,
but Collared Doves are less common visitors and seem to prefer
the area west of Meuse and Sambre.

It is already more than half a century since the Eagle Owl last
nested in Belgium, and it is now an extremely rare straggler. Tengmalm's Owls nested once (1965) in the province of Liège and though
there is a slight tendency for this species to extend its breeding range
to the west it is unlikely to become a regular visitor. Little and

Long-eared Owls may be found nesting in this region but rather surprisingly the Tawny Owl does not seem to like the woodlands of the Ardennes.

Along the streams and rivers one may look for the Kingfisher, whose numbers vary greatly, depending upon the severity of the winters. Grey Wagtails (though nowhere abundant) and Dippers appear to be less susceptible. The Dippers of the Ardennes belong of course to the central European form, which has a darker belly.

Woodpeckers are fairly common in the woodlands of Upper Belgium, among them the Black Woodpecker, whose loud hammering can be heard in early spring.

The Wood Warbler is very common in the deciduous woods, where the Pied Flycatcher has recently extended its breeding range, particularly in the province of Luxembourg. Crested Tits, Goldcrests and Firecrests show preference for coniferous woods, where the Crossbill is sometimes found nesting, mainly in spruce plantations. With a few exceptions the Ardennes are the only part of Belgium where the Treecreeper nests, whereas the Short-toed Treecreeper is to be found all over the country.

In the southernmost part of the province of Luxembourg, the Belgian Lorraine, one may occasionally see Great Grey and Woodchat Shrikes and also Serins, but the Cirl Bunting only breeds irregularly in this area.

Luxembourg

Ko Zweeres

Buzzards

Bird protection measures in the Grand Duchy are well organised and are in many ways similar to those used in Germany and the Netherlands. Field work is supervised by the Luxemburger Landesverband für Vogelkunde und Vogelschutz, which publishes the periodical *Regulus* six times annually. Information can also be obtained from the Conseil Supérieur de la Nature, Direction des Eaux et Forêts (25 rue Philippe 11, Luxembourg).

There is no ringing centre, so if one finds a ringed bird in Luxembourg the ring should be sent to the country of origin.

LUXEMBOURG

Luxembourg, the smallest of the Benelux countries, has an area of about 1,000 square miles, almost 30 per cent of which is covered in woodland, both deciduous and coniferous. Most of these woods are on the northern plateau, which rises in some places to nearly 1,700 feet and is intersected by a few deep river valleys. The climate of this part of Luxembourg is a little harsher than that of the southern part, but it is still mild enough for some wine-growing.

Luxembourg has a surprising population of birds of prey, both in the north and in the south. The most abundant is the Buzzard, though its numbers have decreased recently. The Honey Buzzard is also seen quite frequently but the Goshawk and Sparrowhawk less often. The Peregrine and the Hobby no longer nest in Luxembourg, but there are still fair numbers of Kestrels.

Black Kites are seen mainly in the southern areas and, where the river Mosel forms the eastern border with Germany, they can often be seen scavenging along its banks, sometimes in small parties, particularly when they have just returned from their winter quarters. The Red Kite is much rarer, but a few pairs may still nest in the south. Here, too, one should be able to find the Great Grey, Woodchat and Red-backed shrikes all of which nest in this country, though only the last can be said to be common.

Serins can be heard singing even in the parks of the capital, often in company with Goldfinches and Black Redstarts. These three birds are also to be found elsewhere in the country, as are Hawfinches and Bullfinches, the latter often showing some preference for older coniferous woods, where Crossbills also occur. Yellowhammers and sometimes Corn Buntings can be heard in areas where the woods are interspersed with farmland.

Woodpeckers thrive in this well-wooded country. Apart from the commoner Green, Great and Lesser Spotted, it is possible to see the Black Woodpecker and occasionally the Grey-headed and Middle Spotted Woodpeckers, though the last two are not common.

Rather surprisingly the Nuthatch does not seem to be confined to deciduous woods, but may be seen in coniferous woods as well, and has even been found nesting in holes in rocky outcrops. Treecreepers and Short-toed Treecreepers also occur.

In orchards, especially in the southern parts of the country, one may hear and even see the Golden Oriole, whose bright colours do not prevent it from being well camouflaged. Here, too, there is a chance to see the Hoopoe which is, however, far from common.

Woodpigeons are quite common throughout the country, but Stock Doves far less so. Turtle Doves are to be found in fair numbers and Collared Doves have become established in the last decade.

As might be expected, waders, gulls and terns are hardly to be found in Luxembourg, nor are herons and grebes. The Hazel Grouse occurs in the northern woods but there is little chance of seeing one. Warblers and thrushes are plentiful, as are most of the other woodland birds, including the Crested Tit.

France

R.-D. Etchécopar

Flamingos

including the Channel Islands

E. D. H. Johnson

The three main ornithological societies are La Société Ornithologique de France (Musée National d'Histoire Naturelle, 55 Rue de Buffon, Paris 5e), which publishes *L'Oiseau* (quarterly) and *La Revue Française d'Ornithologie*; La Société d'Etudes Ornithologiques (34 Rue Hamelin, Paris) which publishes *Alauda* (quarterly); and Le Groupe des Jeunes Ornithologistes (129 Boulevard Saint-Germain, Paris) which is mainly concerned with detailed field studies and with educational aspects.

Le Laboratoire d'Ornithologie du Musée National d'Histoire Naturelle has the second largest collection of skins in Europe. Le Centre de Recherches sur la Migration des Mammifères et des Oiseaux (same address) studies migration, and La Ligue pour la Protection des Oiseaux is concerned with bird protection. There are several research stations which can often assist visitors. These include the Laboratoire des Eyzies de Tayac, the Musée de la Mer in Biarritz, the Laboratoires Maritimes de Banyuls et Dinard, La Tour du Valet in the Camargue and the Station Ornithologique d'Ouessant.

Bird-watchers planning to visit France are advised to get in touch with the Laboratoire d'Ornithologie du Musée National d'Histoire Naturelle, 55 rue de Buffon, Paris 5e, which can give detailed advice.

If one finds a ringed bird in France, the ring should be sent to the same address.

FRANCE

France is a country of great geophysical variety, having almost all the diverse habitats found in the countries covered in this book. It is exceeded only by Finland and Sweden in the extent of its forested area, and it boasts many fine and often spectacular rivers, including the Sâone/Rhône, one of the few great north-south valleys of Europe. With the influence of the Atlantic and Mediterranean, the country offers a great variety of climatic conditions, which naturally affects the bird populations. Within a relatively restricted area one can see typical northern European birds and, especially south of the Loire, species characteristic of the Mediterranean area. France therefore is extremely interesting to the bird-watcher, not least because it is relatively sparsely populated.

The important mountain systems are the Alps, Jura, Vosges, Pyrenees and the large southern-central complex, the Massif Central. Next to these mountain masses there are low-lying plains and some fertile regions, such as La Beauce (centre at Vendôme) and La Brie (east-south-east of Paris), and desert-like areas such as La Crau (at the mouth of the Rhône and just east of the Camargue).

Though diminished over the centuries there are still forested areas which retain their original characteristics, and indeed a notable feature of the country is the great variety of the woodland vegetation. Old Hercynian masses like the Auvergne (Massif Central) and Brittany harbour a type of wild life hard to find today except perhaps in certain remote parts of Scotland.

The striking variation in landscape is matched by the diversity of its vegetation. Typical scrub (maquis), flat country (campagne), regions of scattered woodland (bocage) and wasteland (garrigue) are all to be found in France, which also has areas of good agricultural country. Such regions as the Camargue, the Cevennes and Les Landes are examples of quite different types of wild habitat.

The coast varies from the cliffs and rocks of Brittany, to the dunes of Les Landes, and the lagoons and marshes of Languedoc and the Rhône delta. With a coastline of some 2,000 miles, France offers good opportunities for the observation of sea birds and their migration.

Destructive sports are a real menace to the birds of France. About two million French people shoot, the highest concentration in Europe, and there are as many people shooting wildfowl in France as in all the rest of the Continent. The game warden service is well organised, especially in the northern part of the country, but unfortunately it still tends to destroy systematically the birds that prey on game, and some species would already have died out were it not for the refuge provided by the extensive barren and uninhabited areas in the south and centre of the country.

France has a number of different types of reserves. Some such as the Camargue, Les Sept-Iles and Le Cap-Sizun are strictly reserves, while others are areas designated as of national interest where forestry and agricultural development are carried on but bird life is completely protected, as in the Le Mercantour sanctuary. There are also smaller reserves such as the sanctuary at La Pointe d'Arçay, the aim of which is to provide stopping places and shelter, especially during the breeding season. Some of the sporting associations organise temporary reserves by dividing their territory into three parts, each part in rotation being left dormant for three years. The following is a list of some of the sanctuaries of most interest to bird-watchers.

La Mare Sainte-Opportune (Marais Vernier, Seine-Maritime)

A small reserve of 371 acres, created by the Conseil Supérieur de la Chasse in 1956, and directed by Monsieur Dubos, 37 Quai de la Douane, Harfleur, Seine-Maritime. Its particular aim is to protect the breeding of wildfowl.

Rocher de Tombelaine, Ile des Landes, Grand Chevret

These are small coastal reserves along the Gulf of Saint Malo. The Rocher de Tombelaine is not far from Mont Saint-Michel and the other two are close to the summer resort of Dinard. Contact the Laboratoire Maritime de Dinard for permission to visit.

Les Sept-Iles

The Ile Rouzic in Les Sept-Iles, lying off the Station de Perros-Guirec in the Côtes-du-Nord, is the oldest sanctuary in France, created in 1912. This island belongs to the Conseil Supérieur de la Chasse, but the sanctuary is administered by the Ligue pour la Protection des Oiseaux. Although it covers only forty-three acres, its contour makes it a splendid breeding place for such pelagic birds as Razorbills, Guillemots and Puffins. These nest hardly anywhere else in France except on the Breton coast. Irresponsible collecting had reduced the Puffins to a few hundred birds but this sanctuary has been so effective that they had increased to about 35,000; unfortunately the Torrey Canyon oil then reduced them to 400 pairs. The situation of these islands must be particularly favourable as the Gannet has its southernmost European breeding area here. There are now three colonies, totalling over a thousand pairs. Another northern species, the Fulmar, has within the last decade established itself on this island.

Le Cap-Sizun (Finistère)

Among the points on the Breton coast which have a bird life similar to that of Les Sept-Iles is Le Cap-Sizun, where a small reserve of 124 acres was set up in 1958 by the Société pour l'Etude et la Protection de la Nature en Bretagne, Faculté des Sciences, Avenue de Gorgeu 29N, Brest.

The sanctuary in the Golfe du Morbihan

Farther south but still in Brittany, this important bird sanctuary provides a winter resting place for protected species such as the Brent Goose and the Shelduck. This is a good place to watch magnificent winter flights of duck, especially Wigeon, and the extensive mud banks at low tide encourage many migrating shore birds to stop. This sanctuary is administered by the Fédération Départementale des Chasseurs du Morbihan.

La Pointe d'Arçay (Vendée)

Farther south on the Atlantic coast, this reserve of 1,359 acres was created on the mud banks of La Pointe d'Arçay to provide a resting place for migratory birds. This is one of the best areas to see waders and waterfowl. It is directed by the Conseil Supérieur de la Chasse and the Fédération Départementale, 17 Rue Lafayette, La Roche-sur-Yon.

The Camargue

This is one of the best places for bird-watching in Europe, at least for certain rare species. The Camargue is a vast expanse of saline lagoons and freshwater marshes between the two branches of the Rhône, penetrated from the south by the sea over much of its area and with the fresh water of the Rhône flowing in from the north. Unspoilt until recently, this great delta is becoming more popular with tourists and seems to be losing something of its character but at least part of it will be preserved thanks to the creation of a large reserve covering 52 square miles or almost a third of the delta. This sanctuary was created in 1928 by the Société Nationale d'Acclimatation. A pass to visit the reserve must be obtained in advance. Hospitality is organised for visitors and they can find accommodation at Salin de Badon or at La Capellière, provided that they make arrangements with the director in advance.

The Camargue is all the more remarkable because it is often possible to see there species which are rare in Europe. It is one of the only two places where the Greater Flamingo now breeds in Europe. Several thousand nest in the Camargue and, although access to their colony is understandably not easy, a visitor would be very unlucky if, during a spring day, he did not see a group of these beautiful birds fly overhead. A fine colony of Bearded Tits is established opposite 'La Capellière', a house owned by the Société pour la Protection de la Nature. Fan-tailed Warblers can be located everywhere by their unmistakable song and undulating song-flight. More difficult to identify but relatively common are Moustached Warblers, which are not easily distinguished from Sedge Warblers. Cetti's Warblers are very common wherever there is thick undergrowth near water. Although the colonies of Bee-eaters seem to be on the decrease, these birds are still relatively common, much more so than Rollers, which seem to have deserted most of the delta. The marshes, where one frequently hears Bitterns without seeing them, are inhabited by numerous Purple Herons and Marsh Harriers. It is in the Camargue that one can most easily see Red-crested Pochards, which nest in large numbers on the banks of the Etang de l'Impériale. With a little luck one can see Mediterranean and Slender-billed Gulls. In certain places the visitor may come across nesting colonies of Pratincoles. This brief list shows that the Camargue provides an opportunity for seeing, over a relatively small area, many species which are fairly rare in Europe. There are also several heronries near the reserve, where Little Egrets, Night Herons and a few rare Squacco Herons nest together, and there is a small colony of Lesser Kestrels at the Abbey of Montmajour, near Arles.

Having described various areas of particular interest, we now go round France mentioning species worth watching for because of their rarity elsewhere or because they are typical of the country.

Leaving the Camargue in the direction of the Pyrenees one can look out for warblers all over Languedoc; Sardinian Warblers are fairly common and easier to observe than the Subalpine, Spectacled and Dartford Warblers, which are all very secretive and thus much less rare than a casual observer might think. Hoopoes can be seen in open woodland. The Egyptian Vultures, which in the past used to fly over the delta on their way from the Alpilles to the north of the Camargue, are unfortunately becoming very rare like most of the larger birds of prey. Fifteen years ago, at the edge of Causses, on the Aude and Hérault boundaries, in a bare and rugged landscape, Bonelli's and Booted Eagles could still be seen regularly, and Eagle Owls could be heard every evening. Ornithologists who frequent these areas consider that the situation at the moment is most alarming and very few representatives of these three species remain. To the south of Banyuls the foothills of the Pyrenees are frequented by species which like dry areas, such as Black and Black-eared Wheatears and Rock and Blue Rock Thrushes, and sometimes a little higher up by Choughs.

La Lozère and particularly the Gorges du Tarn and the Cevennes National Park are good areas for birds of prey. The Golden Eagle survives here and Short-toed Eagles, Red Kites and Buzzards can be seen.

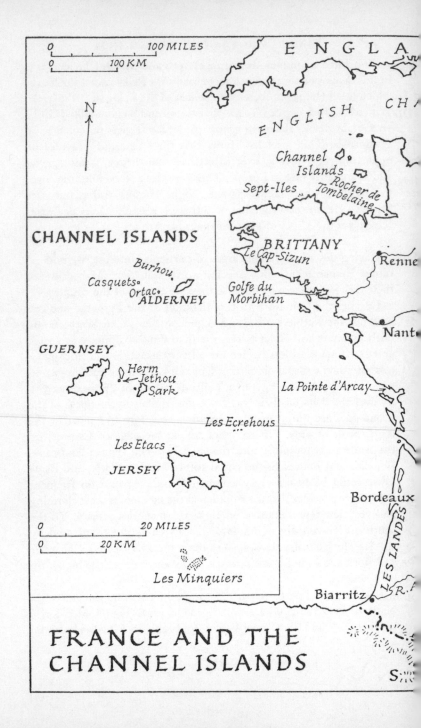

FRANCE AND THE
CHANNEL ISLANDS

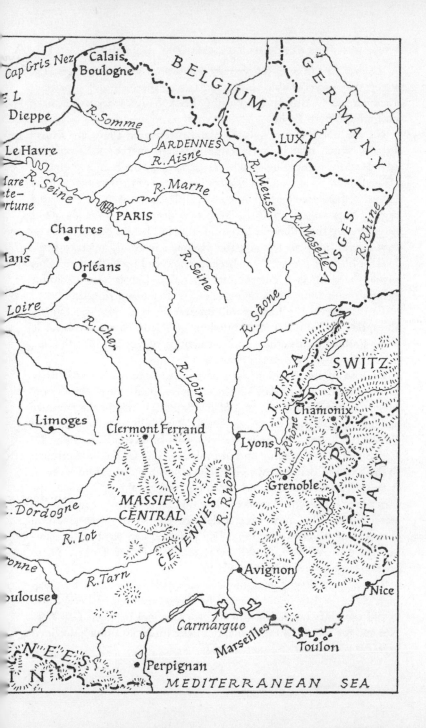

The visitor to the Pyrenees may see Griffon Vultures and, if very lucky, may even be able to observe two or three surviving pairs of Lammergeiers. Unfortunately, the Black Vulture seems to have disappeared from France.

On the north-west slopes in the Biarritz area there are Storm Petrels, which nest in fairly large numbers on the small offshore islands. Any ornithologist who is passing through in October is strongly advised to watch the operation of one of the famous 'palombières' which are very characteristic pigeon-traps of the Basque region. Nets are set up at the head of a deep valley. Woodpigeons migrating up the valley are lured down to net height by beaters who toss special 'bats' in the air; the pigeons apparently mistake these bats for birds of prey, fly low for cover, and end up in the nets. This pigeon-trapping is a commercial operation but is also used for research with some birds being released after being ringed.

Farther north, the Landes will interest the bird-watcher. During the spring and autumn large numbers of Turtle Doves can be seen here. Farther north still, the Noirmoutier region has Bluethroats, which breed nowhere else in France.

Because of its situation as a peninsula, Brittany is particularly favourable for sea birds. As already mentioned, the Fulmar now breeds on the Ile Rouzic, one of the Sept-Iles, and in the summer sizeable concentrations of Gannets, Razorbills, Guillemots and Puffins can be seen. A similar variety of sea birds can be found at Le Cap-Sizun at the extreme end of Finistère. The Golfe du Morbihan in the south of Brittany, which can be crossed by boat from Vannes, is an area particularly suited to winter bird-watching. The shallow water over certain mud banks at low tide attracts a great number of water birds. The most spectacular are the Brent Geese, several thousand of which winter here. Ducks are numerous; besides Mallard there are Wigeon, Pintail, Shovelers and Tufted Ducks. There are also large concentrations of Coots.

The Seine valley, the right bank of which is bordered by steep high cliffs, used to be frequented by a good number of Peregrines, as did the cliffs bordering the English Channel between Cap Gris Nez and the mouth of the Seine, but these birds have much declined in recent years.

Going farther north, the Baie de Somme should be interesting at the migration period, for its extensive mudbanks lie on one of the frequented routes, but the large numbers of duck and waders which pass here tend more and more not to stop because of excessive shooting. Bar-tailed Godwits and Whimbrel may be seen in large flocks and, among ducks, Shelduck, Teal and Garganey pass through in some numbers, to mention just a few of the birds to be found here.

In the north of France the Ardennes region is more or less the only place where there is some possibility of seeing Hazel Grouse, which are very secretive everywhere else. The Black Woodpecker seems to be on the increase everywhere, unlike the Red Kite which is declining like the other birds of prey.

On the heights near Chamonix one can find Alpine Swifts, Alpine Accentors, Snow Finches, Alpine Choughs and Ravens, and the snow-covered conifer forests have Black Grouse, Capercaillies and Nutcrackers. Nutcrackers are disconcerting, for sometimes they disappear suddenly from a part of the forest where they have been common.

One bird which I have often been asked about is the Wallcreeper. I have seen it in winter on a plain, and sometimes even in spring or in autumn in the middle of a town or on a village church steeple, or in the Hérault screes. It nests on very steep slopes in the mountains and it is certainly to be found in La Vanoise, the national park in the Savoy Alps.

Mention must also be made of the barren areas of Champagne and of the very numerous marshy regions inland which are spread all over the country but are of particular interest in Brenne and in the Dombes. This area to the north of Lyons is rich in areas of water, mostly artificial, and reed beds. A great variety of marsh and water birds can be seen here. In the spring and summer Savi's and Grasshopper Warblers can be found not far from each other and their songs can be compared. With luck one can also find Ferruginous Ducks.

La Sologne is famous for its great shoots but the absence of cultivation and the vast semi-wooded expanses continue to favour many interesting birds such as Stone Curlews and Nightjars. The marshy ponds have a variety of water birds and harriers breed in this region.

The bird-watcher whose visit to France is limited to a few days in Paris can still see an interesting variety of birds, especially in the spring. A few years ago I entertained a professor from Tel Aviv who wanted to hear the song of certain birds which were known to him only on migration. As he had only one morning free I suggested a walk in the Bois de Boulogne on the very outskirts of Paris. On that April morning we observed no less than forty-seven species (including a Smew which had probably been injured).

The Channel Islands
E. D. H. Johnson

If one finds a ringed bird in the Channel Islands, the ring should be sent to: La Société Jersiaise, Ornithological Section, 9 Pier Road, Jersey, Channel Islands.

The Channel Islands comprise the two self-governing bailiwicks of Jersey and Guernsey, which each owe allegiance to the British Crown. They lie between latitudes 48° 56′ and 49° 43′ North and longitudes 1° 55′ and 2° 43′ West; some eighty miles from southern England and, in places, less than twelve miles from the coast of Normandy. The Jersey group contains, in addition to the main island of forty-six square miles, the outlying and widely scattered reefs of Les Ecrehous and Les Minquiers. Guernsey, twenty-five square miles, administers the smaller islands of Alderney (including Burhou, Ortac and the Casquets), Sark, and its own off-shore islands of Herm and Jethou which are let to private tenants. British airlines operate frequent and regular services to Jersey and Guernsey and there are local air links with Alderney and several places in Normandy and Brittany. There is also a good service of ships, car ferries and hydrofoils between England, the two main islands and France. Sark is only accessible by sea; there is a regular boat service for most of the year between Guernsey and Herm, where hotel accommodation is available; visits to the smaller reefs are by private arrangement or charter only and, due to tidal hazards, are usually extremely difficult to arrange. Public transport is excellent in Guernsey, rather inadequate in Jersey and limited to taxis in Alderney; Sark and the remaining islets are easily walkable.

The islands' climate is mild, temperate and maritime with warm, prolonged summers. Winters are mild with, very occasionally, short periods of severe frost. All the islands are characterised by extremely rugged, steep, rocky coastlines, alternating with bays of varying size and broad expanses of sand. Tides of up to 39 feet or more preclude the formation of coastal marshes, and wetlands are comparatively scarce. Jersey and, to a lesser extent, Guernsey are intersected by wooded valleys, the greater part of the usable land being devoted to small-scale mixed farming. Guernsey has an extensive glasshouse industry and is rather more regularly built over than Jersey. The smaller islands are correspondingly less populous and less intensely cultivated. The maximum altitudes are 435 feet in Jersey and 344 feet in Guernsey.

For the visiting bird-watcher, the islands' main interest lies in the sea bird colonies, the opportunities for observing migration through a variety of habitats and a few species which are comparatively common although rarer and less easily observed elsewhere.

The Gannet colonies on the stacks of Ortac and Les Etacs, off Alderney, support between them some 1,000 pairs; they originated in the early 1940s. Nearby Burhou holds what was, and may still be, one of the largest Storm Petrel populations in Europe, as well as substantial numbers of Puffins. Fulmars have been prospecting the islands for many years and have been seen on the cliffs of Alderney, although breeding has not yet been confirmed. Small groups of Razorbills and rather fewer Guillemots (now absent from Jersey) breed throughout the islands. Shags are extremely common on the reefs and some cliffs and Cormorants occupy a few of the offshore stacks and rocks. Scattered groups of Common Terns breed on the reefs, principally off Jersey and Herm, as do Sandwich Terns in diminishing numbers; Little and Black Terns are fairly regular autumn passage migrants. The Herring Gull increases annually, the Lesser Black-backed Gull breeds in small numbers, mainly in the Guernsey-Sark-Alderney group and the Great Black-backed Gull in widely scattered pairs, mainly on the reefs. The only colony of Kittiwakes is on the stacks of Les Autelets, Sark. The Black-headed

Gull is a very common winter visitor but the Common Gull occurs only infrequently in very small numbers and mainly in certain favoured localities in Jersey.

The Kentish Plover breeds in Guernsey, Alderney and Herm and Oystercatchers nest commonly throughout on the shores and reefs. A non-breeding summer population of Turnstones remains among the rocky gullies to the south-east of Jersey. Most European waders are seen on migration, although seldom in large numbers. Dunlin, Ringed Plover, Grey Plover, Golden Plover, Bar-tailed Godwit, Lapwing, Turnstone, Sanderling, Redshank, Curlew, Woodcock, Snipe and Jack Snipe are regular and common winter visitors.

Wintering Brent Geese are a feature of Jersey, where they are usually to be found in two flocks in St Aubin's Bay and Grouville Bay to a total of some 800. There is also a small group between Guernsey and Herm. The only regularly breeding duck is the Mallard, although the Garganey occasionally breeds in Jersey. Most of the European ducks are recorded offshore in winter and to a certain extent on inland waters, but numbers are usually small.

The Red-breasted Merganser is, however, quite common offshore, especially in the gullies to the south of Jersey. Scattered grebes and divers occur offshore in winter, throughout, and a very few Little Grebes breed on inland waters.

The Kestrel is common in all the islands and the Peregrine, which declined in recent years as elsewhere in Europe, may still breed occasionally. The Sparrowhawk, once scarce throughout, no longer breeds. The Barn Owl is the only breeding owl and the Short-eared Owl an irregular passage migrant.

The Great Spotted Woodpecker colonised Jersey in the early 1950s and is expected to be proved breeding in Guernsey at any time. The Collared Dove arrived in Jersey in 1961 and had spread to Alderney by 1966. Cetti's Warbler has been present in winter for several years in Jersey and bred, probably at two localities, for the first time in 1973, as did the Serin. The Dartford Warbler is fairly common, though not always conspicuous, among the gorse of the larger islands and the Stonechat is a feature of the commons, heaths and headlands, especially in Jersey. The Chiffchaff is common throughout, but the Willow Warbler, Garden Warbler and Blackcap are restricted to certain wooded areas, mainly in the valleys of Jersey and Guernsey, and the Whitethroat has declined sharply in the last few years. The Lesser Whitethroat bred for the first time in 1972, in Jersey. The resident treecreeper is the Short-toed Treecreeper and the only breeding flycatcher is the Spotted Flycatcher. The Cirl Bunting is scarce and very local and the Yellowhammer is confined to certain areas of the larger islands. While the Swallow breeds commonly throughout, the House Martin is found only in well-defined parts of the major islands and the Sand Martin maintains a precarious breeding status in the three main islands, mainly by exploiting the somewhat ephemeral nest sites presented by working sandpits. A few pairs of Ravens nest on the cliffs of the main islands and on Herm.

Bluethroats, Aquatic Warblers, Grasshopper Warblers, Lesser Whitethroats, Hoopoes, Golden Orioles, Tree Pipits, Ring Ousels and Spotted Crakes are more or less regular on migration.

The recorders of La Société Jersiaise and La Société Guernesaise Ornithological Sections will gratefully acknowledge well-documented records sent in by visiting bird-watchers.

Spain

and the Balearic Islands

Francisco Bernis

H.J.S.

Lammergeiers

During recent years there has been a welcome increase in the interest in avifauna, but for many Spaniards birds are still primarily for shooting. The game laws have, however, helped to protect much of the rich avifauna. The Spanish Ornithological Society (Sociedad Española de Ornitología, 80 Calle Castellana, Madrid) publishes the periodical *Ardeola*.

At present there are three National Parks on the mainland: the Parque Nacional de Ordesa (over 4,800 acres), the Parque Nacional de Aiguës Tortes y Lago de San Mauricio (about 25,200 acres) in the southern Pyrenees, and the Parque Nacional de la Montaña de Covadonga (almost 40,800 acres) near the north coast. There are also several state game reserves, controlled by the Ministerio de Agricultura, and information, publications and maps relating to these can be obtained from the Servicio Nacional de Pesca Fluvial y Casa (Goya 25, Madrid), the Subsecretaria de Turismo (Avenida del Generalísimo 39, Madrid), and Patrimonio Forestal del Estada (Calle Mayor 83, Madrid). In general, the parks and reserves are open to anyone, but one has to keep to the roads and paths.

The Coto Doñana and the Marismas de Hinojos are scientific reserves. One-day permits are issued for some parts but for others permission to enter is only given if the applicant is involved in research which aims to further knowledge of the reserve. Applications for permits should be sent to the Estación Biologica de Doñana (Paraguay 1, Sevilla).

The author's *Prontuario de la Avifauna Española* deals with the birds of the mainland, and of the Balearic Islands, the Canaries and Portugal. The visitor to the Balearic Islands will also find useful *The Naturalist in Majorca* by James D. Parrack (David & Charles).

If one finds a ringed bird in Spain, the ring should be sent to Central Migration Aves, Castellana 80 (Museo), Madrid 6, Spain.

SPAIN AND THE BALEARIC ISLANDS

Spain covers an area of about 190,000 square miles, while the Balearic Islands have an area of 1,935 square miles. The countryside of Spain is quite thinly populated, for a high proportion of the population lives in the larger cities.

The Balearic Islands, lying off the eastern coast of Spain, consist of a north-eastern group, Mallorca, Minorca and seven smaller islands; and a western group, Ibiza, Formentera and four small islands. Mallorca, the largest island, is about fifty miles long from north to south and about the same from east to west. Mallorca, especially, but a few of the other islands as well, are very popular tourist resorts. This has harmful effects on the numbers and variety of bird species. Nevertheless there are still areas that are almost unspoilt, particularly in the mountains. There are excellent sea and air connections with Barcelona, Valencia and Alicante.

There are four very different climatic zones on the mainland of Spain. The interior experiences climatic extremes. On the north and north-western coasts the summers are warm and the winters mild, with a lot of rain, but frost and snow are rare. The south coast has hot, dry summers and warm, humid winters, while the east coast has a typical Mediterranean climate, with little rain.

The central highlands or sierras with their hot, dry summers have a relatively poor avifauna, but in general Spain has a fascinating collection of birds, including some species which are found nowhere else in Europe, while others occur in larger numbers than in any other European country. The special birds include: Cattle Egret, Black Stork, Greater Flamingo, Ruddy Shelduck, Marbled Duck, White-headed Duck, Goshawk, Imperial Eagle, Lammergeier, Black Vulture, Eleonora's Falcon, Barbary Partridge, Andalusian Hemipode, Purple Gallinule, Crested Coot, Pratincole, Slender-billed Gull, Audouin's Gull, Black-bellied Sandgrouse, Pin-tailed Sandgrouse, Great Spotted Cuckoo, Red-necked Nightjar, Red-rumped Swallow,

Lesser Short-toed Lark, Black Wheatear, Spanish Sparrow, Spotless Starling and Azure-winged Magpie.

Because of its mild climate several North European nesting birds spend the winter in southern Spain. Many parts of the country have been little investigated ornithologically, so it is still possible to add to our knowledge of the Spanish avifauna.

This was shown, for instance, when British ornithologists began to note swifts with white rumps in the province of Cadiz in the early 1960s. At first they thought these were Little Swifts (*Apus affinis*), a species which has colonised Morocco, Algeria and Tunisia since about 1925. Naturally it was assumed that this species had crossed the Straits of Gibraltar, but when the first photographs of these birds were published, there were doubts about the correctness of the dentification. Further investigations, including the capture of one of the birds in a mist-net, established that this new addition to the Spanish avifauna was the White-rumped Swift *Apus caffer*, another African species which has now been found also in Morocco but which at that time was not known to occur nearer to Spain than Nigeria. These birds nest in the Sierra de la Plata and one or two other places in the province of Cadiz.

Northern Spain

Spain is a country of contrasts. The countryside in the north is in many ways similar to the adjoining parts of Europe, with extensive deciduous woods (oak, beech, birch) and fertile fields. Here we find the Cuckoo, and many different songbirds, such as Robin, Tree Pipit, Whinchat, Yellowhammer, Song Thrush, and Bullfinch. The woodlands have Black Woodpeckers and Woodcocks and the mountain slopes harbour the occasional Capercaillie. In the Pamplona area there are more exciting species such as Hoopoe, Calandra Lark, Short-toed Lark, Tawny Pipit, Woodchat Shrike, Bonelli's Warbler, Melodious Warbler, Ortolan Bunting and even Rock Sparrow, which often nests under bridges.

The north of Spain also has the Parque Nacional de la Montaña de Covadonga and the Reserves of Somiedo and Riano, which are near the northern coast and south of the road running from Bilbao, via Santander, to Oviedo. Covadonga consists of the north-western part of the Picos de Europa, whose highest point is the Peña Santa de Castilia (8,490 feet). This has the Golden Eagle and Griffon Vulture and many other mountain birds, as well as Brown Bears, Wolves and Wild Boars.

The Somiedo Reserve (about 247,000 acres), lying on the boundary between the provinces of Oviedo and Léon, is well worth a visit. This is best done from Pola de Somiedo or La Plaza, which have simple inns where one can hire the horses needed to visit this vast reserve.

The reserves of Riano and Los Picos de Europa together cover an area of nearly 440,000 acres. They lie south of Covadonga and have a similar avifauna.

The Orveda Reserve (at least 4,900 acres), on the slopes of the Pyrenees opposite Gavarnie, is one of the few places where one has a reasonable chance of seeing the Lammergeier, although often only from a distance. Griffon Vultures also occur, and the mountain birds include the Goshawk, Peregrine, Rock Nuthatch, Rock Sparrow and Alpine Chough.

There is also a chance of seeing the Lammergeier in the valleys of the Río Gállego and the Río Aragón and here the species include Egyptian and Griffon Vultures, numerous Red and Black Kites, Booted, Bonelli's and Short-toed Eagles, Scops Owl and an occasional Eagle Owl.

The large national reserve of Aigües Tortes, with an area of at least 24,700 acres and several lakes, has a similar avifauna.

Central and western Spain

The rest of Spain has a typical Mediterranean character. The valleys of the Ebro and Guadalquivir and parts of the central highlands are still quite unspoilt and only slightly hilly. The flat parts are almost without trees and often very dry. Here there are steppe and desert birds such as Little and Great Bustards, Stone Curlew, Black-bellied and Pin-tailed Sandgrouse, Calandra, Short-toed and Crested Larks and Black-eared Wheatear.

Many of the sierras appear barren and inhospitable and they have relatively few bird species, but these are of great interest: Red-legged Partridge, Spectacled Warbler, Black-eared Wheatear and

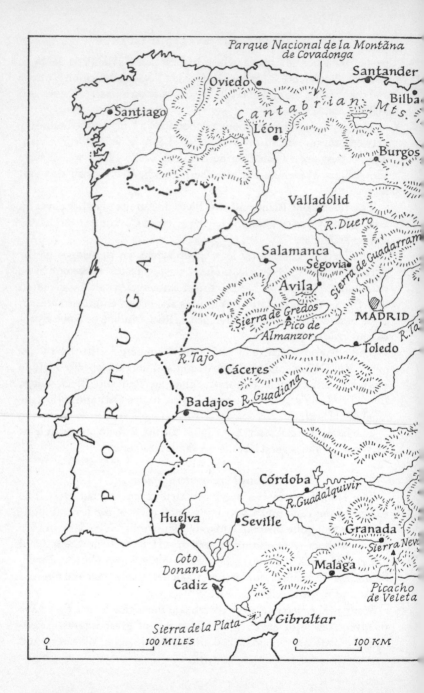

Parque Nacional de la Montãna
de Covadonga

Santander

Oviedo

Bilba

Santiago

Cantabrian Mts.

León

Burgos

Valladolid

R. Duero

Salamanca

Segovia

Sierra de Guadarram

Avila

Sierra de Gredos

Pico de
Almanzor

MADRID

R. Ta

Toledo

R. Tajo

Cáceres

Badajos

R. Guadiana

Córdoba

R. Guadalquivir

Huelva

Seville

Granada

Sierra Neva

Coto
Donana

Malaga

Picacho
de Veleta

Cadiz

Sierra de la Plata

Gibraltar

PORTUGAL

0   100 MILES   0   100 KM

SPAIN AND THE BALEARIC
ISLANDS

Thekla Lark. There are many more species in areas where the slopes of the hills are covered in woodland: Griffon, Egyptian and Black Vultures, Red and Black Kites, Buzzard, Booted, Short-toed and Golden Eagles, as well as Stone Curlew, Scops Owl, Alpine Swift, Hoopoe, Crag Martin, Tawny Pipit, Orphean Warbler, Bonelli's Warbler, Black Wheatear, Rock Bunting, Alpine Accentor and Chough.

There should still be Lammergeiers in the Sierra Nevada, though this is a very rare nesting bird, even in Spain. Egyptian and Griffon Vultures are very common here, and there are also Golden Eagles, Peregrines, and Lesser Kestrels. One can travel by road from Granada quite high up the Picacho de Veleta (altitude 11,350 feet), and have a reasonable chance of seeing, or at least of hearing, Alpine Swift, Roller, Hoopoe, Crag Martin, Woodchat Shrike, Melodious, Sardinian and Subalpine Warbler, Black Wheatear, Rock Bunting, Azure-winged Magpie and Chough.

The Coto Nacional de Cazorla y Segura, a reserve of 247,000 acres, lies just north of the Sierra Nevada, and contains the source of the Guadalquivir. Here Lammergeiers can usually be found, and certainly other kinds of vulture. There is a large reservoir with waders and ducks, but not in very large numbers except during the migration periods. Great Crested Grebes nest here in summer, and the small islands have nesting Black-winged Stilts, Gull-billed Terns, Little Terns and sometimes Pratincoles.

The Cazorla y Segura Reserve is not easily accessible. It is owned by the Patrimonio Forestal del Estado (the Spanish State Forestry Service) to whom application should be made for an entry permit. In addition to the species already mentioned this sierra has Alpine Accentor (often above the tree line), Rock Thrush, Blue Rock Thrush, Wallcreeper, Ortolan Bunting and Alpine Chough (only in the north and north-east).

The Sierra de Guadarrama, with peaks rising to almost 6,000 feet, is not far from Madrid. White Storks nest in the villages at the foot, and also Lesser Kestrels and many songbirds. This area is famous for its nesting birds of prey which include Honey Buzzard, Red and Black Kites, Goshawk, Sparrowhawk, Booted, Bonelli's, Imperial and Golden Eagles, Black and Griffon Vultures, Peregrine, Hobby and Kestrel.

Western Spain has a population of Black Storks, widely separated from the main breeding grounds in eastern and south-eastern Europe and in Asia Minor. The best chance of seeing these is in the area between Merida and Badajoz, on the Madrid-Lisbon road, near the Portuguese frontier. There are vast irrigation works along the Río Guadiana, east of Badajoz, which attract all sorts of birds from the very dry area of the Estremadura. Great and Little Bustards nest here and there on the sierras, which are not irrigated. The irrigated areas have Black and White Storks, as well as Roller, Bee-eater, Hoopoe and Spotless Starling. Any sighting of the Bluethroat in this area should be reported immediately to the Spanish Ornithological Society; it is just possible that this bird may nest here.

In the area between Badajoz and Merida it is also worth exploring other valleys, such as those of the Rio Zatapon and Rio Burdalo, where there is chance of seeing Night Heron, Cattle Egret, Corncrake, Pratincole, Red-rumped Swallow, Tawny Pipit, Woodchat and Great Grey Shrikes, Melodious Warbler, Black-eared Wheatear and Ortolan Bunting.

The Sierra de Gredos with the Pico de Almanzor (altitude 8,470 feet) is also worth exploring for it has Griffon and Black Vultures, Red and Black Kites, Firecrest, Crossbill and Rock Bunting. In the valley of the Rio Tietar there is a chance to see Quail, Stone Curlew, Bee-eater, Hoopoe, Thekla Lark, Woodchat Shrike, Cetti's, Melodious, Orphean, Dartford and Fan-tailed Warblers, Black-eared Wheatear, Spotless Starling, Golden Oriole and Azure-winged Magpie.

The east coast

On the east coast birds still hold their own, in scattered areas, in spite of the invasion of tourism. On the Costa Brava at the mouths of the Rio Fluvia and Rio Ter there are reed beds in among the rice-fields, with Cetti's, Savi's and Fan-tailed Warblers. Purple Herons and Little Egrets can be seen searching for food in the rice-fields, and during the migration season and the winter months many kinds of waders appear. Along the Costa Brava there are small areas of maquis in which Marmora's Warbler is said to live; the distribution of this species deserves attention. Other species which can be expected on the Costa Brava are Bonelli's Eagle and Eleonora's Falcon (a species never seen nesting here), Black Kite, Lesser Kestrel, Scops Owl, Red-rumped Swallow, Lesser Grey Shrike, Great Spotted Cuckoo, Bearded Tit and many songbirds.

The delta of the Ebro, half-way between Tarragona and Castellon de la Plana, has sand dunes, bogs and rice-fields which are worth exploring. There is a large colony of nesting Purple Herons, and other birds to be seen include Spoonbills, Avocets, Black-winged Stilts, and Whiskered, Gull-billed, Little and Roseate Terns; the Lesser Short-toed Lark also breeds here.

Red-crested Pochards and Ferruginous Ducks nest in the lagoon just south of Valencia and this area also has Coots, Crested Coots and Bearded Tits.

There are still many areas, even along this intensively exploited coast, where a few hours or even days can be spent in looking for characteristic Mediterranean species.

Andalusia

In Andalusia the famous marismas along the Guadalquivir offer surprises in every season. The Coto Doñana and especially the Coto del Rey are famous for their heron colonies, with Night, Purple and Squacco Herons, Cattle and Little Egrets, White Storks and Spoonbills. Flamingos are there almost throughout the year although, as in the Camargue, they do not always breed. Other nesting birds include Ruddy Shelduck, Marbled Duck, White-headed Duck, Crested Coot, Purple Gallinule, Black-winged Stilt, Pratincole, Whiskered Tern and even the rare Slender-billed Gull.

The cotos are particularly rich in birds of prey, with Booted, Imperial, Bonelli's and Short-toed Eagles and various vultures. Many areas have been made into reserves with restricted entry and before attempting a visit it is absolutely essential to consult the biological station in Seville well in advance. Other species to be seen, even on a short visit, include Azure-winged Magpie, Red-rumped Swallow, Pintailed Sandgrouse, Pratincole and an occasional Glossy Ibis.

In the sierras the White-rumped Swift (p. 190) normally breeds in the nests of the Red-rumped Swallow, to which it carries feathers which can be seen protruding from the entrances.

The country as a whole

The Lesser Kestrel is the commonest bird of prey in Spain. It can be seen almost everywhere, sitting on telegraph poles along the roads, or hovering over mountain slopes and fields. It often nests in large buildings, sometimes in ruins, in the small towns and villages (except in the north and north-west). Red Kite, Buzzard and Booted Eagle are common in most woods and Short-toed and Bonelli's Eagles are widespread throughout the country, although often rather localised. Golden Eagles are only seen high up on mountains, but Egyptian and Griffon Vultures are common almost everywhere; the Black Vulture is much rarer, though Lammergeiers still occur in a few places. The Peregrine has also become rather rare.

The Little Owl is the most abundant of the owls, and the Barn Owl is also seen in every town and village. The Tawny Owl can be found in almost all the larger areas of woodland, while Scops Owls appear to prefer parks and orchards, where they are quite common. Most of the more inaccessible mountain areas will have one or more pairs of Eagle Owls.

The Azure-winged Magpie, restricted in Europe to Spain and Portugal, prefers holly and cork oak, but it can also be seen in mixed woods, and at harvest time in orchards. It is not found in northern and eastern Spain, but is common to the east of Madrid. Ravens are common in rocky, desolate areas. The Rook is a winter visitor.

Although they attract much attention in spring with their loud shrieks, Great Spotted Cuckoos are nowhere numerous. They are summer migrants which arrive quite early in the spring. Nightjars can be seen on the plateaus as well as on the inland sierras, and also in the northern districts. Red-necked Nightjars are quite common in low-lying areas in the centre, west and south.

Red-rumped Swallows nest in almost all parts of Spain, but they can only be found intermittently, and they clearly prefer uninhabited areas, where they nest up against cliffs and under bridges, but now and again in houses like Swallows do. Precise information on the distribution of the Red-rumped Swallow, especially in the north, is always welcome.

Dartford Warblers nest in quite small patches of heather throughout the country and Whitethroats, Garden Warblers and Blackcaps are common nesting birds in the woods of the north and in the mountains of central Spain. Subalpine Warblers evidently prefer dwarf oaks and cistus bushes in the central, eastern and southern parts of the country. The Sardinian Warbler is remarkably common among bushes in the east and the south, and also in fruit-growing districts.

Songbirds are not very abundant in the undergrowth of the dry valleys and the plateaux. The Nightingale and the Melodious Warbler are the most characteristic species, and the Olivaceous Warbler frequents tamarisk bushes along the rivers in the south and east and can also be heard in parks and town gardens in the south. Cetti's Warbler and Fan-tailed Warbler are widespread, the former especially in bushes near rivers, streams and lakes, the latter in slightly smaller numbers although it can be found fairly frequently in grassy valleys, along the banks of lakes and on the edges of bogs. These two species do not migrate and Cetti's Warbler can be heard in every month of the year. Great Reed Warblers and Reed Warblers nest in almost every patch of reeds, but Moustached and Savi's Warblers only settle in areas with well established reed beds.

The Woodchat Shrike is common in woods and orchards in central, western and southern Spain, and the Red-backed Shrike in the northern districts. The Great Grey Shrike does not migrate. The Lesser Grey Shrike can be found only along the northern part of the Costa Brava.

The Short-toed Treecreeper is common throughout the country, but the Treecreeper is found only in the northern mountains, where both these closely related species nest.

The Corn Bunting is the most numerous of the buntings, particularly in low-lying fields. The Cirl Bunting nests commonly in river valleys and well irrigated fields, and the Rock Bunting is abundant on mountain slopes with rocky outcrops or bushy vegetation, and also near to sea level.

Curiously enough, Spanish Sparrows are quite rare, being found only in a few places in the south and south-east and near the east coast. They prefer small woods with poplar or eucalyptus, but can also be found in holly and cork oak. They often build their nests in the lower parts of the nests of White Storks and birds of prey.

Two species of starlings can be seen in winter, for the ordinary Starling then comes south to Spain, and the Spotless Starling is a resident. The latter can be seen in all parts of the country, except in the east, and it can be found nesting under the roofs in village houses as well as in trees.

White Storks nest in many villages in central, east and south-west Spain, and so do Swifts and occasionally one or two pairs of Pallid Swifts.

Balearic Islands

During the holiday months of July and August, Mallorca might appear to be rather lacking in birds, but this will not be so in April, May or even June. Then it is not uncommon to see Black Vultures flying while one is eating one's breakfast on a hotel terrace.

The boggy area of La Albufera (about 6,200 acres), on the north-east coast, not far from the Bahia de Alcudia, is seriously threatened, because there are plans to drain the whole area and build a tourist centre. The vast reed beds there still harbour Purple Heron, Little Egret, Bittern and Little Bittern, Water Rail and Spotted Crake and at times a surprising number of birds of prey, including Black Vulture, Red Kite, Marsh Harrier, Osprey (which nests on the Balearic Islands), Hobby, Red-footed Falcon and often large numbers of Eleonora's Falcons. The waders there include Kentish Plover, Grey Plover, Wood Sandpiper, Black-winged Stilt and Ruff. Some of these birds are migrants or winter visitors.

Nightingales are very common nesting birds on Mallorca and so are Cetti's Warblers; other breeding species include Moustached, Great Reed and Fan-tailed Warblers. The Blue Rock Thrush occurs in the north of the island, near Cabo de Formentor. Manx and Cory's Shearwaters nest on some of the Balearic Islands and can be seen feeding; the former are of course of the distinctive Balearic race.

Puig Mayor (altitude 4,608 feet), the highest peak in Mallorca near the north-western coast, and Galatzo (3,350 feet), which is near Palma, both have many birds of prey, including Egyptian and Black Vultures, Bonelli's and Booted Eagles, Peregrine and Kestrel.

Little Egrets and Black-winged Stilts can be seen on and near saltpans, for example the one at C'an Pastilla, just outside Palma and Salinas de Levanto near Campos, and there are also Black, White-winged Black and Whiskered Terns, and Mediterranean and Audouin's Gulls. Eleonora's Falcons often come here to hunt dragon-flies. These beautiful little falcons nest late in the summer and to feed their young they hunt small songbirds which are then starting to move south. Quails can often be heard calling in the fields, and there are also Red-legged Partridges.

Other interesting species on Mallorca, and on other islands in the group, include Short-toed and Thekla Larks, Grey Wagtail, Wood-chat Shrike, Sardinian, Subalpine and Marmora's Warblers, Fire-crest, Stonechat, Cirl and Corn Buntings, Crossbill, Goldfinch, Serin, Raven, Hoopoe, Bee-eater, Stone Curlew, Scops Owl, Crag Martin and Tawny Pipit. During the winter months there are so many Chiffchaffs and Willow Warblers on these islands that the inhabitants know them collectively as 'pájaros de nieve' (snow birds).

Portugal

R. O. Vicente

Black-winged Kites

In the past, ornithological work has been almost entirely restricted to the zoological departments of the Universities of Lisbon, Coimbra and Oporto; their zoological museums contain the most important collections of Portuguese birds. The bird reserve near Mindelo (about 1,400 acres), controlled by the zoological department of Oporto University, is on the coast about fifteen miles north-west of Oporto. Here birds, especially Turtle Doves, are caught for ringing. This migration work is hampered by lack of assistants, and help from volunteers is welcome.

Bird protection and the regulation of shooting is under the Forestry Department of the Ministry of Agriculture which also controls a number of state reserves. In these, shooting is subject to severe restrictions, and the birds enjoy a certain amount of protection throughout the year. The park on the Serra do Gerez (altitudes up to 5,000 feet) deserves a special note, because eagles and other birds of prey can sometimes be seen there.

There is a Society for the Protection of Nature and also a Portuguese Ornithological Society.

If one finds a ringed bird in Portugal, the ring should be sent to: Sociedade Portuguesa de Ornitologia, Faculdade de Ciències, Universidade do Porto, Oporto, Portugal.

PORTUGAL

Portugal is rectangular in shape, with the long sides running approximately north and south and measuring about 330 miles; the western side faces the Atlantic Ocean. The average distance between the Atlantic and the Spanish border is about 125 miles. The country can be conveniently divided into three regions by the river Douro in the north, and the Tagus in the centre. The Douro flows through the town of Oporto and the Tagus forms a large estuary at Lisbon. The coastal parts, facing the Atlantic, are quite distinct from the inland areas close to the Spanish frontier.

Portugal is mainly agricultural with one of the highest population densities for any agricultural country in Europe. Most of the land has been developed for farming or, where unsuitable for this, for forestry. The numerous hills, ranging between 300 and 1,000 feet, produce characteristic scenery, especially south of the Tagus, where they are covered with cork oaks or used for growing corn. The hills and mountains in the north are mainly covered with pine woods.

The higher mountains are situated north of the Tagus, with the highest peak at 6,600 feet in the Serra de Estrela, which is covered with snow for a few weeks during the winter. North of the river Douro there are several mountains ranging from 3,000 to almost 6,000 feet. Two interesting mountains, both nearly 3,300 feet high, are the Serra de S. Mamede, just south of the Tagus, and the Serra de Monchique, which divides the two southern provinces of Alentejo and Algarve.

The climate of the country is mild, particularly along the coast, where there are orange and olive groves, but snow lies for a few weeks every year in inland areas near the Spanish border.

The country presents a variety of biotopes, which can be easily seen as one drives through any part of Portugal.

There are marshes at the mouths of the rivers in the Algarve (especially near the town of Fáro), and in the estuaries near the towns of Setúbal and Aveiro. The valley of the Tagus, around Santarém, also has some marshes. There are only a few natural lakes and most of them are situated along the Atlantic side, but some at Serra da Estrela. There are several artificial lakes, created by dams, along the tributaries of the Douro and the Tagus, and some of these support appreciable populations of ducks (up to two thousand in winter) and waders. The dams are shown on the road map published by the Portuguese Automobile Club.

The coastline alternates between rocky cliffs and sandy beaches, and there are only two groups of offshore islands worth mentioning. Berlengo, the main island of one group, is about eight miles from the fishing village of Peniche; the other group of islands, Farilhoes, lies about twelve miles north-west of Berlengo. Thousands of sea birds nest on these islands, and from May till July one can find nests of Herring Gulls, Shags, Guillemots and Cory's Shearwaters in all parts of the islands, including the cliffs, which are about 300 feet high. Swifts and Black Redstarts also nest there.

There are numerous islets along the southern coast, from Fáro to Cape St Vincent, where Little Egrets, Swifts, Rock Doves and Jackdaws nest.

The spring and autumn migrations of many northern European species can be observed along the coast; some particularly good vantage points are the capes of St Vincent, Sines, Espichel and Carvoeiro (near Peniche). Sandwich and Arctic Terns and Gannets fly past in small groups, but Curlews, Whimbrels, godwits and Turtle Doves pass in flocks that often number several hundred birds.

The whole of the southern coast is very rewarding for any ornithologist wishing to observe bird migration; Swallows can be seen arriving in January and Bee-eaters in April. The autumn migration of passerines is sometimes very noticeable during September, and it is still not known whether they fly straight to Africa (when they leave the coast of the Algarve) or fly eastwards to reach the coast of Spain near Gibraltar.

Along the coast it is possible to observe the spectacular diving of Gannets during the winter months, and the feeding of Little and Common Terns during their nesting season in summer. The Black Tern is also a summer visitor to the marshes and rice fields.

The lakes and estuaries have Grey Herons during the winter, and Purple Herons nest there in the summer. Cranes have been seen regularly in winter, mostly in Alentejo, and Glossy Ibises in summer, but there are few records, and the same applies to Spoonbills and Flamingos. The White Stork is common and its numbers do not seem to have diminished, as has happened in northern Europe. The Black Stork is known in Alentejo, but its exact range is not well defined.

The best places to observe waders, in summer or winter, are the river estuaries near Aveiro, Lisbon and Setúbal. Thousands of Avocets, Redshanks, Grey and Golden plovers, Lapwings and the smaller Plovers, such as the Ringed and Kentish, can be seen on the Tagus estuary.

Little and Cattle Egrets, Bittern and Night Heron nest in Portugal and can be seen in a few marshes along the river estuaries. There is a remarkable nesting area for all these species near the small village of Golega on the Tagus.

Ducks are fairly common, particularly Mallard, Wigeon, Tufted Duck, and Common Scoter. The Purple Gallinule has been seen in Portugal, but there are no reliable observations of its nesting. Coots and Moorhens are common.

The numbers of birds of prey vary according to the species. The Kestrel is still common over most of the country, and Buzzards may be seen in the upper valley of the Tagus and in other districts. The town of Évora has an interesting population of Lesser Kestrels living on the church spires. Peregrines are scarce, but Red and Black Kites and three species of harriers can be seen in marshy areas. The Black-winged Kite is known to breed in Portugal but there are only a few nesting pairs; unfortunately, they seem to have been affected by the use of toxic chemicals on the farms.

In the valley of the river Guadiana and in Bragança, the northeastern district of Portugal, one can see vultures, especially Griffon and Egyptian Vultures—sometimes up to half a dozen at a time. The district of Bragança is particularly good for bird-watching because its rivers carry water even during the summer months, and so it has a larger bird population than other parts of Portugal.

The five European species of swallows and martins all appear in

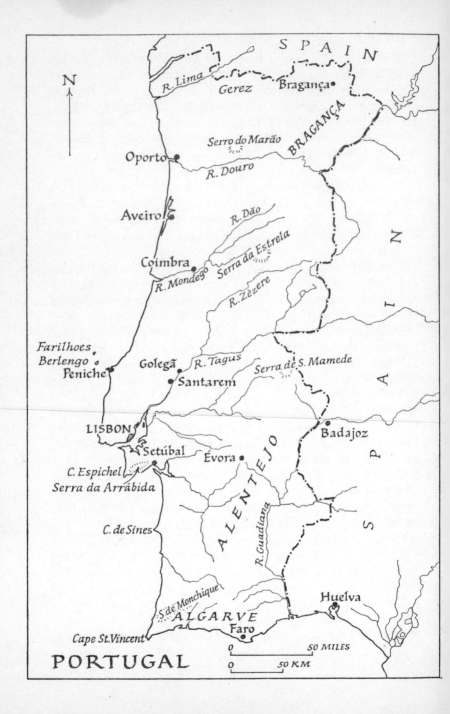

N

S P A I N

R. Lima
Gerez
Bragança

BRAGANÇA

Serro do Marão

Oporto

R. Douro

Aveiro

R. Dão

Coimbra

Serra da Estrela

R. Mondego

R. Zêzere

Farilhoes
Berlengo
Peniche

Golegã
R. Tagus
Serra de S. Mamede

Santarem

LISBON

Badajoz

Setúbal
Evora

C. Espichel
Serra da Arrábida

ALENTEJO

C. de Sines

R. Guadiana

S. de Monchique

Huelva

ALGARVE

Cape St. Vincent
Faro

50 MILES

PORTUGAL

50 KM

Portugal. The Red-rumped Swallow was first recorded in Bragança, but it has also been observed in Alentejo, and the Crag Martin is known in several localities. House Martins, Swallows and Sand Martins are very common. The Alpine Swift appears in small numbers in such places as the capes of St Vincent and Espichel and has also been seen in Bragança. The Swift is very common, particularly in the town of Setúbal.

Eagles are rare but some of them can be seen in the higher mountains, such as the Serra do Marão, where the Golden Eagle is known to nest. The Imperial Eagle appears along the Spanish border. Other eagles, such as Bonelli's and Booted, can be seen on Serra de Monchique. The Osprey has been observed along the southern coast but there are no reliable reports of its breeding. The numbers of birds of prey have steadily decreased during recent decades.

The province of Alentejo provides a suitable habitat for Great and Little Bustards, and also for Black-bellied and Pin-tailed Sandgrouse. The numbers of Great Bustards are diminishing because of hunting and corn cultivation. Huge flocks of Woodpigeons can be seen in this province during the winter.

Pratincoles and Black-winged Stilts are both summer visitors that nest along the Tagus valley and in the marshes of the Algarve.

Snipe, Jack Snipe and Woodcock are winter visitors and much hunted. Among the waders, the Redshank is abundant and there are smaller numbers of Greenshanks and Ruffs, especially in the south. Many of the smaller waders are common in winter, particularly those that nest in northern Europe, and it is possible to see flocks of Sanderlings, Knots and Dunlins. Yellow and White Wagtails are common on the marshes and along the rivers.

The commoner gulls are the Black-headed and the Lesser Black-backed during the winter, and the Herring Gull in summer; the last may be seen roosting on the cliffs. The winter flocks of Lesser Black-backed Gulls generally include about 10 per cent of Great Black-backed Gulls. There are a few records of other gulls, such as the Mediterranean and the Slender-billed.

The commonest game birds are the Red-legged Partridge and the Quail. The mountains north of the river Douro used to have numerous Partridges but they were much hunted for a time; their numbers are increasing in the state parks as a result of the protection afforded by the forestry services.

The Eagle Owl can be seen on the Serra da Arrábida, near a cement factory. Here, too, one can see Blue Rock Thrushes, Black-eared Wheatears and Black Redstarts, all species that can be found on cliffs and mountains throughout the country.

The Nightingale is a common summer visitor in all parts of Portugal, and the Bluethroat and Rock Thrush are also seen in summer but only in the area between the rivers Tagus and Douro. Barn and Little Owls are abundant throughout the country, the latter particularly in the Algarve.

Bee-eaters appear as summer visitors in all parts of the country, and are fairly abundant in the Bragança district. Rollers appear in the inland districts close to the Spanish border.

Hoopoes are common in the summer but have also been observed during the winter months—a point which requires further investigation. The Cuckoo can be heard throughout Portugal but the Great Spotted Cuckoo is rare, though it can be seen, for instance, along the upper valley of the Tagus, where it lays in Magpie nests. The Nuthatch can also be found along the same stretch of the Tagus.

The commoner woodpeckers are the Green and the Great Spotted, particularly in the area north of the Tagus. The Wryneck appears during the summer and has been observed north of the Douro and also in Alentejo.

Crested and Skylarks are common, the latter especially in winter, and the Short-toed Lark is a summer visitor. Calandra and Thekla Larks are residents but their distribution is not well known, although both appear in Alentejo (near S. Mamede) and in Bragança.

The river Tagus provides a convenient limit to the distribution of the Magpie and Golden Oriole, for both are more abundant to the north of this river. The Azure-winged Magpie appears south of the Tagus, mainly in pine woods along the coast.

Choughs and Jackdaws are very localised, both occurring at Cape St Vincent, though there are also Jackdaws at Marvão (Serra de S. Mamede) and on a small island (Ilha do Pessegueiro) off the coast, just south of Cape Sines. Ravens are still common everywhere and they can be seen nesting on the cliffs. Carrion Crows are also common, but not in large numbers. The Spotless Starling is common, but is not so numerous in towns as the Starling is in northern Europe, whereas the latter is a winter visitor to Portugal.

The marshes along the rivers have several warblers, such as the Great Reed, Cetti's and Fan-tailed. Sardinian Warblers are resident, but local: they occur, for instance, near Lagoa S. André just north of Cape Sines. Rufous Bush Chats are also very local and confined to areas south of the Tagus.

The Great Grey Shrike is common, especially north of the river Tagus, and the Red-backed Shrike appears in the Bragança district. Rock Sparrows and Rock Buntings are localised in the more mountainous parts of northern Portugal. Blackbirds occur throughout the country but Mistle Thrushes are not so common. Fieldfares and Redwings are winter visitors staying near open country and in open woodland.

The Chaffinch, Goldfinch, Greenfinch, Siskin and Serin are common in gardens and on mixed farms, and so are various tits (Great, Coal, Blue and Long-tailed), but the Hawfinch is localised, appearing among the pine woods, and the Crested Tit is more frequent north of the Tagus.

The numbers, status and distribution of some of the species mentioned are not very well known, owing to lack of detailed observations; numbers have also fluctuated appreciably during recent decades owing to increased land utilisation. In general, however, Portugal can be said to offer excellent opportunities for the ornithologist.

Switzerland

U. N. Glutz von Blotzheim

Black Kites

The Swiss Ornithological Station (Schweizerische Vogelwarte) at Sempach, north-west of Lucerne, is the only scientific institute dealing with the ecology, breeding biology, distribution and migration of birds. It is helped in its work by many amateur ornithologists, who are members of one or more of the four main ornithological societies: Ala, Schweizerische Gesellschaft für Vogelkunde und Vogelschutz; Nos Oiseaux, Société Romande pour l'Etude et la Protection des Oiseaux; Parus, Schweizerische Verband für Vogelschutz, Vogelkunde und Vogelliebhaberei; VSV, Verband Schweizerische Vogelschutzvereine. Each society has its own publication; of these *Der Ornithologische Beobachter* and *Nos Oiseaux* are the best known. Many museums have fine bird collections and those in the Museum of Natural History at Bern (with beautiful dioramas) and in the Saint Gallen Museum are well worth seeing. Of the scientific collections in the museums of university towns the most important are at Basle and Geneva. There are also many local collections such as those of the National Park Museum in Chur and of the Convent College in Einsiedeln.

If one finds a ringed bird in Switzerland, the ring should be sent to: Vogelwarte Sempach, Sempach, Lucerne, Switzerland.

SWITZERLAND

Switzerland lies about 300 miles from the North Sea and some 90 miles from the Mediterranean. The Alps, around which the country has evolved, form a notable barrier between the northern and southern climates of Europe, and the weather is often very different in different parts of the country's small area of 15,700 square miles. The highest peak is Monte Rosa (15,153 feet) and the lowest point is the level of Lake Maggiore (633 feet). Contrary to popular belief, Switzerland is not entirely mountainous. Indeed, two-fifths of its area is made up of lowlands, hills and mountains up to 3,000 feet in height, and its many valleys provide interesting and variable changes in landscape and fauna. There is a well-marked division into three main areas, the Jura, the Mittelland and the Alps.

The Jura consists of a mountain chain formed during the Tertiary era, at about the same time as the Alps. Its folds, deposited in the Jurassic and Cretaceous periods, are particularly apparent in the south-west where the mountains reach a height of about 5,500 feet; in the north-east the maximum is about 3,000 feet. Rain seeps through the Jura's limestone strata and emerges farther down in the form of springs in the valleys, while the higher parts remain rather dry. In more low-lying parts with loamy soil the plentiful rainfall (47–55 inches per annum) produces moorland conditions with a climate not unlike that of northern Europe. Large parts of the Jura, where human habitation has not yet encroached too much, are covered with deciduous and mixed forests of beech and silver fir.

The Mittelland, a strip about 20–35 miles wide, separates the Jura from the Alps and extends from Lake Geneva to Lake Constance. In the south-west it has the character of a plateau with canyon-like valleys, while the rest is hilly with a few more prominent peaks (Napf 4,578 feet, Hornli 4,251 feet). It is drained by many streams and rivers, all flowing in a north-westerly direction, either into the River Aare or directly into the Rhine. The flat shores of several lakes formed during the Ice Age provide ideal breeding places for water-fowl and shore birds. Unfortunately, however, these areas are continually threatened by the tremendous pressure of an increasing human population and the reclamation of land for industry, agriculture and recreation, so that few really good parts remain for birds. Even the wooded areas have been reduced and their character changed by large-scale planting of spruce in the formerly deciduous forests.

The Alps, which form three-fifths of the total surface area of Switzerland, have been much less altered by man than either the Jura or the Mittelland. Nevertheless, the upper limit of the forests has been lowered to provide more pasture land, hydro-electric schemes have changed the character of many of the higher valleys, and the numerous roads, funiculars, ski-lifts and so on, which have been built to increase tourism, have all left their scars on the land-scape and affected the wildlife. The Alps are important not only because of the large area they cover, but also because of their considerable climatic and hydrographic influence on the rest of the country.

The Swiss laws concerning the hunting and protection of birds are among the best in Europe, but much effort is still necessary to maintain certain habitats, especially those of waterfowl and of shore and marsh birds. Some 500 nature reserves total about 220 square miles, or 1·4 per cent of the whole country. Most of these are so small that access is not possible without disturbing the birds, but there are larger and more easily accessible reserves and other protected areas in the Alps. These include several of the most beautiful parts of Switzerland, such as the Swiss National Park in the Upper Engadine, the areas around the Aletsch Glacier and Zermatt, and the well-known virgin forest of Derborence which can be reached via Conthey near Sion. The scenery and the chance to see Marmots, Chamois or even Red Deer or Ibexes will compensate the bird-watcher who, in some parts of the Alps, may be a little disappointed by the lack of diversity in the avifauna.

The Alps are accessible by train and funicular, or, in summer, by good roads, but accommodation can be a problem in the tourist season and visitors should make inquiries well in advance. Camping, especially in the lower regions, is closely controlled and the many well-equipped camping sites now available should be used whenever possible. Typical alpine birds can be seen almost everywhere in the Alps, but it is better to choose a part where highland and lowland species meet. This happens in the Engadine, Tessin and many other places either on the northern side of the Alps (Bernese Oberland, the area south of Lake Lucerne, Glarus and Toggenburg) or in the main alpine valleys (those of the Rhône and Rhine).

A summary of Swiss breeding birds is best given by dividing the country into the four main altitudinal zones: hilly, mountainous, subalpine and alpine. The hilly zone comprises the lowlands and reaches altitudes of up to about 1,800 feet north of the Alps, 2,200 feet in the Alps and more than 2,500 feet in the southern parts. Its most attractive habitats are the lakes and marshes. Mallard and Coot are abundant on the lakes south of the Jura and in the Mittelland, and Great Crested Grebes breed in the shallow parts in large colonies, sometimes up to five hundred pairs. Little Grebes, Moorhens and Water Rails are widespread, but Black-necked Grebes, Teal, Garganey and other species are sparsely scattered. Red-crested Pochards prefer Lake Constance, especially the eastern part. Mute Swans, first introduced in the seventeenth century, have become one of the commonest species of waterfowl. Reed Buntings, Reed Warblers and Great Reed Warblers are found in all the reed beds and now and then one may see a Savi's Warbler, a Little Bittern or, on the south-eastern shore of Lake Neuchatel, perhaps even a Purple Heron.

In coniferous woods near the lakes and rivers, colonies (or single nests) of Grey Herons are widespread, but more striking is the large number of Black Kites, especially over and around the western lakes. Two big colonies of five hundred or more Black-headed Gulls breed on the Kaltbrunn marshes (between Lake Zürich and the Walensee) and on the marshes about nine miles north of Zürich; a few pairs also nest regularly in the reserve at the south-eastern corner of Lake Neuchatel, on artificial islands in the Klingnau reservoir, on the eastern part of Lake Constance near the mouth of the Rhine. Little Ringed Plovers breed on the Rhine and the Rhône, but seldom elsewhere. Common Sandpipers are not confined to the hilly zone,

SWITZERLAND

0   50 MILES

0   50 KM

G

Basle

SOLOTHURN

R. Doubs

R. Aare   Solothurn

R. Emme

J U R A

N

R. Aare

Bern

Mittelland

Lake Neuchâtel

Fribourg

FRIBOURG   Thuner See

Brienzer See

Interla

Jungfrau

Lake Geneva

BERNESE OBERLAND

R. Rhône

Geneva

Simplo

L

Zermatt

Mont Rosa

A

Matterhorn

St. Bernard P.

F

R

I

T

but are found at higher altitudes up to 4,400 feet or even 5,500 feet.
Goosanders favour similar habitats in the western lowlands. Curlews
are becoming much scarcer and can now be found only in a few
places on the Versoix marshes and near Lakes Hallwil, Zürich and
Pfäffikon.

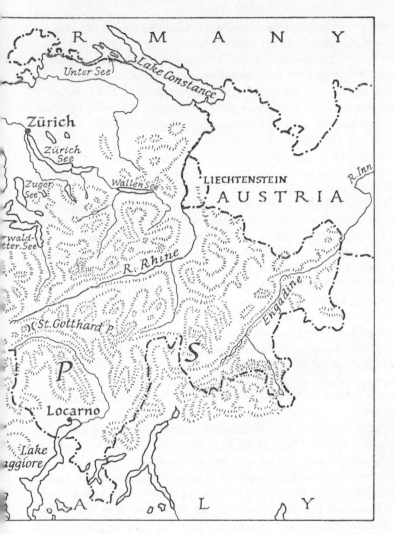

Collared Doves have spread rapidly since 1955 and can often be seen in the towns and larger villages. Swifts breed everywhere under tiled roofs, and there are colonies of Alpine Swifts in at least thirty towns and villages, but these also nest in natural sites on the cliffs similar to those occupied by Crag Martins. Parks, and especially cemeteries, have a high density of breeding birds: Blackbird, Greenfinch, Serin, Great Tit, Goldfinch, Redstart and Linnet are the most numerous and the Hawfinch can also be seen in such places. Starlings and Tree Sparrows are common in orchards and hedgerows and around farm buildings. Fieldfares nest in colonies at the edges of woods, in groves, copses or orchards. Wherever there are Fieldfares, Great Grey Shrikes are seldom far away, but Red-backed and Woodchat Shrikes have a rather patchy distribution. Lesser Grey Shrikes are largely confined to the Venoge valley (western part of Lake Geneva) and the Broye plain, though it is sometimes possible to find a few pairs in the vicinity of Basle.

A very striking and widespread species, particularly in the eastern and central parts of the Mittelland, is the Pied Flycatcher, which lives in the same habitats as the Grey-headed Woodpecker. The twittering song of the Corn Bunting is heard everywhere in the grassy lowlands. Cirl Buntings are faithful to the vineyards, while Ortolans inhabit the sunny slopes along the shores of Lake Geneva and the Rhône up to altitudes of 3,000 or even 5,000 feet. Among birds of prey, apart from the Black Kites, Buzzards and Kestrels can be seen. Sparrowhawks are widespread throughout the year, though perhaps more evident in winter when they hunt around farm buildings and in the vicinity of villages, and Hobbies like the neighbourhood of lakes and rivers. Barn, Little and Tawny Owls are all common, while the Scops Owl is confined to warm, dry valleys and is most numerous in the Rhône valley between Brig and Martigny.

The mountainous zone stretches from the highest vineyards up to 3,600 feet in the foothills of the Alps and in the Jura, up to 4,300 feet in the central Alps and up to 5,000 feet in the southern parts. It is dominated by woodland, some deciduous (especially beech), some coniferous (silver fir and pine) and some mixed. Few species live in the beech woods, but Marsh Tits are seldom missing and a loud 'drydrydrydry' usually reveals a Black Woodpecker; the Wood Warbler is also heard. The pines grow on the dry and sunny slopes, and provide a habitat for Bonelli's Warblers, Scops Owls and, where the trees are thinly scattered, even Rock Buntings. The density of the breeding birds is much higher, however, in the mixed woodland and in the pure silver fir forests; here the typical species include

Chiffchaff, Robin, Wren, Dunnock, Song Thrush, and Bullfinch as well as various tits and treecreepers, Nuthatch, Goldcrest and Fire-crest. With luck one can find the nests of Buzzard, Honey Buzzard and Sparrowhawk. Red Kites breed in the north and west, and Pere-grines nest on steep cliffs, often near to Ravens.

The subalpine zone comprises the mountain peaks of the south-western Jura and the section between 4,300 feet and the upper limit of the forests in the northern and central Alps (about 5,500 and 7,400 feet respectively). Here spruce is the dominant tree, though in the drier, innermost mountain chains it is sometimes replaced by larch or various species of pine. This coniferous woodland alternates with more or less heavily grazed pastures. Lowland species such as Black-bird, Jay and Marsh, Blue and Great Tits disappear and are replaced by Citril Finch, Redpoll and Crested and Willow Tits. In the spring, long before the snows begin to melt, the song of the Ring Ouzel is heard in the forests and Water Pipits sing above the pastures. Great Spotted and Black Woodpeckers are always present, and here and there a Three-toed Woodpecker may reveal its presence by its characteristic slow drumming. In the early morning Black Grouse can be heard near the upper edge of the forest and sometimes even a male Capercaillie.

In June Wheatears are common on the pastureland, while stables and byres provide homes for Black Redstarts. In the subalpine grass-land, which is not cut until late in the summer, Whinchats have a better chance of rearing their young than in the heavily cultivated lowlands. The abundance of Nutcrackers is particularly striking when they start carrying pine cones or hazel nuts over great distances to their winter storage places. The subalpine zone also provides breeding sites for Wallcreepers, a species which descends in winter to the cliffs and larger buildings in the lowlands. Golden Eagles are not difficult to find, and indeed most of the Swiss eyries are in this zone. On the other hand, Eagle Owls have become so scarce that one should refrain from any risk of disturbing them, but Tengmalm's Owl is fairly widespread and, with luck and experience, one may even find a Pygmy Owl.

The Alpine zone has only a few species which will be new to the visitor. Rock Thrushes and Rock Partridges are probably at their highest density here, though they also breed on suitable sunny slopes in the subalpine and mountainous zones. More restricted to these highest parts are Alpine Accentors and Ptarmigan. Snow Finches are widespread, though somewhat local, and are easy to find because they nest alongside House Martins under the roofs of alpine buildings in, for example, the Grimsel, Furka and Gotthard Passes and on the Gornergrat. Alpine Choughs are difficult to approach at their nesting sites in rocky caverns high up in the mountains, but vagrant flocks can be seen in the tourist areas and even in the lower valleys at all times of the year. Incidentally, the red-billed Chough is one of Switzerland's rarest breeding birds, occurring only in some lateral valleys of the Rhône and in the Lower Engadine.

Outside the breeding season the lakes, rivers and hydro-electric schemes provide very favourable habitats for birds. In March and April many dabbling ducks and waders concentrate in certain extensive, flooded plains, and later in the season these birds become more and more attracted to the wetland areas near lowland lakes. The following areas can be recommended for spring excursions: the plain of the River Orbe between Bavois and Yverdon; the huge wetland areas and arable land in the south-eastern corner of Lake Neuchatel; the plain of the River Aare between Bienne and Soleure; the marsh near Neerach and other marshes and small lakes in the vicinity of Zürich; and the plain of the River Linth between Walensee and Zürichsee, and the marshes near Kaltbrunn. The Rhine delta at the eastern end of Lake Constance is also one of central Europe's most important resting places for waders and, although just over the frontier, is easily accessible from eastern Switzerland.

In summer and autumn waders are most conspicuous in places where there are stretches of mud left by a drop in the water level; such places are the Rhine delta, Unter See between Constance and Stein am Rhein, the Klingnau reservoir near Koblenz, the mudflats at the upper and lower ends of Lake Neuchâtel and the Etangs de Bavois.

In the autumn, too, many passes and other places high up in the Alps or in the higher parts of the Jura are ideal for watching bird migration. The best known of these are Cou and Bretolet, where on any day between mid-September and mid-October one may see some 40,000 to 80,000 birds flying through, occasionally even up to 300,000. These two passes are accessible only by a tiring walk of two to three hours and it is difficult to find accommodation at the small bird observatory, even if it is booked well in advance at the Vogelwarte Sempach. Visitors may therefore prefer to go to one of the other passes which are easily reached by car or funicular, such as Wasserscheide on the northern slope of the Gantrisch, Hahnenmoos (near Adelboden) and Forclazpas.

In winter the plains and woods are largely devoid of interesting passerines, although some non-migrant alpine species, such as Wallcreeper, Snow Finch and Alpine Accentor, descend to the lower zones and become a little easier to find. Instead, ornithologists are more attracted to the large lakes (which do not usually freeze), and to some reservoirs and large rivers, where waterfowl are abundant at this season. Even the most experienced bird-watcher may be impressed by the huge gatherings of dabbling ducks, Tufted Ducks, Pochards, Goldeneyes and Goosanders, as well as by the regular appearance of rarer species such as divers, Slavonian and Black-necked Grebes and Arctic Skuas on Lake Geneva, on the hydro-electric schemes of the River Aare (Niederried, Holderbank, Klingnau), on Unter See (off Ermatingen) and on the Upper Rhine (Stein am Rhein, Eglisau, Bern, Riburg, Augst). Geese, patricularly Bean and White-fronted Geese, are regular winter visitors in small numbers in a few open areas from late December to early March. Cormorants gather in certain places at the upper end of Lake Geneva, in the south-eastern corner of Lake Neuchâtel and on Lake Constance.

Ornithological discoveries are always possible in Switzerland, especially in the subalpine and alpine zones. Although the country is small, several valleys and mountain areas have seldom or never been visited by ornithologists. For instance, the distributions of such secretive species as the Three-toed Woodpecker and the Pygmy Owl are not at all well-known, while the Melodious Warbler was first discovered only a few years ago in southern Tessin where it is now known to be a regular and widespread breeding species. The Dotterel is an extremely rare breeding bird in the eastern part of the Swiss Alps.

Italy
with Corsica, Sardinia, Sicily
AND OTHER ISLANDS IN
the Western Mediterranean

Sergio Maria Frugis

Hoopoe

Information on birds can be obtained from the Museo Civico di Storia Naturale or the *Rivista Italiana di Ornitologia*, both at Corso Venezia 55, Milan, from the Laboratoria di Zoologia applicata alla Caccia, Via S. Giacomo 9, Bologna, and from the Associazione Italiana per il World Wildlife Fund, Via Micheli 62, Rome.

If one finds a ringed bird in Italy, the ring should be sent to: Laboratoria di Zoologia applicata alla Caccia, Via S. Giacomo 9, Bologna, Italy.

ITALY
WITH CORSICA, SARDINIA, SICILY
and other islands in
THE WESTERN MEDITERRANEAN

The boot-shaped peninsula projecting into the northern Mediterranean is screened almost continuously at its northern borders by the Alps. The much longer chain of the Apennines, curving from the knee to the toe of the boot, makes the backbone of the peninsula south of the Po valley which is Italy's only extensive area of lowland. The maximum length of the country is from Mount Bianco to the south-eastern tip of the Salentina peninsula (700 miles) and the maximum width is from the French border to Yugoslavia (about 400 miles). The avifauna is rich, with 450 species, of which 232 breed, and yet Italian ornithology is in a poor state. A few serious students do their best to encourage a small number of bird-watchers and hunters with some ornithological interest, but there are many gaps in our knowledge of the distribution and ecology of the breeding species.

It has often been stated that bird life is very scarce in Italy because of the heavy toll taken by hunters and netters, but in many areas this is far from true. No one would deny the damage done by over a million hunters with very little control, nor the effect of netting on passerines, but most of the decline in many bird populations is due to land reclamation and excessive, unplanned urbanisation; moreover, modern agricultural methods, water and land pollution have made much land unsuitable for wildlife. Paradoxically, until very recently it has only been the hunters and their organisations which have been aware that hunting restrictions and habitat conservation were badly needed if there was to be any chance of their sport surviving. In 1967, however, the Italian National Appeal of the World Wildlife Fund was founded and a practical programme for the establishment of a network of wildlife sanctuaries has been started. Two such reserves are already operating along the western coast, in Tuscany, and more details of these will be given later.

The numerous game reserves, most privately owned, are scattered throughout the peninsula and in many of the islands. These provide safe wintering, breeding or resting places for a great number of species as only game birds can be shot in them. It should, however, be noted that 'game birds' includes waterfowl and waders (of which only snipe are regularly shot) and that among the birds of prey only the smaller species are safe; this is partly due to an odd law which protects almost every diurnal and nocturnal feathered predator, except in game reserves. These places are therefore among the best for bird-watching but are often difficult of access and in any case permission to visit has to be obtained from the owner. There are, however, many other opportunities for bird-watching in the Alps and Apennines. The country roads and railways are generally well developed so that many places are easily accessible. For profitable bird-watching it is advisable to choose the breeding season, although the period of migration also offers good opportunities, particularly in the islands (the smaller ones are often better than the larger), the eastern Alps, the southernmost Apennines, the southern coasts, the Po delta, and the Venetian lagoons. Two very important national parks are well worth a visit and these are dealt with in the following pages.

Even with our scanty knowledge it is possible to make a rough, provisional division of the Italian peninsula into four main avifaunal zones. This may help the visitor to know in advance the types of habitats and the kinds of birds that may be seen on different trips.

These main areas correspond quite closely with the four main vegetational zones which, in turn, almost coincide with Italy's four main geographical features, namely the Alps, the Po valley, the Apennines and the coastal areas. In describing the bird life of these zones, I shall stress the need for more knowledge.

The alpine chain is still relatively unspoilt, and in several places offers some of the most beautiful scenery in Italy. Firs, larches and other conifers are often present in mixed evergreen forests, while larches alone tolerate the higher altitudes, together with a dwarf race of pine. The tree line generally does not go above 6,000 feet and above it alpine pastures alternate with scrubby growths of alder and rhododendron. Higher up lie the great peaks and the bare rocks of the true Alps with their snowfields and permanent glaciers. The western section of the alpine chain has a number of interesting places easily reached by car, not so easily by train. In the Alpi Marittime, starting for example from Cuneo, the best trips are to Tenda, Maddalena and the mountains in between. From Turin visits could be made to the Alpi Cozie (Sestrières, Val Pellice and Val Germanasca). In the relatively uninhabited Alpi Graie a note should be taken of the altitudinal distribution of even the common species. Here, for instance, the ranges of House and Italian House Sparrows come close to one another and may possibly overlap; although similar, the males are easily recognised in the field and every note of their occurrence would be of value. From Aosta trips can be made to Courmayeur and Cogne, part of which is included in the Gran Paradiso National Park, an area of some 170 square miles of mountains and valleys centred round Gran Paradiso (altitude 13,100 feet). This park was formerly a game reserve of the Italian kings but is now a complete wildlife refuge where a good population of Ibex survives, and Chamoix, Marmot, Stoat and other wild mammals are still abundant.

Bird life is also abundant though no species are restricted to the area. One of the best sights is that of the Golden Eagle majestically soaring in search of prey. Many facilities are afforded to the visitors to the park, and the Tourist Office in Cogne (Aosta) will provide information.

The Alpi Pennine include two wonderful peaks, Cervino and Monte Rosa, and several interesting places which can only be reached by road. I also recommend trips to Champoluc and Breuil, Gressoney la Trinitè and Macugnaga, where glaciers begin just above the tree line.

The central section starts in the west with the Alpi Lepontine where excursions can be made eastwards from Domodossola in the Val Vigezzo and up to the mountains around Malesco. The Valtellina area, including the Adda valley up to Bormio and Stelvio is rewarding (another large national park is planned here). Madesimo and Livigno are also worth a visit.

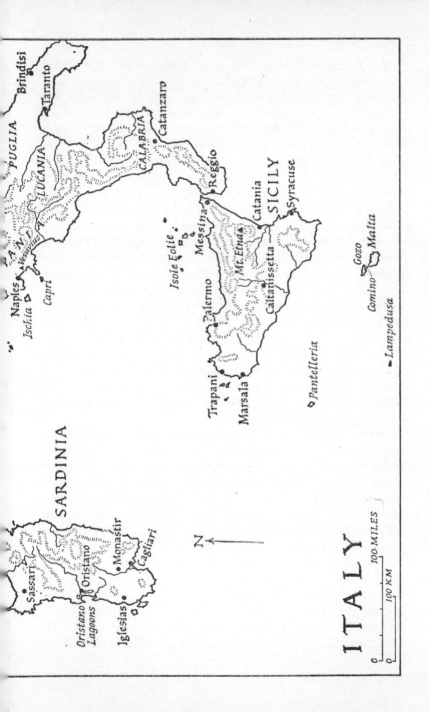

ITALY

N

100 MILES
100 KM

SARDINIA

Sassari
Oristano
Oristano Lagoons
Iglesias
Monastir
Cagliari

PUGLIA
Brindisi
Taranto
LUCANIA
Vesuvius
Naples
Ischia
Capri
CALABRIA
Catanzaro
Reggio
Isole Eolie
Messina
SICILY
Catania
Mt. Etna
Syracuse
Palermo
Caltanissetta
Trapani
Marsala
Pantelleria
Gozo
Comino Malta
Lampedusa

The eastern section has four main divisions: the Alpi Atesine, Dolomitiche, Carniche and Giulie.

Among the numerous species breeding in the Alps the most interesting are Nutcracker, Chough (western Alps only), Alpine Chough, Crested Tit, Willow Tit and Treecreeper (in Italy almost exclusively a mountain bird), Wallcreeper, Dipper, Ring Ouzel, Rock and Blue Rock Thrushes, Bonelli's Warbler, Alpine Accentor, Water Pipit, Great Grey Shrike (note every possible instance of actual breeding), Siskin, Redpoll, Citril Finch, Serin, Snow Finch, Crag Martin, Black, Three-toed, White-backed and Grey-headed Woodpeckers (the last two apparently only in the eastern section), Alpine Swift, Tengmalm's, Pygmy and Eagle Owls, Rock Partridge, Hazel Grouse, Black Grouse, Ptarmigan and Capercaillie (the last apparently absent from the western Alps), Goshawk, Honey Buzzard and (in the eastern Alps) Griffon Vulture. Information is needed on the distribution of the woodpeckers, owls, tits and treecreepers.

The Po Valley

This is the only extensive area of true lowland in Italy and, although rather varied, it may be described as a zone of deciduous forest, intensive cultivation and an abundance of water, including lakes, rivers, rice-fields and brackish lagoons. The main river is of course the Po itself.

On the whole, the larger lakes are less interesting than the smaller ones, but Lake Garda has a colony of Herring Gulls whose breeding grounds are not known, and on Lake Como Black Kites are common throughout the year (more so in summer); they breed on inaccessible cliffs near the rocky shores. In the town of Como itself the cathedral has a breeding colony of Alpine Swifts, which also nest on some buildings in Pallanza (Lake Maggiore). Collared Doves are common in Milan and also in other towns such as Saronne, Bologna and Trieste. Milan is a good starting point for motor trips to the rice-growing areas to the west and south of the town. Almost any rice-field between Novara and Vercelli and between Vercelli and Pavia may have Little Egrets, Grey, Purple, Night and (much rarer) Squacco Herons, of which there are several scattered colonies. The same areas have several small breeding colonies of Black Terns, while the hedgerows and woods surrounding the fields may produce Marsh Warblers and Lesser Grey Shrikes. In winter, harvested rice-fields and the permanently flooded meadows are frequented by large numbers of Snipe, Lapwings, Fieldfares and resident larks; during the autumn migration Water and Meadow Pipits are abundant, and in spring there are ducks (mostly surface-feeding species) and waders such as sandpipers, godwits, Ruffs, Redshanks and Spotted Redshanks. Poplar plantations and wooded areas along the numerous streams and along the Po itself produce many species, including Red-backed and Woodchat Shrikes, Nightingale, Whitethroat, Lesser Whitethroat, Garden and Marsh Warblers, Hoopoe and Golden Oriole. Reedy places have Reed, Great Reed and Sedge Warblers (the latter being rare), Little Bittern, Little Grebe, Moorhen, Coot (rare), Water Rail and Spotted Crake. On gravelly and sandy shores Common and Little Terns, Little Ringed Plovers and Stone Curlews are common.

Muddy shores along the main streams are frequented from July to the end of October by numerous waders ranging from Dunlins and Little Stints to Greenshanks and Ruffs but apparently the only breeding species are Redshanks and Common and Green (rare) Sandpipers. Savi's Warbler is often heard locally (e.g. near Pavia), and in recent years Cetti's Warbler has appeared along the Ticino (especially between the Magenta and Vigevano bridges) and has spread eastwards to the Po: its characteristic call note and song may be heard all the year round. Glossy Ibises nest in small numbers near Vercelli and Verrua Savoia. However, this bird, together with Black-winged Stilts, Avocets, Pratincoles, Whiskered and White-winged Terns (the latter apparently only on passage), Oystercatchers and many other waders can be more easily seen in the rice-fields near the mouth of the Po and in the Valli di Comacchio. The latter is famous for its waterfowl (especially for ducks on passage) and the small muddy islets have nesting Herring and Black-headed Gulls, Little and Common Terns, Shelducks, Mallard and Teal, while Coots, Great Crested Grebes, Penduline and possibly Bearded Tits breed among the reeds and other water plants. There is a large colony of breeding herons (Grey, Purple and Night) and Little Egrets in the nearby Punta Alberete district, and the salt-pans of Cervia have breeding groups of Black-winged Stilts, Avocets and Kentish Plovers.

The brackish, freshwater and sometimes truly marine lagoons which form a network north and south of Venice, known by the misleading name of Valli Venete, are among the best places in Europe for wildfowl (particularly from late autumn to late spring) but, as in the case of Comacchio, access is rather difficult, as most of the land is privately owned. As a consequence, recent information on bird life is scanty and observations are needed. Practically nothing is known of the breeding distribution in the Po valley of the rails and crakes or of the Sedge, Moustached, Grasshopper and Aquatic Warblers.

An old park, open to the public, near the town of Mantova, the so-called Bosco Fontana, still supports a small breeding colony of Black Kites which spread out to neighbouring districts and feed mainly around the Laghi di Mantova, freshwater lagoons created around the town by the river Mincio. Although subject to heavy pollution the Laghi themselves are good spots for bird-watching.

Orphean, Subalpine and Melodious Warblers can be seen in several places, but particularly in the region of Pavia, especially around the village of Broni where there are also small scattered colonies of Bee-eaters.

The Short-toed Lark breeds in small numbers along the river Taro (Parma) and every year a few pairs of Montagu's Harriers are seen where this river joins the Po. The Barred Warbler is also seen in this area, but it rarely breeds and its range in Italy is almost unknown.

The Apennines

Although deforested in many places (especially in the north) the Apennines still have much relatively unspoilt woodland. From altitudes of over 3,000 feet down to the coast the forests are predominantly deciduous with oaks, chestnuts and poplars; higher up, there is a mixture of beech and white and red firs (as on the lower slopes of the Alps) and as a result the bird life is very varied. The avifauna does not include unusual species but some alpine forms can still be found, such as Water Pipits, Snow Finches, Alpine Choughs and Alpine Accentors, while the Rock Partridge is widespread; the members of the grouse family are absent. Beech woods are generally richer than conifer forests in tits and warblers (look for Orphean, Subalpine, Melodious, Wood and Bonelli's); Short-toed Treecreepers and Spotted and Collared Flycatchers are quite common, but it is not known whether the last occurs with the Pied Flycatcher, which is the common breeding species north of the Po. Black and Black-eared Wheatears are seen (particularly in the Ligurian Apennines) but little is known of the present distribution of these species. Black-eared Wheatears are, however, found breeding in very small numbers around the marble and other stone quarries in the mountains north of Brescia.

It is difficult to recommend any particular place for bird-watching in the Apennines, though a few well-known localities are worth mentioning. In Tuscany every beech wood should be visited for warblers, flycatchers and finches, while the Goshawk still occurs in conifer and deciduous woodland above 3,000 feet from Tuscany through Umbria to Lazio Campania and Calabria. Bearded Tits, Sedge, Reed and Great Reed Warblers, Great Crested and Little Grebes breed at Lake Trasimeno near Perugia, while migrating waders, gulls, terns and wildfowl rest on the shores or on the water. Interesting passerines on passage such as Bluethroats (both races), Red-throated Pipits and Red-breasted Flycatchers can be seen among coastal vegetation. Between the true Apennines and the coast there are several smaller hills with sparse vegetation (frequently very poor pasture) in Tuscany, Latium and Campania, and the area between Monte Amiata (south-west of Trasimeno) and Monte Aurunci (north of Gaeta) has such birds of prey as the Peregrine, Lanner and Egyptian Vulture, but it is not certain whether they breed. By far the most interesting part of the Apennines, however, lies in the Abruzzi, where glaciers can still be found. The Parco Nazionale degli Abruzzi includes the upper valley of the river Sangro, an area of outstanding beauty as well as an unusual fauna. Here there are completely isolated populations of Chamoix, Bear, Wolf and possibly Lynx. Birds are plentiful and include breeding Dotterels (rare), Choughs, Alpine Choughs, Snow Finches, Golden Eagles and—a recent discovery—the White-backed Woodpecker. No special permission is needed for bird-watching in the park; there is accommodation at Pescasseroli and the park administration buildings are here too.

The Sila mountain range in Calabria has Collared Flycatchers as well as Firecrests and many other passerines (look for Subalpine and possibly Spectacled Warblers). There are also Black Woodpeckers and, very rarely, Black-headed Buntings. On the lower slopes towards the coast, where the Black-headed Bunting breeds, the passage of raptors, especially Honey Buzzards, is said to be spectacular, although this must have been severely affected by hunting. Very little is known of the Apennines of Lucania where ornithological trips might prove very fruitful (look out for Egyptian Vultures).

The Coasts

The coasts of Italy have an irregular strip of relatively uniform vegetation which is usually referred to as 'macchia'; when less dense this becomes 'garigue' or 'gariga'. In many places almost the only tree left from the original vegetation is the olive, and this is now under cultivation. The evergreen oak is very seldom found nowadays in true forest communities because much of the Mediterranean coastal vegetation has been reduced by man's activities to a degraded form where shrubs and smaller plants predominate. Cork oak and umbrella pine (the latter perhaps introduced into the Italian peninsula) are also characteristic of this zone but have a patchy distribution on the mainland. The larger and smaller islands are also covered to a great extent by macchia. In Apulia, in Tuscany, along the river Arno, and in northern Italy around some of the larger lakes, this type of vegetation occurs farther inland than elsewhere.

The Mediterranean macchia is the favourite habitat of Sardinian, Subalpine, Spectacled, Dartford and Marmora's Warblers (whose presence in Italy has been disputed), Tawny Pipits, Short-toed and Calandra Larks, Corn, Cirl and Black-headed Buntings (this is rare and mainly between Calabria and Apulia), Lesser Kestrels, Rollers, and so on. The towns and larger villages have Pallid Swifts breeding, sometimes with Swifts. Along the Tyrrhenian coast in Liguria look for Black-eared and Black Wheatears, and for the Short-toed Eagle. Certain areas of coastal marshland are good places to look out for waterfowl and for Fan-tailed and Cetti's Warblers.

Three such places deserve special mention. The first is Bolgheri (just south of Leghorn) where the President of the World Wildlife Italian Appeal, the Marquis Mario Incisa della Rocchetta, established the first WWF bird sanctuary in Italy. Here there is a freshwater marsh of some 120 acres where large numbers of waterfowl and waders winter and rest on passage. The marsh (which in summer has a very low water level) is divided from the sandy shore by a strip of macchia whose main features are a wood of very old umbrella pines and a small beech wood; here human interference is limited to watching animals and even this is very strictly controlled. One of the most impressive sights is the assembly on a winter afternoon of thousands of Woodpigeons and Starlings, coming in to roost in a few favourite trees. At peak season (usually January) more than six thousand ducks (mostly surface-feeding) frequent the area with as many Coots, while the surrounding grass fields have numerous Lapwings, Golden Plovers and Curlews. The rarer visitors include Greylag Geese, Goosanders, Great White Egrets, Glossy Ibises, Avocets and so on, while Black-winged Stilts, though not breeding, are frequently seen.

The second place is the Lago di Burano, ten miles south of Monte Argentario. This is the second WWF reserve, and it too is mainly devoted to the protection of migrating and wintering waterfowl and waders. In contrast to Bolgheri, Burano is essentially a brackish lagoon. A rather dense belt of reeds harbours many rails including, it seems, Baillon's, Little and Spotted Crakes, whose status as breeding birds needs to be confirmed. Reed and Great Reed Warblers, as well as Cetti's and Fan-tailed Warblers appear to breed there. Pochard, Tufted and Ferruginous Ducks and Wigeon are more numerous as winter residents here than at Bolgheri, while a few Red-crested Pochards and Goldeneyes are seen every winter.

The belt of macchia dividing the lagoon from the seashore is very rich in bird life particularly during the spring migration when one can see Hoopoes, Rollers, Bee-eaters, Great Spotted Cuckoos, Turtle Doves, many birds of prey (Sparrowhawk, Osprey, Honey Buzzard and Buzzard, Merlin, Hobby, harriers and kites) and many small passerines such as Subalpine Warblers and Lesser Grey Shrikes. In the surrounding fields there are Crested, Calandra, Short-toed Larks and Skylarks, as well as pipits and wagtails. In winter the rich fish population of the lagoon attracts a flock of Cormorants from the neighbouring breeding grounds.

The third place is the promontory of Monte Argentario, united to the mainland by two sandy strips averaging a quarter of a mile in width, which enclose the Orbetello lagoon. Black-winged Stilts and Montagu's Harriers breed there regularly. In addition to the species mentioned for the previous two localities, this area has many more waders, among which the Marsh Sandpiper deserves special mention; it has been observed quite regularly in recent years. The Red-rumped Swallow has also established itself as a breeding species among the villas and cottages along the roads near Monte Argentario, between Porto Ercole and Porto Santo Stefano.

Between Rome and the tip of the peninsula there are many places worth a visit. Little is known of the birds there and they will be more numerous and interesting in the less inhabited zones; the same can be said of the Ionian coast. In the coastal marshes and the hills around Sibari (Calabria) the northward passage of many migrants is said to be spectacular. Quails, Turtle Doves, waders, Garganey and other ducks can often be watched coming ashore from the sea in the mornings. In winter, thrushes and Woodcock are abundant although much hunted.

On the Adriatic coast the best opportunities for bird-watching are in Apulia. Besides good patches of the typical macchia there are several small to medium-sized brackish lagoons and coastal marshes which have many interesting species at all seasons. Three areas deserve special mention: the Lago di Lesina and the Lago di Varano to the north of the Gargano promontory and the coastal strip along the Gulf of Manfredonia, from the town of Manfredonia to Barletta. Once a paradise for birdlife, the marshes and lagoons of Manfredonia are now much reduced in extent owing to land reclamation and water pollution. However, they still have a number of interesting breeding species, including Bearded and Penduline Tits, Pratincoles, Cetti's, Sedge and Fan-tailed Warblers and Little Bustards (rare and now protected); Short-toed and Calandra Larks are also seen. In winter and during migration a great many more species are found (finches, doves, dabbling and diving ducks, waders and so on). This is also the only known regular wintering station in Italy for White-fronted, Bean and (now very rare) Greylag Geese. The drastic reduction of wet habitats has greatly reduced the number of geese, which at present do not exceed four thousand in normal winters.

Visitors to these Apulian marshy grounds in summer (especially in June and July) should carefully scan every small area of water for waders for, although these are mostly arctic breeders, many spend their first summer in a southern country, when they are usually already in full breeding plumage.

I cannot close this section without mentioning the Gargano promontory which, with its hilly grounds, forms the spur of Italy. This is an outcrop of calcareous rock rising to heights of 1,650–2,700 feet. It is covered partly with macchia and partly with pine woods, except near the summits where there is the still untouched Foresta Umbra consisting of limes, sycamores, chestnuts and oaks, as well as some centuries-old beeches. Here the little-known avifauna includes White-backed Woodpeckers (very rare and probably occupying a different ecological niche than the far commoner Great and Lesser Spotted Woodpeckers), Black-headed Buntings, Red-rumped Swallows, Lanners, Red Kites and Black and Black-eared Wheatears.

Corsica

Of the three main islands in the western Mediterranean, Corsica holds the most diversified habitats, as vegetation ranges from true mountain species (pine, birch) in the higher parts to Mediterranean ones along the coasts. Correspondingly, bird life is very varied and relatively rich in raptors. Among the species of interest are: Bonelli's Eagle, Red Kite, Lammergeier (rare and in the most inaccessible mountains), Goshawk, Raven (often occurring in flocks), Bee-eater, Citril Finch, Cirl and Corn Bunting, Blue Rock Thrush, Subalpine, Spectacled, Sardinian, Dartford, Marmora's, Cetti's and Fan-tailed Warblers, Spotted Flycatcher (by far the commonest and most wide-spread breeding bird), the Corsican race of the Woodchat Shrike, Short-toed, Calandra and Woodlarks, Tawny Pipit, Stonechat, Spotless Starling, Rock Sparrow and Pallid Swift. Breeding on islets off the coasts are the Mediterranean races of Manx and Cory's

Shearwaters, Shag (young Shags are markedly whiter below than young Cormorants), and Herring and Audouin's Gulls (the last mainly in the south-east). Two wetlands along the eastern coast provide excellent opportunities for bird-watching—among many interesting species, for example, will be found such very rare birds as the White-headed Duck. These are Bigulgia Lagoon and the Reserve Nationale de Casabianda, which has recently been established as a bird sanctuary covering an area of 5,371 acres stretching from the Tyrrhenian coast to the mouth of the river Tavignano. The Corsican Nuthatch deserves special mention. Once considered conspecific with the Red-breasted Nuthatch of North America, it has now been shown to be a separate species, restricted to this Mediterranean island. It is a rare bird, confined to very old conifer stands (most of which are exploited for timber) and is on the verge of extinction. Bird-watchers are asked to cause as little disturbance as possible and not to give any information which might enable selfish bird collectors to take this or any other rare bird. Although protected by French law, there is unfortunately little control on the island.

Sardinia

Sardinia has a characteristic avifauna, for even species well represented on the continent, have here, in isolation, reached subspecific status. Many of these subspecies are also found in Corsica, but in general they cannot be identified in the field and the situation is further complicated during migration and in winter when the local populations are joined by continental birds of the same species. Among the few species recognisable in the field are the Sardinian Hooded Crow (grey parts with diffused brown tinges) and Citril Finch (upper parts with distinct brown streaks). Dartford, Sardinian, Spectacled and Marmora's Warblers are common (though the last species has a somewhat patchy distribution). Bee-eaters, Rollers and Hoopoes are especially common during spring migration but they also breed. Short-toed and Calandra Larks are found everywhere in suitable habitats. Bonelli's Eagles, Lammergeiers and Black and Griffon Vultures are still found in the central mountain ranges, which are very difficult of access and not always safe places for tourists. On the western coast the Oristano Lagoons have many interesting species, such as Purple Gallinule and Ferruginous Duck, but land reclamation and rice cultivation have partly destroyed the habitat. In winter, however, large numbers of waders and wildfowl provide food for small numbers of Eleonora's Falcons which breed on the island, while in the north and west there are still breeding colonies of Shags, Audouin's Gulls and both species of shearwaters. Herring Gulls are common breeders, of course, but the status of the Slender-billed Gull is uncertain; it is certainly present in winter but probably also present as a breeding species. Sardinia (together with Gibraltar) is the only place in Europe where Barbary Partridges are found. Spotless Starlings are common and Starlings are also present (chiefly in the north), and the Italian House Sparrow is replaced by the Spanish Sparrow.

Sicily

Although a considerable amount of collecting and observation was formerly carried out in Sicily, little is known of the present distribution of birds in this island, apart from a few articles in foreign journals. Here again, several species have evolved local races, though to a lesser extent than in Sardinia and Corsica; these races are generally indistinguishable in the field. Land reclamation, even in the most arid zones, has profoundly altered the original habitat distribution, and the bird life. In fact, there are now no extensive areas of wetland.

Sicily is very mountainous, the highest peak being Mount Etna (over 9,000 feet), which is partly covered with snow all the year round. The vegetation is predominantly Mediterranean, although there is still some mixed woodland with pine, beech, chestnut and poplar, particularly in the north-east. Coastal roads are generally good but those in the interior are often in poor condition. The best places for bird-watching are in the more central, less inhabited districts, though these are usually difficult of access. On field trips care should be taken to carry an adequate supply of drinking water. Many interesting species may still be found, including Bonelli's Eagle, Red Kite, Lanner, Egyptian Vulture, Sicilian Rock Partridge (which in some places is very pale in colour), Spotted Starling and Little

Bustard. The Griffon Vulture which used to be present in some numbers appears to have been exterminated through poisoning of carcasses, but as in other parts of southern Italy the plaintive call of the Scops Owl is frequently heard; Red-necked Nightjars are certainly present but almost nothing is known of their distribution. Very good opportunities for bird-watching are offered during migration, particularly on the eastern and southern coasts where one may see large numbers of such birds as the Caspian Tern, Avocet and Black-winged Stilt.

Other Islands in the Western Mediterranean

The Tuscan Archipelago comprises a group of small islands of which Elba is the largest. Regular boat services connect the island with Livorno and Piombino. Of the smaller islands only Giglio is reached by a boat service from Porto S. Stefano and Pianosa, Capraia and Gorgona by the boat service for Elba. For Montecristo and Giannutri it is necessary to hire a boat (in general rather expensive). All these islands, except Elba, are rather poor in resident species but these include Spectacled and Marmora's Warblers. At migration times, however, such places are usually visited by good numbers of birds, some of which belong to species seldom found on the Continent. These remarks may be applied to all the many other islands scattered along the coasts of Italy.

The Neapolitan Archipelago comprises Ischia, Procida, Capri and, farther to the north-west, Ventotene, Ponza and Zannone. The first three islands are so crowded with people and so heavily hunted that very little bird life is left, although on Capri there is a very active Swedish Ornithological Station where many interesting species are ringed. Zannone is very interesting during both autumn and spring migration but unfortunately it is not regularly served by boat.

North of Sicily, the Isole Eolie are easily reached from Naples and Messina. These volcanic islands have been little studied until very recently and most is known of the species that winter there (including large numbers of passerines) and the passage migrants. The species known to breed include Peregrine and Eleonora's Falcon (the latter on Alcudi and Filicude), Buzzard, Dartford, Sardinian and

Subalpine Warblers, Blue Rock Thrush, Linnet, Goldfinch and Herring Gull. It is not known whether either Manx or Cory's Shearwaters still breed.

Boat services connect Palermo and Ustica, while other interesting islands are Pantelleria (reached by boat from Trapani) and the Pelagia group (Linosa, Lampedusa and the rock of Lampione). The latter islands are still relatively little inhabited and they provide good breeding sites for such species as Manx and Cory's Shearwaters, Peregrine and Eleonora's Falcon, Storm Petrel and Herring Gull. On Lampedusa, the passage of migrants is spectacular and may frequently include Red-breasted Flycatchers, Rufous Bush Chats and Trumpeter Finches.

The Maltese islands, situated in the central channel connecting the eastern and western basins of the Mediterranean Sea, consist of Malta, Gozo, Comino and the uninhabited rocks of Cominotto and Filfla. Resident birds are very few and comprise Blue Rock Thrushes, Barn Owls, Spectacled Warblers, Manx and Cory's Shearwaters, Rock Doves and possibly the Spanish Sparrow. A few other species arrive here to breed, but far more species are observed on passage.

In the Adriatic part of the Mediterranean, the Tremiti islands can be reached by boat from Termoli and Rodi Garganico. The island of S. Domino has a beautiful pine wood frequented on autumn passage by a large number of birds, among which the Woodcocks and thrushes are heavily hunted. The breeding species include Manx and Cory's Shearwaters, Peregrine, Pallid Swift, Blue Rock Thrush and Sardinian Warbler.

Hungary

Zóltan Tildy

Great White Egret

The National Bureau for Nature Conservation (Egyetem Sér 5, Budapest V) is the official body in the field of bird protection. Scientific institutions are only allowed to collect birds or their eggs if this body has given them permission to do so, while private citizens are forbidden to collect either eggs or birds. The establishment and management of reserves is also under the jurisdiction of the National Bureau for Nature Conservation. Normally these reserves are not open to the public, except with special permission from the Bureau. In the protected areas every form of collecting is forbidden, while in the breeding areas of rare species photographing or filming are also not allowed.

The National Bureau for Nature Conservation also manages the Hungarian Ornithological Institute (Garus U. 14, Budapest II) which is the oldest body concerned with ornithology in the country, having been in existence for over 75 years. The scientific staff of this institute works in close co-operation with a large number of amateur ornithologists.

If one finds a ringed bird in Hungary, the ring should be sent to: Ung. Ornithologisches Institut, Madartani Intezet, Kolto U. 21–23, Budapest XII.

HUNGARY

Hungary is situated in the basin enclosed by the Carpathians and the eastern end of the Alps. It measures 300 miles from west to east and 150 miles from north to south, and covers an area of 35,000 square miles. The Hungarian basin has been cultivated for centuries, and this has had a decisive influence on the present vegetation; what remains of the original vegetation and fauna is preserved.

Transdanubia, the area to the west of Budapest, has natural borders formed by the rivers Danube and Drava and the eastern extensions of the Alps. It is characteristic of the varied topography of this area that, in addition to mountains and cultivated parts, it also has the largest lakes in the country: Balaton, Velence and the Hungarian part of the Neusiedler See.

The bird protection and nature conservation area nearest to Budapest is at Lake Velence, about 37 miles south-west from the capital; it extends over approximately ten square miles; an entrance permit is required. The reed beds, which cover over 570 acres, provide undisturbed nesting places for various herons at the western end of the lake. Great White Egrets, Grey and Purple Herons and Spoonbills nest regularly in the area, and others which nest commonly in the reed-bed area include Greylag Geese, Ferruginous Ducks, Little Crakes, Moustached Warblers, Bluethroats and Bearded Tits; Penduline Tits and Savi's Warblers nest occasionally. In the Velence hills, 1,140 feet high and situated north of the lake, Bee-eaters are frequent and regular nesters and Rock Thrushes breed sporadically. Lesser Grey Shrikes can also be seen in the cultivated areas. The nearest town is Székesfehérvár, about 7½ miles away.

Székesfehérvár is also the nearest town for the most important nesting areas of Transdanubia at Sarrét and Mezőföld, respectively 46 and 80 miles from Budapest. In addition to the cultivated areas there are numerous waterlogged meadows, marshes, reed beds and saltpans at Sárkersztúr and Sárszentágota. The most common nesting species in the area are Ferruginous Duck, Bluethroat, Lesser Grey Shrike and in some places Purple Heron, Savi's Warbler, Penduline Tit, Redshank and Red-footed Falcon. The salt-pans at Sárszentágota provide the only known Transdanubian nesting place of Avocets and Kentish Plovers.

About 62 miles from Budapest, following the south-west road by Lake Velence, is the beginning of Balaton, the largest lake in central Europe, which extends about 48 miles from south-west to north-east and has a surface area of approximately 230 square miles. The greatest width is nine miles, the narrowest only one mile, and the average depth only nine feet. The Balaton area is the best known and most frequently visited resort in the country. During summer there is comparatively little to be seen from an ornithological point of view, but during the spring and autumn migration several species gather on the large water surface and on the long shorelines. A little way south of Lake Balaton are several fish ponds which form important nesting places for aquatic birds. Black-headed Gulls and Common Terns nest in colonies and Ferruginous Ducks are common. During migration there are about fifteen duck species, including rare visitors, as well as numerous gulls and waders.

At the western end of Lake Balaton, near the estuary of the River Zala, lies Little Balaton, Hungary's best known nature conservation area. An entrance permit has to be obtained if one wants to visit it. Little Balaton attracts the same birds as Lake Balaton (with the exception of the Rock Thrush), as well as such others as Little Egret, Squacco Heron, Night Heron and Cormorant. Redshanks and Black-tailed Godwits nest frequently and Curlews breed in the meadows. Other common nesters in the Balaton area are Lesser Grey Shrikes and Syrian Woodpeckers, and Bee-eaters, Rollers and Red-footed Falcons also breed there. Keszthely (118 miles from Budapest) is the nearest town to the nature conservation area, being about 8½ miles away.

On the southern side of Transdanubia are the isolated highlands of Mecsek; the highest peak is 2,220 feet. The forests of this mountain chain consist mainly of beech, oak and hornbeam. Several birds of prey breed, although not in large numbers: Black Kite, Honey Buzzard, Booted Eagle and Saker as well as Ravens. Rare species are

Lesser Spotted Eagle and Imperial Eagle. Black Woodpeckers and Collared Flycatchers also breed in this area. The nearest town, Pécs, is situated at the foot of the mountains, 122 miles south-south-west of Budapest.

About 96 miles south of the capital is the Gemenc game preservation area, which is famous all over Europe. The forests in this part of the Danube valley have luxuriant vegetation and an abundant avifauna, including White-tailed Eagle, Black Stork, Saker and, more sporadically, Lesser Spotted Eagle. Black Kites, Night Herons, Purple Herons and Black Woodpeckers also breed there. In cultivated areas around the forests Syrian Woodpeckers, Bee-eaters and Rollers nest regularly and Lesser Grey Shrikes occasionally. Other areas with similar conditions and bird populations can be found farther south along the Danube. The nearest town to Gemenc is Szekszárd, about 5½ miles away, and 89 miles from Budapest.

Hanság, in the north-western part of Transdanubia, is an area of heathland interspersed with meadows, reeds, marshy alder woods and canals. The last include the Hanság canal which crosses the area longitudinally and is supplied by numerous smaller canals. There are also some lakes in the area. The bird life of Hanság is rich and varied. Including also the cultivated area outside Hanság, the most important nesting species are Great Bustard, Grasshopper Warbler, River Warbler, Savi's Warbler, Penduline Tit, Red-footed Falcon, Lesser Grey Shrike and Barred Warbler. Great White Egrets do not nest in the area but visit here in the summer and autumn from the Neusiedler See. The following species breed sporadically: Night Heron, Curlew, Black-tailed Godwit, Redshank, Bearded Tit, Black Kite, Montagu's Harrier, Lesser Spotted Eagle, Greylag Goose, and one or two pairs of Booted Eagles and Black Storks. The nearest towns to the area are Gyor (approximately 22 miles) and Mosonmagyarovar (approximately 3 miles).

The Visegrád hills, north of Budapest and on the right bank of the Danube, are of volcanic origin. The rich bird life in the valleys of this mountain range gives a good idea of the avifauna of central Europe. The few Dippers and Grey Wagtails are characteristic mountain species. Several birds of prey nest in the higher parts of the mountains, including Peregrine, Saker, Red Kite, Black Kite, Goshawk,

Sparrowhawk, Kestrel and Hobby, and, rarely, a pair of Short-toed Eagles. Collared Flycatchers may be found in the oak woods, Red-breasted Flycatchers in the beech woods, and the Black Wood-pecker nests sporadically. Scops Owls breed occasionally in the orchards of villages along the Danube and the Eagle Owl has nested in three quarries only. Visegrád, via Szentendre, is 24 miles from Budapest. The mountain roads are well signposted. Tourist hostels and restaurants ensure enjoyable excursions.

Pilis, about 24 miles south-east of Budapest, is a dolomite and limestone mountain area of the Triassic period. Its bird life is fairly abundant, though water is scarce on the peaks. The wooded parts have Chaffinch, Hawfinch, Starling, Tree Pipit, Nightingale, Rock Thrush, Stonechat, Wheatear, Blackbird, Song and Mistle Thrush, Roller, Hoopoe, Golden Oriole, and a few Buzzards, Sakers and Hobbies. The distance from Budapest to Esztergom is 28 miles, and one can motor round the whole mountain via Szentendre, Pomáz, Pilisszentkereszt and Dobogókö.

Börzsöny mountain is on the left bank of the Danube, 31 miles north of Budapest. Although one cannot take a car on the mountain itself there is a fairly good road around the base and several places where one can stay. This steep mountain is covered with oak and beech forests, with numerous springs and brooks. The valleys have Grey Wagtails and Wrens, and some Dippers. Red-breasted Fly-catchers occur among the hornbeams and Collared Flycatchers can be seen in the oak woods. In the upper regions Mistle Thrushes, Black Woodpeckers, Woodcocks, Hazel Grouse and White-backed Woodpeckers can be observed, while Sakers and occasionally Peregrines breed in the rocky parts. One or two pairs of Imperial Eagles and Lesser Spotted Eagles also nest.

The Cserhát range consists of gently sloping hills, with clay and sandy soils, few forests and little water. The highest peak is Naszály (2,130 feet) rising above the town of Vác. Rock Thrushes and Wheat-ears can often be seen in the quarries, and small colonies of Bee-eaters can occasionally be found in the soft sandy banks. Red-backed Shrikes, Whitethroats and Barred Warblers are frequent among the bushes, and Scops Owls are always common in the old walnut trees.

Mátra is at the centre of the north-central mountain range, with

Kékestető (3,320 feet) as the highest peak of the country. Galyatető (3,150 feet) is a mountain health resort with several hotels. The avifauna consists mainly of songbirds, with Black Redstarts and House Martins around inhabited places and Lesser Whitethroats and Whitethroats in the garden hedges. Yellowhammers and Red-backed Shrikes frequent the stony pastures whilst Rock Thrushes and Wheatears prefer the quarries. Nightingales, Song Thrushes, Blackcaps, Barred Warblers, Golden Orioles, Rollers, Hoopoes and Turtle Doves can be seen in the forests, and Robins, Wrens, Cuckoos, Redbreasted Flycatchers and Collared Flycatchers in the valleys. Among the woodpeckers, Great Spotted Woodpeckers are most frequent, and Syrian Woodpeckers are common in inhabited places. A motorway passes through the Mátra area, and most of the tourist hotels are accessible by car.

The Bükk massif is composed of sedimentary limestone with a depth of several hundred feet. It is 12 miles long and the wide plateau has an altitude of about 2,600–2,900 feet. The slopes are covered with extensive oak and beech forests. The bird life differs from that of Mátra in that the cliffs are particularly favoured as nesting places by Peregrines and Sakers. Birds nesting in the pine woods of the plateau include Dunnock, Goldcrest, Coal Tit and Mistle Thrush, while Woodlarks are common in the meadows. The mountain streams have Dippers and Grey Wagtails. To get a good idea of this region the best route from Budapest is via Gyöngyös to Eger (80 miles), and then via Felsőtárkany, Rapashuta and Lillafured to Miskolc (43 miles).

The mountains near Zemplén and Tokaj are composed of andesite and rhyolite. Here, extensive areas of forest and cliff provide homes for such birds of prey as Imperial Eagle, Peregrine, Saker, Red Kite, Black Kite, Lesser Spotted Eagle, Booted Eagle, Goshawk and Sparrowhawk, and in the pine woods Crested Tits also breed. The best route to follow is from Miskolc via Szerencs, Sarospatak, Satoraljaujhely, Pálháza, Kemencepatak and Kőkapu (180 miles from Budapest).

The Great Hungarian Plain, with an area of about 19,000 square miles, covers the central and eastern part of the country. It is bordered to the west by the Danube, to the north by the northern

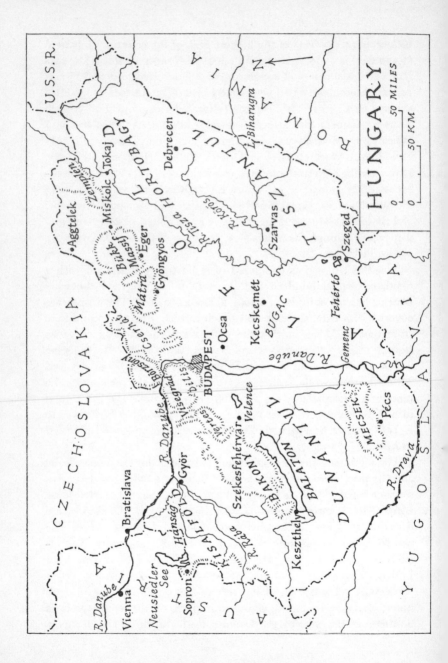

mountains and to the east and south by the Rumanian and Yugoslav frontiers. This area is divided into two separate regions by the River Tisza. The area between the Danube and Tisza is now almost entirely under cultivation, but between Kecskemet and Szeged there is more or less flat steppe country with sand dunes, salt-pans, marshy meadows and alder woods, each with its characteristic bird life.

The typical birds of the area can best be seen by following the main Budapest-Szeged road. The grassy country steppe, broken up by salt-pans, marshy forest and dunes starts about 24 miles from Budapest. Ócsa is an area of about 1,230 acres with alder woods and marshy meadows. The characteristic birds of the marshy grasslands are Great Bustard, Curlew, Black-tailed Godwit, Redshank, Montagu's Harrier and, rarely, Short-eared Owl. A few pairs of Red-footed Falcons breed in deserted crows' nests in the alder woods. Grasshopper Warblers and River Warblers are also common nesting birds in the woodland clearings, and a few pairs of Rollers can be found at Ócsa.

The Apaj-Ürbő steppe area lies 9 miles south-west of Ócsa, and here the nesting species include Great Bustard, Kentish Plover, Black-tailed Godwit, Redshank, Avocet, Pratincole and Stone Curlew. Bearded Tits, Bluethroats and Savi's Warblers breed among the reeds in the fish ponds. During spring and autumn migration this area is visited by many waders and ducks.

Lake Fehértó (White Lake) near Szeged is the southernmost of the salt lakes in the area between the Danube and Tisza and is one of the country's most important reserves for waterfowl; an entrance permit is necessary to visit it. Birds occurring here include Avocet, Black-winged Stilt, Kentish Plover, the odd Pratincole, and several thousand pairs of Black-headed Gulls and Common Terns. Purple Herons nest in large colonies among the reed beds of the fish ponds, and Black-necked, Great Crested and Red-necked Grebes also breed.

The Tisza valley is an important migration route, and Lake Fehértó is one of the main assembly points for birds which follow the river in spring and autumn. Thousands of waders collect along the shores, and on the water surface there are large numbers of ducks and geese. Szeged Museum has the richest regional collection of the varied avifauna of the Lake Fehértó area.

Approximately 4 miles north-east of Lake Fehértó, in the valley of the Tisza, is the Sasér reserve. Willow and poplar woods broken up by meadows and streams give this area a very characteristic appearance. The heron family is particularly well represented, for each year there are breeding colonies of 60–100 pairs of Little Egrets, 10–12 pairs of Squacco Herons, 100–150 pairs of Night Herons and 20–40 pairs of Grey Herons. Among the birds of prey, Black Kites breed regularly, and White-tailed Eagles and Red-footed Falcons sporadically. Rollers and Syrian Woodpeckers are also common in this reserve.

The area to the east of the River Tisza is characterised by the Kardoskút–Fehértó, an area of about 370 acres situated between Hódmezővásárhely and Orosháza, with an avifauna similar to that of the Szeged-Fehértó region. It is of importance mainly as a meeting place for various waders. Perhaps the most interesting sights here are the migrating Cranes, which come over the eastern border of Hungary in spring and autumn and stay on the lake for several weeks.

Lake Biharugra lies between the Sebes-Körös area and the eastern frontier of the country, and borders on extensive fish ponds covering an area of about 7,400 acres. Among the reedy islets several waterfowl breed, including Greylag Goose, Mallard, Garganey, Gadwall, Pintail, Shoveler, Pochard and Ferruginous Duck. During the autumn and spring migration Lake Biharugra is also the assembly place for hundreds of thousands of ducks and also for White-fronted, Lesser White-fronted and Bean Geese. After Hortobágy this area is Hungary's second largest wintering place for birds.

In the woods near the town of Debrecen there are some pairs of Levant Sparrowhawks, which first bred in Hungary in 1962.

Between the Debrecen heathland and the River Tisza lies the largest continuous salt steppe of the lowlands, the famous Hortobágy region, covering an area of some 49,000 acres, interspersed with cultivated land, forests and large fish ponds. The reed beds around the fish ponds shelter a colony of 50–150 pairs of Spoonbills. One or two pairs of Great White Egrets nest here as well, although not every year.

Hortobágy is world famous in ornithology mainly as a migration point. Its almost limitless, open barren country is the most important area for wild geese in Europe. During the autumn thousands of geese fly into this area and several species of ducks also gather here in enormous numbers, mainly on the deep fish ponds.

Ohát Forest, a nature reserve in the western part of the lowlands, has Hungary's largest colony of Red-footed Falcons, consisting of about two hundred pairs.

Each of the more interesting ornithological areas of the lowlands mentioned above is accessible by car. The most distant point from Budapest is Lake Biharugra, about 185 miles away. All the areas mentioned here are within an hour's travelling time from the nearest towns offering adequate accommodation for the visiting bird-watcher.

Rumania

Dan Munteanu

White Pelicans

Ornithological work is carried out under the auspices of the Ministry of Education (Museum of Natural History in Bucharest, Universities of Cluj and Iaşi, and the Biological Institute at Pîngărţi) and of regional museums, such as those at Timisoara, Oradea, Piteşti, Bacău, Sibiu, Craova and Tulcea. The Institute for the Protection of Plants in Bucharest studies the relationship between birds and agriculture and the Central Ornithological Bureau co-ordinates ringing. The Institute for Forest Research in Bucharest pays particular attention to species which come under the shooting laws, and the Commission for Nature Monuments (controlled by the Rumanian Academy in Bucharest), concerns itself with protected species and the management of reserves.

At the moment Rumania has no separate ornithological periodical. The results of ornithological research are published in general biological periodicals, and sometimes abroad.

If one finds a ringed bird in Rumania, the ring should be sent to: Centrala Ornitologica Romana, Bd Ion Ionescu de la Brad 8, Bucharest I, Rumania.

RUMANIA

A look at the map of Rumania or, better still, a visit reveals a surprising variety of natural conditions for a country whose area is a little less than that of Great Britain. Central Rumania, or Transylvania, forms a plateau 600 to 1800 feet above sea level and almost encircled by mountains, some of which are over 7,800 feet (the Eastern Carpathians, the Southern Carpathians or Transylvanian Alps, and the Western Carpathians). The Dobruja area in the southeast includes the Danube Delta and the remains of some of the most ancient mountains in Eurasia, while in the south there are slightly undulating plains, most of which provide fertile agricultural land.

There are numerous rivers, the majority of which drain into the Danube, which in turn takes their waters to the Black Sea. The number of lakes has been reduced by settlement and drainage, but in recent times a number of reservoirs have been constructed in various parts of the country. The Rumanian part of the Black Sea coast has a length of about 150 miles.

The climate of Rumania is temperate-continental, with warm summers and relatively hard winters. January is the coldest month with an average temperature just below freezing point in the plains and much colder in the mountains; July is the warmest in most of the country with an average of over 20°C in the plains. Rainfall is at its lowest (about 15 inches) on the Black Sea coast and highest (40–60 inches) in the mountains, and most of it falls in the spring. The moderating Mediterranean influence is felt in the south-west of the country.

The avifauna is similar to that of Central Europe, but the situation of the country in the south-east of Europe introduces some special characteristics. First, there is the penetration, particularly in the southern regions, of Mediterranean species such as Egyptian Vulture, Black-winged Stilt, Mediterranean and Slender-billed Gulls, Pratincole, Alpine Swift, Crag Martin, Calandra Lark, Woodchat

Shrike, Sombre Tit, Moustached and Olivaceous Warblers, Black-eared Wheatear, Black-headed and Cirl Buntings, Spanish Sparrow and perhaps also Rock Partridge. Secondly, there are several Asiatic species with a range that extends into this part of Europe; these include White and Dalmatian Pelicans, Pygmy Cormorant, Great White Egret, Spoonbill, Ruddy Shelduck, Pallid Harrier, Saker, Red-footed Falcon, Marsh Sandpiper, Black-winged Pratincole, Pied Wheatear, Rose-coloured Starling and Paddyfield Warbler. At the same time several northern species, such as Mute Swan, Tufted Duck, Crane and Dotterel nest as far south as Rumania.

Apart from breeding birds, numerous migrants pass through the country, both from central and northern Europe and from western Asia. Many species that breed farther north spend the winter in Rumania.

The mountainous regions of Rumania offer some of the wildest and most beautiful scenery in Europe. In the Southern Carpathians the alpine zone is particularly well represented at Retezat, Paring, Fagaras, Bucegi and Piatra Craiului, and in the Eastern Carpathians at Ceahlau, Calimani and Rodna. Among the birds typical of these alpine regions are Alpine Accentors and Water Pipits, as well as Dotterels in the Cibin, Lotru and Bucegi Mountains, and probably also in the Rodna Mountains. Other species include Dunnock, Black Redstart, Ring Ouzel, Raven and, more sporadically, Partridge and Skylark. A few Shore Larks were recently found in summer in the Cibin and Tarcu Mountains. The Lammergeier has recently disappeared and the Golden Eagle is becoming very rare. The calcareous rocks of the mountain zone form a suitable habitat for Wallcreepers, which even extend to the barren alpine regions, and for Rock Thrushes.

The Retezat National Park in the Southern Carpathians is the only national park in Rumania. It covers an area of about 32,000 acres, and includes both barren alpine country and forests of conifer and beech. Part of the park is a scientific reserve established to protect the Chamois, various eagles and numerous interesting plant species, and for this the visitor will need a permit from the Commission for Nature Monuments.

The conifer forests cover a large area in the mountains, especially in the Eastern Carpathians, but the avifauna there is no richer than in other parts of Europe. The commonest birds are Coal Tits and Firecrests, and, at least in the north of the country, Goldcrests, Ring Ouzels, Willow and Crested Tits, Crossbills, Bullfinches and Nutcrackers are found everywhere; also Willow Warblers and Siskins nest in the north. Among the woodpeckers, the Three-toed and Black are characteristic. There are Capercaillies in all the dense forests but Black Grouse are scarce and restricted to some places in the north of the country, such as the Rodna and Calimani Mountains, Cirlibaba and Eastern Maramures. Among the birds of prey there are Buzzards, Lesser Spotted Eagles and Tawny, Ural and Tengmalm's Owls.

The mixed mountain forests, with spruce, fir, beech, hornbeam and birch, cover a large area and are particularly well represented in the Southern and Western Carpathians. Their avifauna comprises species characteristic of both conifer and deciduous forests.

The deciduous forests stretch over the lower zones of the mountains and into the sub-Carpathian region and occur in more restricted areas on the plains and even in the Danube Delta, at Letea and Caraorman. Some of the birds common to both conifer and deciduous forest include Cuckoo, Great Spotted Woodpecker, Tree Pipit, Robin, Blackbird, Song Thrush, Chaffinch and Jay. Others such as Hazel Grouse, White-backed Woodpecker, Wren, Collared and Redbreasted Flycatchers, Chiffchaff and Mistle Thrush prefer the beech forests at somewhat higher altitudes. Some species from the conifer forests, such as Black Woodpecker, Dunnock and Bullfinch, also extend into these forests.

Many other birds are widespread in the deciduous forests, where Garden Warblers, Blackcaps, Wood Warblers, Spotted Flycatchers, Redstarts and Great Tits are all common, together with five species of woodpecker: Great Spotted, Middle Spotted, Lesser Spotted, Green and Grey-headed. Nuthatches are also very numerous and Woodlarks are often seen flying above the trees. The call of the Turtle Dove is heard frequently, but Stock Doves and Woodpigeons are rarer. Blue, Marsh and Long-tailed Tits are also quite numerous, as are Icterine Warblers and, in the south, Olivaceous Warblers. Hoopoes and Wrynecks are found particularly among

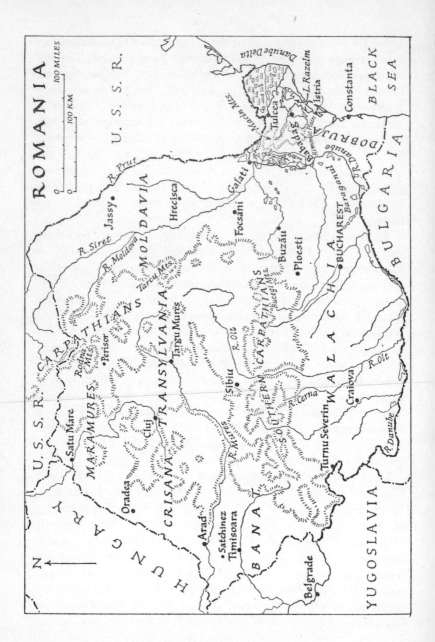

ROMANIA

N

100 MILES

100 K.M.

BLACK SEA

U.S.S.R.

HUNGARY

YUGOSLAVIA

BULGARIA

Danube Delta

Macin Mts.

L. Razelm

Istria

Constanta

Tulcea

Rîmnicu Plain

DOBRUJA

R. Danube

D.R.D.

Baraganul

BUCHAREST

Ploesti

Buzău

Bucegi Mts.

Focsăni

Galati

Hrecisca

R. Prut

Jassy

R. Siret

R. Moldova

MOLDAVIA

Tarcu Mts.

Persani

Rodna Mts.

CARPATHIANS

TRANSYLVANIA

Targu Mures

Sibiu

R. Olt

R. Olt

SOUTHERN CARPATHIANS

R. Cerna

Craiova

WALACHIA

Turnu Severin

R. Mures

Cluj

MARAMURES

Satu Mare

Oradea

CRISANA

Arad

Satchinez

Timisoara

BANAT

Belgrade

R. Danube

willows, as are Starlings, Golden Orioles and Hooded Crows. Pheasants occur in the undergrowth of many forests at low altitudes. Among the birds of prey which prefer deciduous forests, Black Kites, Booted Eagles and Hobbies are relatively common, as well as Sakers (particularly along the Danube), while Goshawks extend from the mountains to the sea.

Many of the deciduous forest birds occur in woodland along the rivers, and of these River, Marsh and Barred Warblers, Lesser Whitethroats, Nightingales and Thrush Nightingales are particularly characteristic.

In town parks, apart from some of the woodland birds, there are three species which have recently appeared in Rumania: Collared Dove, Syrian Woodpecker and Serin. The first two are common in localities where Swallows, House Martins, House and Tree Sparrows and Jackdaws have also bred. Swifts occur in some towns, and Black Redstarts and Serins are found particularly in mountain villages, while White Storks nest quite commonly in villages on the plains, especially near rivers and ponds.

The avifauna of the extensive plains is less diverse but it includes some interesting birds. Great Bustards occur in the south of the country and in the plains of the west. The Little Bustard, which used to nest in Baragan, now probably occurs only as a migrant. Quail are to be found over many parts of Europe, but here as everywhere else they continue to diminish. The Partridge, which has become much reduced in numbers, is now protected. Among the larks, the commonest are the Skylark and Crested Lark, but in the southeast they are joined and even replaced here and there by the Calandra Lark and Short-toed Lark. Corncrakes, Tawny Pipits and Yellow Wagtails are numerous. Red-backed and Lesser Grey Shrikes are numerous in bushes and clumps of trees, and Great Grey Shrikes breed in Transylvania and northern Moldavia. Yellowhammers and Corn Buntings are common throughout Rumania, as are Whitethroats, Whinchats and Stonechats. Ortolan Buntings are more numerous in the south. Rollers, Greenfinches and Goldfinches are frequent along the roadsides.

There are large colonies of Rooks in tall trees. Sometimes their abandoned nests may be occupied by Red-footed Falcons, Kestrels or Long-eared Owls; Magpies too are common. Among the birds of prey which prefer the plains, the Black Kite, Imperial Eagle and Pallid and Montagu's Harriers all nest in Rumania in small numbers.

In the mountain regions there are Dippers and Grey Wagtails along the streams, and at all altitudes there are Little Ringed Plovers, Common Sandpipers, Kingfishers and White Wagtails along the rivers. Colonies of Sand Martins and Bee-eaters nest in cliffs and steep river banks in the hilly regions and on the plains. In backwaters, marshes and pools, the avifauna is in general similar to that found in the Danube Delta, but poor in the rarer species.

Up to recent times there were extensive marshes at Banat in the west of the country. The ornithological reserve of Satchinez (160 acres) has been established in the small area that remains unspoilt. Grebes, herons, ducks, Coots, Bluethroats and many others nest here, but the most important species is the Little Egret, which nests in mixed colonies with Squacco and Night Herons.

In the interior of the country, high-altitude lakes, which still preserve something of the rich aquatic avifauna of earlier times, are found in Crisana (Carei, Otomani, Cefa), in central Transylvania (Sic, Geaca, Taga, Zaul de Cimpie, Taureni), in the Rimmic Plain (Balta, Alba, Amara, Ianca, Jirlau) and in north-eastern Moldavia; there are also lakes on the plains along the Danube (the majority of which are now settled) and along some of the larger rivers.

To see the numerous rare aquatic species, however, one must visit the Dobruja, a region with an extremely interesting and rich bird life. The Danube Delta and Razelm lagoon complex forms one of the largest water bird areas in Europe, comparable with the mouth of the Guadalquivir, the Camargue and the Volga Delta. Tulcea is the main town of the Delta and the starting point for visitors. Steamers transport visitors along the large canals and, using small boats and the help of local fishermen, bird-watchers can explore the backwaters and lakes and penetrate the dense reed beds. Authority from the Commission for Nature Monuments is needed to visit the reserves.

Here the White Pelican has its only large colonies in Europe. These are not always in the same place, sites being deserted and new colonies started, but in recent years there has been a growing colony near Lake Rosca. Dalmatian Pelicans also nest near here, but in smaller colonies. The Great White Egret nests in reduced numbers, but, as a result of protection, the Little Egret has become one of the common species of the Delta. Spoonbills, on the other hand, have disappeared from the Danube pools and now nest in only a few places in the Delta and at Lake Cerna (western Dobruja). There are numerous mixed colonies of Pygmy Cormorant, Night and Squacco Herons and Little Egret. The Glossy Ibis is common and is the most numerous species in many of the heronries. Purple Herons are also common, but the numbers of Grey Herons and Cormorants have been reduced. Among the ducks the commonest are Mallard and Ferruginous Duck, but seven other ducks nest here, as do Greylag Geese and a small number of Mute Swans. Of the four species of grebes the commonest is the Great Crested Grebe. The Coot is one of the most abundant birds of the Delta and in the reed beds there are also Bitterns, Little Bitterns, Water Rails, Moorhens, Savi's, Reed and Great Reed Warblers, Bearded and Penduline Tits and Reed Buntings. Overhead are Black and Common Terns and, in smaller numbers, Black-headed and Herring Gulls and Whitewinged Black Terns. Among the birds of prey are Black Kites, Lesser Spotted and White-tailed Eagles and Marsh Harriers.

In the Razelm lagoon area (Razelm, Golovita, Zmeica, Sinoe), shallow stretches of water alternate with wide areas of marshland and the more open vegetation supports an avifauna differing from that of the Delta proper. The most notable species is the Shelduck, which nests mostly in Istria (about 300 pairs). The Ruddy Shelduck is much rarer and has almost disappeared. Black-winged Stilts nest in the Murighiol reserve and in a few other places, and Avocets occur to the north of Razelm. Other common species here include Little Ringed and Kentish Plovers, Lapwing, Redshank and Pratincole. Black-winged Pratincoles, Oystercatchers, Curlews and Marsh Sandpipers occur less commonly. Terns nest here in large numbers, the most abundant being the Black, White-winged Black, Whiskered and Common. Gull-billed and Caspian Terns are found in small numbers. The commonest gull is the Black-headed, followed by the Herring, Mediterranean, Slender-billed and Little (breeding pairs are scarce, but there are numerous immature birds). Black-tailed

Godwits are seen everywhere in summer, but it has not yet been confirmed that they nest here. After nesting, many birds of the Delta come to the lagoons and in spring (March-April) and particularly autumn (August–October) great flocks of migratory birds pass through the Delta and Razelm complex.

Within the Delta there are three great reserves, the Rosca-Buhaiova-Hrecisca (which also includes the old botanical reserve of Letea Forest), the Perisor-Zatoane and the Periteasca-Leahova, with a total area of about 84,000 acres. There are also four small reserves or refuges, at Murighiol, Plopul (Beibugeac), Istria and on the island of Popina.

The shores of the Black Sea have a number of littoral lakes, such as Corbu, Tasaul, Siutghiol, Agigea, Techirghiol, Costinesti, Tatlageac and Mangalia, where the bird life is similar to that of the Razelm complex. However, the number of breeding birds is smaller, although the rare White-headed Duck has been found to breed at Lake Agigea. The whole of this region is visited by numerous migrating waterfowl.

In winter the wetlands of Dobruja and the shores of the Black Sea support large numbers of waterfowl, such as Black-throated Diver, Whooper Swan, White-fronted and Red-breasted Geese, Teal, Wigeon, Pintail, Tufted Duck, Goldeneye and Goosander.

The mainland of Dobruja is relatively less known, although many interesting birds are found here including several which occur only rarely in other parts of Rumania, such as Alpine Swift, Woodchat Shrike, Egyptian Vulture, Stone Curlew, Pied Wheatear, Rose-coloured Starling, Spanish Sparrow and Black-headed Bunting. Many species typical of the plains or steppes are also present. In the north of Dobruja there are the Macin Mountains, rising to 550 feet, and the Babadag Plateau. In the last century the woodlands of Babadag were renowned for great numbers of nesting birds of prey, particularly Black Vultures, but these and the Griffon Vultures are now rare and only occur as vagrants both in the Dobruja and in the Carpathians. A number of mountain birds such as Black and White-backed Woodpeckers, Sombre Tit, and Rock Bunting are found here.

Bulgaria

James Ferguson-Lees

Black-headed Wagtails

Ornithology in Bulgaria is at present largely the province of the Academy of Sciences, the Zoological Institute and the Agricultural Scientific Research Institute. There is no ornithological society, however, and there are very few serious ornithologists; amateur interest is confined to elementary teaching in schools. Nevertheless, the Natural History Museum at Sofia contains an interesting collection of mounted specimens and the Bulgarian public is beginning to take advantage of national parks and wildlife sanctuaries. There are four sanctuaries on the Danube and three on the Black Sea Coast, and a number of reserves for migratory birds. Nearly all species and their eggs are protected by law and even more comprehensive legislation is envisaged. Shooting is well regulated by comparison with many European countries, while the netting of birds and the commercial exploitation of eggs for food are now completely prohibited.

If one finds a ringed bird in Bulgaria, the ring should be sent to Musée de Zoologie, Centre d'Ornithologie, 1 Boulevard Rouski, Sofia.

BULGARIA

Bulgaria is a roughly rectangular country, rather more than 300 miles from west to east at its widest and averaging about 150 miles from north to south. It can be divided conveniently into five main regions: the fertile Danube plain in the north; the Stara Planina mountains forming a belt across the middle and rising to 7,800 feet; the central plain and valleys of the Maritsa and its tributaries immediately to the south of this belt; the high and heavily wooded Rila, Rodopi and Pirin mountains rising to 9,600 feet in the extreme south and south-west; and in the east the Black Sea coast and its adjacent hinterland which, in the north-east, includes the southern part of the steppe country of the Dobrudja. Bulgaria is thus made up of four alternating layers of lowland and mountain held together, as it were, by a coastal strip down one side.

Bulgaria is an agricultural country and the lowland areas have largely been turned over to farmland. It is difficult, therefore, to find really unspoilt parts and in the north-east, for example, the fields and vineyards extend almost to the cliff edges or beaches. Land reclamation and hydro-electric schemes have been major factors in the general reduction of breeding marsh birds. This is particularly noticeable around the Black Sea lakes at Varna and Burgas where intensive agriculture has caused big changes in bird populations over the last forty years. The mountains, on the other hand, are relatively unspoilt. Main roads are good throughout Bulgaria (and comparatively free from traffic), but secondary roads can be very poor and are often unmetalled, with the result that the heavy thunderstorms which are a feature of the hot summers in this part of Europe can make them temporarily almost impassable.

For a closer examination of Bulgarian birds it seems best to consider first the last of the five main areas, the Black Sea coast, as this is the part in which people from western Europe are most likely to stay. Unfortunately, although facilities for tourists here are now easier and cheaper than ever before, the enormous increase in visitors is resulting in a mushroom growth of hotels which is helping further to destroy what is left of the natural habitats. Among the most interesting sections are Lakes Burgas, Mandra and Atanosov which are all within easy reach of the town of Burgas. Not so long ago these used to be the nesting places of a wider variety of water birds than now, but an interesting selection still breeds there and they are also dormitories and feeding areas for large numbers of non-breeders and immatures and a focal point for waders and terns at the migration seasons.

White Pelicans may be seen at these lakes in tens or even hundreds in summer, as well as Purple and Squacco Herons, Little Bitterns, Little Egrets, the odd Great White Egret or Black Stork, numbers of White Storks, and a few Spoonbills and Glossy Ibises. There are grebes, including Red-necked and Black-necked, and up to a dozen species of ducks at a time, among them Ferruginous Ducks and Ruddy Shelducks. Marsh Harriers nest and the visitor may also be lucky enough to see a White-tailed Eagle or an Osprey. Variable numbers of non-breeding Mediterranean and Little Gulls are present throughout the summer, and a few of the former sometimes nest. Little Ringed and Kentish Plovers, Black-winged Stilts and Avocets breed by these lakes and possibly Pratincoles also. Common and Little Terns both nest, and Gull-billed and Black have done so. Short-toed Larks, Tawny Pipits and Black-headed Wagtails are dotted about in suitable areas.

Some of these species are commoner on spring or autumn passage. Cranes may also be seen in large numbers in March and October. Migrant waders (including Marsh and Curlew Sandpipers, Ruffs, Little Stints, Spotted Redshanks, Black-tailed Godwits, and a few Broad-billed Sandpipers) pass through in hordes. In April–May and August–September fluttering parties of Black, White-winged Black, Whiskered and Gull-billed Terns may be seen. In winter these lakes provide quarters for Greylag, White-fronted and Lesser White-fronted Geese (and the odd Red-breasted), Whooper Swans, and a whole variety of ducks including White-headed, Goosander and Smew.

Many of these birds may also be seen on the saltpans and open water at Pomorié, farther north at Lake Varna (often comparatively disappointing) and at Lakes Shabla and Blanitsa at the edge of the Dobrudja, The shoreline is worth watching for waders and terns, as well as Shags (Cape Kaliakra), Cormorants, occasional Manx Shearwaters and, in winter, divers and various seaducks. Great Crested, Red-necked and Black-necked Grebes are likely to turn up on both sea and fresh water. The cliffs around Varna and Balcik provide homes for several interesting species. One of the rarest, but quite common here, is the Pied Wheatear, in Europe confined to the coasts of north-east Bulgaria and south-east Rumania. Here, too, are Rock Thrushes breeding at sea level in the niche occupied by the Blue Rock Thrush farther west in Europe, as well as Rollers and the odd pair of Eagle Owls, while Rose-coloured Starlings may be seen in tens or even hundreds (though their numbers vary enormously from year to year). Nor should the interesting colonies of cliff-nesting House Martins and Tree Sparrows be overlooked.

At the edges of the coastal towns, especially in the extensive hotel gardens at Varna, it is possible to hear the jingling song of the Cirl Bunting (here at almost the northern limit of its range in eastern Europe) and, at night, the monotonous and melancholy whistle of the Scops Owl, though both are commoner on the lower slopes of the mountains in the southern part of the country. A cliff overlooking Balcik holds one of the few coastal colonies of Swifts and Alpine Swifts (the latter are more numerous in the mountains). In the towns Collared Doves are common and Herring Gulls nest in hundreds on the roof-tops, even above busy streets; on the old houses at Nessebur those gulls may be watched at little more than head height. A bird to watch out for at the edges of any inhabited area, including villages and farms, is the Syrian Woodpecker; the very similar Great Spotted Woodpecker is found more in the real woodland which the Syrian seldom visits. In some villages and wood-edges near the coast Spanish Sparrows outnumber both House and Tree. Open country all along the Black Sea coastal strip produces another speciality of south-east Europe, the Black-headed Bunting, a strikingly coloured little bird which is really very numerous in this part and which can frequently be seen on telephone wires beside the road, along with Rollers, Bee-eaters, Lesser Grey Shrikes and the odd Stonechat or

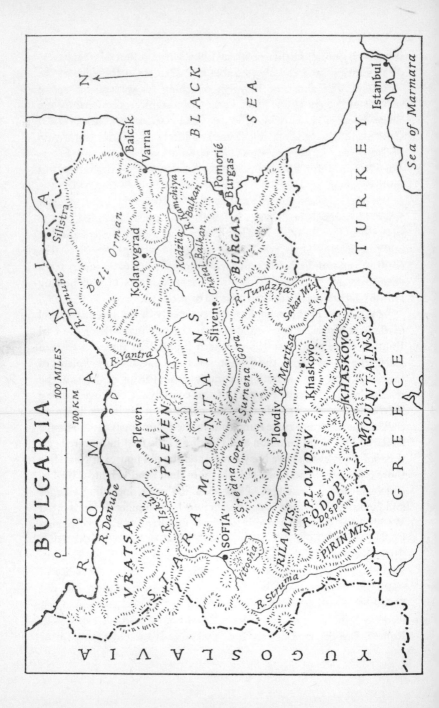

Wheatear. Suitable areas of scrub hold such birds as Olivaceous and Barred Warblers and surprising numbers of Red-backed Shrikes which breed here in almost any rank vegetation.

Bee-eaters, Rollers, Ortolan Buntings, Lesser Grey and Red-backed Shrikes, Tawny Pipits and, of course, Hooded Crows, Wheatears and Crested Larks are widespread throughout lowland Bulgaria and not just confined to the Black Sea section. Skylarks, incidentally, though widespread, are rather thin on the ground. The *quic, quic-ic* of the Quail is a common sound from May onwards and Corncrakes and Nightjars are widespread if scarce, but Stone Curlews are largely confined to the Dobrudja and both Great and Little Bustards are now reduced to the status of scarce migrants or winter visitors, unless odd pairs still nest in the Dobrudja. Other birds of this steppe area are Marsh Sandpipers, Pratincoles and Short-toed and Calandra Larks, the last being particularly abundant.

Undisturbed woodland is becoming increasingly scarce in eastern Bulgaria as coastal development continues, but any concentrations of mixed or deciduous trees are well worth a visit, including the forest areas surrounding the mouths of such rivers as the Kamchiya (south of Varna) and the Ropotamo (between Burgas and Michurin). (Unfortunately, Baltata Forest at the mouth of the Batova, south of Balcik, is but a shadow of its former self as a result of development.) Woodland birds include Sombre Tits, Olive-tree Warblers (apparently extending their range) and Collared Flycatchers of the eastern race, here at their western limit, which lack the white collar and rump and can be easily overlooked as Pied. Surprisingly common is the Hawfinch, so scarce and local in many parts of Europe; this species is even quite numerous in the drier and more stunted woodland on hillsides. Chaffinches, Goldfinches and Greenfinches are also generally widespread as are Jays and Great Tits. Other birds of the woods in summer include Hoopoes, Rollers, Turtle Doves, various woodpeckers (among them Grey-headed and a few White-backed and Middle Spotted), Wrynecks, Long-eared Owls, Woodlarks, Golden Orioles, Nightingales, Redstarts, Penduline Tits (in wetter areas), Nuthatches, Short-toed Treecreepers and Red-breasted Flycatchers.

Most raptors are far scarcer than they were, but open country and wooded areas are among the areas to see them. Some, such as Honey Buzzards and Goshawks, are commoner on the wooded lower slopes of the mountains, but the lowland tree-nesting species include Hobbies and fewer Sakers, Lesser Spotted and Short-toed Eagles, rare White-tailed Eagles and Long-legged Buzzards, many more Buzzards (of the confusing rufous-tailed race), Levant Sparrow-hawks and, of course, Black Kites, though as nesting birds the last are largely confined to the Danube area. Marsh Harriers breed in the Danube and coastal wetlands, and Montagu's Harriers and (probably) Pallid Harriers in the Dobrudja. Egyptian Vultures are scarce, mainly in the lowlands and gorges. Kestrels are widepsread, but nesting Lesser Kestrels are confined to the south, especially in Plovdiv and Pazardjik. Most of the other birds of prey are passage migrants, but one can see occasional Ospreys, Red Kites, Booted Eagles and Red-footed Falcons, as well as Rough-legged Buzzards, Hen Harriers and Sparrowhawks which are also winter visitors. Spotted and Imperial Eagles are much rarer.

The Danube plain tantalisingly reflects the much richer popula-tions of waterbirds to be found in the lower reaches of that river and its delta (which are, of course, in Rumania). Between Rusé and Silistra are several areas where open sheets of water are flanked by vast reed beds and at one of these, Lake Sreburna, there is a small colony of Dalmatian Pelicans. Lake Srehurna also has breeding Red-necked and Great Crested Grebes, Little Bitterns, Purple Herons, Spoonbills (occasionally), Glossy Ibises, Greylag Geese, various ducks (including Gadwall, Garganey, Red-crested Pochard and Ferruginous), Marsh Harriers, Spotted and Little Crakes, and Black, White-winged Black and Whiskered Terns, as well as Kingfishers and a variety of warblers—Savi's, Great Reed, Reed, Marsh and Sedge. Various herons (including Great White Egrets), waders and other birds turn up to feed. The Danube islands of Vadim and Per-sina hold colonies of Cormorants and Pygmy Cormorants, Night and Squacco Herons, Little Egrets, Glossy Ibises and, most interesting of all, Black Storks, The plentiful acacias in the Danube area pro-duce scattered pairs of Penduline Tits, and in the crops and arable fields Calandra Larks especially are plentiful. There are also far too many Magpies here, as in many other parts of Bulgaria.

The other lowland zone, the central plain and the valleys of the Maritsa and its tributaries, west to the eastern edge of the Rodopi mountains, is rather less well-known and could well repay thorough investigation. Apart from many woodland and open country species already mentioned, it is possible that this section holds several other birds which at present are hardly known in Bulgaria, such as the Masked Shrike, Sardinian and Subalpine Warblers, and Blue Rock Thrush (the last two on rising ground). Another reason why this part might well prove of considerable interest in the spring is the suggestion that many migrants on their way north are turned west by the central Stara Planina mountains and so follow this lowland corridor up into Yugoslavia and thence to Hungary. Likewise, the central mountain range has received little attention from ornithologists who have usually been attracted to the higher, more extensive and wilder mountains of the south-west, and if this migration theory is correct, the passage of birds of prey and other birds along this escarpment could be interesting.

The Rila, Rodopi and Pirin mountains of the south are certainly spectacular. The Rila range is the nearest to Sofia and contains both the highest mountain in Bulgaria, Stalin Peak, and the famous Rila Monastery. It is quite easy to get to and beyond such places as Samokov and Yakoruda by car, but the Rila Monastery itself, at nearly 3,900 feet, provides as good a starting point as any for an exploration on foot. Though much of the mountain region would be difficult to reach, there are enough roads and tracks to take the visitor into a wide selection of habitats. Some of the lower slopes are densely wooded with deciduous trees and these are replaced farther up by extensive belts of conifers which in turn give way to rocky slopes and gorges and to the high peaks which are still snow-covered when birds are starting to nest. Mountains are never as thickly populated by birds as lowland areas, but there is still a wonderful selection of species. Wooded slopes hold Hazel Grouse and Capercaillies (both scarce), Woodcock, Long-eared and Scops Owls, Black and Middle Spotted Woodpeckers, Sombre and Willow Tits, Treecreepers, Siskins, Crossbills, Hawfinches and Nutcrackers. More open ground produces Rock Partridges (in the west) or Chukars (in the east), an Eagle Owl if one is lucky, Woodlarks, Ring Ouzels, Black Redstarts,

Rock and Cirl Buntings, and Alpine Choughs (but no Choughs). Alpine Swifts, Red-rumped Swallows, Crag Martins and, in the south-west, a few Rock Nuthatches breed in the rocky faces. Higher still, at 6,000 feet or more, the energetic observer may find Shore Larks, Water Pipits, Alpine Accentors, Rock Thrushes, and here and there a beautiful pair of Wallcreepers. There may even be Snow Finches, though the records are very few. At all levels the rushing mountain torrents provide homes for Dippers and Grey Wagtails. Birds of prey, however, are rather few. There are Golden Eagles and Peregrines, for example, but vultures are desperately scarce, probably as a result of the unfortunate practice of poisoning carcases to kill wolves. There are still a very few Griffon and possibly one or two Black Vultures in the south, but Lammergeiers have apparently gone.

If one is based on Sofia with limited transport, some of the mountain species can be seen on Vitosha which rises to over 7,000 feet and lies only a few miles from the capital. Stalindam, a large sheet of water to the south-east of Sofia, is ornithologically disappointing, but there are other wetland areas in the Sofia basin. One of the best is Aldomirovtsi marsh, which can produce grebes, herons, ducks and waders. The visitor to Sofia itself will note the large number of Collared Doves to be seen in even the busiest streets right in the centre of the city and at the same time how dingy their plumage is compared with those of gardens and parkland farther north and west in Europe. He will also be struck by the way in which the Tree Sparrow outnumbers the House Sparrow in even the most built-up areas; the same situation applies in many other parts of the country in both town and country districts, particularly in the north as far east as Silistra. At the same time, if he does not venture outside the capital, he will be missing some fine scenery and an opportunity of seeing a number of fascinating species in a country where there is still plenty of room for ornithological discoveries.

Yugoslavia

D. D. Harber

Glossy Ibises

The most important ornithological centre in Yugoslavia is in the Biological Institute of Zagreb University, which publishes *Larus*; most of the articles in this periodical have a summary in German and sometimes in English. Ringing is also organised here, although as yet only on a small scale.

Bird protection is still in its infancy, and it looks as though the eagles in the Vojvodina have not as yet profited from the protection which they enjoy, at least on paper. Many coastal birds are still caught in snares and many people go shooting, particularly for Cranes. Vultures and eagles are not only shot but have their eggs stolen, and they are often victims of the poisoned meat put out to control the wolves.

If one finds a ringed bird in Yugoslavia, the ring should be sent to Ornitholoski Institut, Ilirski trg. 9, Zagreb I, Yugoslavia.

YUGOSLAVIA

Yugoslavia, about 560 miles from north-west to south-east and 370 miles from west to east, occupies an area of 98,000 square miles and is thus rather larger than Great Britain. Mountains, usually without much tree cover, occupy some three-quarters of the total area. In the north-west the Julian Alps rise to a maximum of 9,393 feet. From these the Dinaric Alps and other ranges run north-east, parallel with the Adriatic, to link up with the mountains of Montenegro which attain a height of 8,301 feet. The Dalmatian coast, with its arid carboniferous limestone (karst) mountains and its numerous islands, extends along the Adriatic. At the extreme south-east end of this coast lies Lake Skadar, the largest lake in the Balkans, the greater part of which belongs to Yugoslavia, the rest being Albanian. Macedonia, the most southerly part of the country, is also very mountainous but includes the northern ends of two more great lakes, Ochrid and Prespa, and of one smaller one, Dojran. North of Macedonia lies Serbia, which again is mountainous as far as Belgrade where the Danubian plain starts and extends to the Hungarian frontier, forming the so-called Vojvodina. Another extensive, but much narrower, plain runs along the valley of the River Sava from Belgrade to Zagreb in the north and beyond. Between these two plains lie some low hills, the most easterly extremity of which forms the Fruska Gora.

The amount of land suitable for agriculture is thus severely limited and great attention is given to making the best use of that which is available. This has occasioned enormous drainage schemes with disastrous effects on marsh birds, particularly in the flood-lands along the Danube and the other great rivers in the north and in many other regions. Ornithologists will be well advised to seek the most recent information before setting out to visit any area of marsh, since it may, in fact, no longer exist. For example, in Macedonia the internationally famous swamps of the Crna Reke near Bitola, which, even as late as the 1950s held large numbers of nesting herons, pelicans and other birds, have now completely disappeared, while the Neretva marshes on the Dalmatian coast have undergone much the same fate.

Main roads are often very good and improvements are taking place all the time, but other roads may sometimes be hazardous. The field ornithologist will find no restrictions on his activities, except perhaps near frontiers and, of course, military installations and prisons. It should be noted that people living in the country, in particular, are inquisitive, especially in the more remote parts, and it is as well to be able to explain to them that one is a foreign tourist interested in birds. When this is understood they are generally helpful and will not object to one going on their property.

The Dalmatian coast is likely to be the part of Yugoslavia most visited by foreigners, and is also one of the areas of greatest interest to the bird-watcher. It enjoys a Mediterranean climate in contrast to the Continental conditions prevailing over the rest of the country. Breeding species are limited by the barrenness of much of the terrain. However, Olivaceous, Barred, Orphean, Sardinian and Subalpine Warblers nest in the maquis and garrigue areas of the lower slopes while Olive-tree Warblers apparently extend from the south to at least the Dubrovnik area. Rock Partridges and Black-eared Wheatears also occur on these slopes and Black-headed Buntings are abundant in places. Except in the north, Sombre Tits can be found in the usually scattered woodlands, and higher up Rock Nuthatches and Rock Thrushes are often quite common, though Blue Rock Thrushes appear to be scarcer. A few Griffon Vultures survive, even as far north as the island of Krk, and there are still Golden and Short-toed Eagles in the wilder parts. The same may apply to Peregrines and Lanners, though little is known of their present state. Cretzschmar's Buntings and Rufous Bush Chats may nest in the extreme south, and Red-rumped Swallows and Spanish Sparrows certainly do so. The best centre here is Petrovac, from which there is a good road to Lake Skadar. A feature of some of the towns in this part is the abundance of Collared Doves, while at Dubrovnik and Petrovac, for example, one may drink one's Turkish coffee with Alpine Swifts screaming low over one's head. Scops

Owls call at night but are seldom seen. Rock Buntings nest in the mountains in the north and are more widespread in winter. Kentish Plovers are known to nest only at Nin, near Zadar, and south of Ulcinj. Melodious Warblers have nested on Krk and the adjacent mainland.

Much visible migration takes place along this coast with parties of Grey and Purple Herons, Little Egrets, Squacco and Night Herons passing and sometimes coming down to rest on the rocky shores, particularly of the islands. Red-footed Falcons, Rollers, Collared Flycatchers and other interesting birds also pass through, and Mediterranean Gulls may be encountered. Manx Shearwaters occur at sea and doubtless nest on some of the islands as do Shags in the north, but otherwise there are very few sea birds apart from some Herring Gulls.

The few wet areas along this coast are particularly attractive to many migrants and to wintering birds. The lake of Hutovo Blato near Metkovic and the adjacent parts of the Neretva Valley, despite drainage and much shooting, may still hold parties of up to about forty Marsh Sandpipers as well as several other waders, including Temminck's Stints. White-tailed Eagles and Pygmy Cormorants occur, though it is uncertain whether they still breed. Geese, especially Bean, can be seen in hard winters.

Lake Skadar is of particular interest since it may be the last breeding site in the country of the Dalmatian Pelican. Here also are to be seen numerous Squacco and Purple Herons, Little Egrets, Glossy Ibises, Ferruginous Ducks and Pygmy Cormorants. Large numbers of geese, mainly Whitefronts, occur there in winter as do many species of ducks. This huge lake cannot be explored properly without the aid of a boat, but much can be seen from a long causeway which runs from Virpazar towards Titograd. On the plain north of this lake Crested, Short-toed and Calandra Larks can be seen.

Macedonia is an area of great ornithological interest. Titov Veles, on the main road to Greece, makes a good centre for the mountain areas, including the famous Babuna Gorge. More than twenty Griffon Vultures may be seen together in this district and Egyptian Vultures are not uncommon, while Black Vultures and Lammergeiers are said to occur and may perhaps still nest. Golden and Booted

Eagles are to be seen, as is an occasional Long-legged Buzzard. Lesser Kestrels breed and so do a few Black Storks, and Red-rumped Swallows are almost common in places. Both Rock and Blue Rock Thrushes are reputed to occur, as well as Wallcreepers. High up the mountains Alpine Accentors, Alpine Choughs, Nutcrackers, Snow Finches and other alpine birds breed and so does a Balkan race of the Shore Lark. These higher regions, however, are a challenge to the visiting ornithologist with the great distances and limited means of communication.

In the Vardar valley Imperial Eagles, once common, may still breed, and Great Spotted Cuckoos have been shot there in summer. Innumerable Nightingales sing in this area, which also holds Marsh and Olivaceous Warblers, Black-headed Buntings and Penduline Tits. Syrian Woodpeckers are now usual. The commonest shrikes are Red-backed with Lesser Grey second, and Woodchats are scarce except on passage. Bee-eaters and Rollers can sometimes be seen, and Little Bustards may still nest. The area south of Skopje has many White Storks.

Lakes Ochrid and Prespa have mostly steep, rocky shores unsuitable for many birds, but they have marshy areas at their northern ends—though these are subject to increasing human interference. These are important for migrants, the area near Asamati on Prespa being particularly valuable. Various species of herons and Glossy Ibises and Pygmy Cormorants can be seen. Goshawks, Short-toed Eagles, Marsh Harriers and Red-footed Falcons (the last often in quite large parties) may also be seen, and both Black and White-winged Black Terns are at times numerous. Many species of waders occur, Wood Sandpipers and Ruffs being the most common, and a few Marsh Sandpipers can be encountered. Cetti's, Savi's and Moustached Warblers can be heard and Red-throated Pipits are probably not uncommon. Tawny Pipits breed in the vicinity. In addition, pelicans, doubtless coming from Little Lake Prespa in Greece, may at times be seen on Prespa. Lake Dojran still perhaps has a few breeding Dalmatian Pelicans. By car Bitola makes a good centre for Lake Prespa, and Ochrid for the lake of that name.

The dry uplands of Macedonia are more likely to experience a summer invasion of Rose-coloured Starlings than any other part of

Yugoslavia and they have bred there. Eagle Owls are believed to be more numerous in Yugoslavia than in any other European country, though this does not mean that they are easily observed. Many from farther north come to Macedonia in winter when they have been seen hunting in town parks and sitting on roof-tops. Finally, Macedonia still has, despite drainage, large numbers of breeding Black-headed Wagtails, easily the most handsome race of the Yellow Wagtail.

The mountains of southern Serbia, which lie north of Macedonia, are in general somewhat lower and contain all the species which can be seen there, including Imperial Eagle, Levant Sparrowhawk, Short-toed Treecreeper and Bonelli's Warbler.

The Danubian plain north of Belgrade is of great interest and has been well studied by ornithologists. A few miles west of Belgrade is the marshy area of the Obedska Bara, now a nature reserve and hence, one hopes, safe from drainage schemes. In a good year Red-necked and Black-necked Grebes, Pygmy Cormorants, Purple and Squacco Herons, Little Egrets, Little Bitterns, White and Black Storks, Spoonbills, Glossy Ibises, Imperial and White-tailed Eagles, Red Kites, Little and Spotted Crakes and Penduline Tits may nest in this reserve. There is a colony of Red-footed Falcons not far away, and Lesser Spotted Eagles and Whiskered Terns from breeding sites elsewhere in the district are also seen at Obedska Bara. Much the same species, together with, in places, Cormorants, Bitterns and Black-headed Gulls, may be seen in other suitable localities, such as Carska Bara north-west of Belgrade, the vicinity of Novi Sad, and at Kopacki Rit between the Danube and the Drava near Osijek, and here a few Great White Egrets may still breed. It seems doubtful if Greylag Geese now do, at least in any numbers. Only Marsh Harriers seem to nest, though Hen, Pallid and Montagu's Harriers are recorded, as elsewhere in the country, particularly during migration. Marsh Warblers breed and River and Aquatic Warblers are said to do so. Olivaceous Warblers, which have extended their range in recent years, nest in many localities, including the suburbs of Belgrade itself. From the Kalemegdan, the ancient fortress of the capital, Black Kites can often be seen scavenging along the Danube. Sakers still nest in suitable localities along the rivers.

An especially interesting area is the Fruska Gora, a range of lowish hills along the south side of the Danube near Novi Sad. Imperial, Spotted, Lesser Spotted and White-tailed Eagles have nested in recent years and may still do so. Black Storks also breed there. Ferruginous Ducks are widespread and White-headed Ducks have nested recently at Lake Ludas near Subotica close to the Hungarian frontier. Avocets and Pratincoles still attempt to breed on occasions in this area. There is a remarkable sandy district called Deliblatska Peščara, a few miles north-east of Belgrade, where Stone Curlews nest. It must be stressed, however, that for the most part the Danubian plain is now farmland and of relatively lesser ornithological interest, though, of course, such birds as Hoopoes, Wrynecks, Golden Orioles, Great Reed Warblers and Serins may be seen there. Much flooding takes place along the great rivers in early spring with the melting of the mountain snows, and wildfowl are then abundant. Many wildfowl and Cranes also occur in autumn. Visiting geese are usually White-fronted and Bean, with an occasional Red-breasted Goose. Cold weather drives these, together with Mallard, Pintail, Shoveler, Teal, Pochard, Tufted and other ducks, south to the Vardar valley on their way to Greece or to Lake Skadar.

The mountains of Bosnia and Herzegovina, between Belgrade and the sea, are wild, and apart from a few main roads, not easily accessible. Little field work has been done there and it is possible that Cranes may nest in a few remote localities. This part of Yugoslavia might very well repay exploration.

The alpine area to the north of the country is where most foreign visitors tend to arrive, and here the usual alpine species may be found, seen at much lower altitudes, and there is a record of two Wallcreepers in the centre of Zagreb in March. All the European woodpecker species, except the Syrian (which is common in the Danubian plain) are to be found in this area and so are Red-breasted and Collared Flycatchers. Honey Buzzards and Ural Owls occur and Waxwings are frequent in winter. On the fringe of this region White-spotted Bluethroats have been found nesting on the Drava near Koprivnica.

Yugoslavia has many interesting species of birds, though a good deal of the country remains to be explored. The visiting bird-watcher could add to our existing knowledge and might well come across occurrences new to the records.

Greece

the Greek Islands,
European Turkey
and Albania

I. C. T. Nisbet

Spur-winged Plovers

Few Greek ornithologists undertake field work, so we owe most of our knowledge of Greek birds to ornithologists from the north who visit the country in spring and summer. There are large numbers of active hunters and in many areas it is probable that too many waterfowl are being shot. Protection of forests and fresh-water marshes, which are becoming increasingly restricted, is an urgent matter. There is a re-afforestation programme, but public interest in the protection of nature is very slight.

There is no ringing centre so if one finds a ringed bird in Greece, the ring should be sent to the country of origin.

GREECE, THE GREEK ISLANDS,
EUROPEAN TURKEY AND ALBANIA

The scenic grandeur of Greece, which makes such a powerful impression on visitors, is due in large measure to the tragic destruction of its natural resources. The visitor to the classical sites, travelling from town to town along the main roads, sees barren, scrub-covered mountains and parched, windswept plains, but few of the remote areas of forest and marsh which harbour the scattered remnants of its natural fauna and flora.

Greece falls naturally into three geographical areas (excluding the islands whose birds are discussed later). The mountainous mainland extends some 200 miles south from the Yugoslav frontier to the Gulf of Corinth, and some 150 miles from east to west; the still more mountainous Peloponnese is a peninsula some 90 miles square, connected to the mainland only by the narrow isthmus of Corinth; the north-east comprises a lowland strip about 50 miles wide, running east from Salonika for 200 miles between the Bulgarian mountains and the Aegean Sea.

Of the three major habitat divisions of the country the mountains occupy the largest area, more than three-quarters of the country being over 1,000 feet above sea level. The most important ranges are the rugged and inaccessible Pindos mountains (up to 8,400 feet) which form the north-south backbone of the country, the partially isolated massifs of Olympos (9,573 feet) in the east and Parnassos (8,067 feet) near the Gulf of Corinth, and the Rhodope and other mountains which run eastwards along the Bulgarian border. In addition to these, many peaks in the north and west exceed 6,000 feet, as do many in the Peloponnese. The natural forests of these mountains have been largely destroyed by man and his goats, leaving rugged rocky slopes sparsely covered with low scrub.

The lowlands of Greece, although limited in area, comprise a number of different habitats. The foothills of the mountains are mainly bare and scrub-covered, although large tracts of the Mediterranean evergreen forests (stone pines and holm oaks) remain in Attica and along the Gulf of Corinth. Extensive plains are found only in Thessaly and in the north-east, in the valleys of the four major rivers which descend from the north. A narrow strip of fertile country is found around many parts of the coast, being widest on the west side and near the mouths of the larger rivers. Some of the river valleys are barren and dry in summer, but those which are well-watered support olives, vines, citrus fruits and other crops.

Marshes in Greece include a number of lakes in the mountain valleys, especially in the north; a few large and rich lakes in lowland drainage basins; and some extensive coastal marshes, mainly in the west and on the north coast of the Aegean. The lowlands and marshes of Greece are relatively easy to approach and explore, but the roads into the mountains are few and of poor quality.

The mountains are largely barren and the best areas for birds are in general the most remote and inaccessible. The outstanding exception is Delphi, whose wealth of bird life is a fitting complement to its awe-inspiring scenery. Griffon Vultures are constantly in the air, Lammergeiers and Egyptian Vultures appear hourly, and the visitor who stays for two or three days can expect to see Black Vultures, Lanners, Golden and Bonelli's Eagles and many other birds of prey. Rock Doves, Rock Sparrows, Alpine Choughs and Crag Martins live unobtrusively in the cliffs, and the ruins abound with Sombre Tits and Rock Nuthatches. In summer the scrub above and below the village harbours Rüppell's Warblers and Cretzschmar's Buntings, and the fruit trees and olives support Olivaceous and Olive-tree Warblers, in addition to a striking variety of migrants in spring and autumn. A dirt road from Arachova leads up to an extensive fir forest whose breeding birds include White-backed and Black Woodpeckers, Firecrests, Crested Tits and perhaps Eagle Owls, and from there the 8,000-foot summit of Parnassos can be reached in a brisk half-day's walk. Rock Buntings breed around the tree line, and on the upper slopes (forced lower by snow in spring) there are Rock Partridges, Ortolan Buntings, Shore Larks, Rock Thrushes, Black Redstarts and Alpine Accentors; the more fortunate visitors find Snow Finches.

Much the same avifauna occurs in other Greek mountains, although it is hard to find a comparable variety of species in a small area. Vultures live mainly in the more remote ranges, but can be seen from roads in several of the high passes (for instance the Klissoura and Koka passes) and in the Vale of Tempi. Griffon and Egyptian Vultures are much the commonest species, but Lammergeiers can be seen at times at Meteora, in the Brallos Pass, and around the Parnassos massif, and Black Vultures occur in the same areas and in the hills north of Alexandroupolis. The alpine zone is relatively accessible on Mount Killini, and can be reached by the energetic walker high on Mount Olympos and Mount Peristeri; in the northern mountains there are a few Wallcreepers, in addition to the species known from Parnassos. The birds of the Pindus range, however, are little known and need investigation.

Coniferous forests (mostly firs) are accessible on Mounts Parnis, Taygetus, Killini and Mainalou, on the roads from Amphissa to Lamia and from Florina to Kastoria, near Karpenision and in the valleys leading up to the Bulgarian frontier. All these forests are rich in small birds; those in the north are said to contain Tengmalm's Owls, Middle Spotted and Three-toed Woodpeckers and Nutcrackers, but there are few recent records of these species. Deciduous forests are much harder to find, and urgently need exploration before the last accessible areas are cleared. There are chestnut forests at Kastania (Macedonia) and on Mount Dirphis (Euboea), and oak forests are accessible at Daphni (Macedonia) and near Megalopolis. The Collared Flycatcher (represented by the half-collared race which looks more like a Pied Flycatcher in the field) is known to breed at Daphni, and should be looked for in other places. Hillside scrub often contains Rüppell's Warblers, at least in the east and south-east. Rock Nuthatches, Crag Martins, Red-rumped Swallows, Alpine Swifts and Rock Sparrows are widespread but local; they are best sought in steep mountain valleys and ravines, especially where there are perennial streams. Virtually nothing is known about the winter birds of these mountains, but in April and September Red-throated Pipits are common in places.

The common summer birds of the lowlands are similar to those found in other Mediterranean countries, including such characteristic

GREECE

0   100 MILES

0   100 KM

southern species as Lesser Kestrel, Crested Lark, Black-eared Wheatear and Sardinian Warbler. Red-backed Shrikes are abundant throughout the country, but Bee-eaters, Rollers, and Lesser Grey Shrikes are much commoner in the north, where they are the most conspicuous birds of open country in the autumn. Among interesting species, Black-headed Buntings are common from May to August in cultivated areas, Cretzschmar's Buntings are common on scrub-covered slopes (except in the north-east) and Calandra Larks occur locally on open stony slopes. Hawks can be seen occasionally, especially over hill slopes, and are always worth close examination; Short-toed Eagles are fairly common and Booted Eagles are widespread in the north, while Imperial Eagles and Long-legged Buzzards can be seen occasionally. In winter, flocks of larks, pipits and buntings are abundant in open ground and should be searched for Asiatic vagrants; Great White Egrets feed in some flooded fields, and Pallid and Hen Harriers occur sparsely.

Those travelling by car should be prepared to stop whenever they see good areas of cover. Deciduous woodland is rare near roads, and the evergreen forest is not rich in birds, but small areas of scrub, patches of ilex, old olive groves with ground cover, and mature orchards are often rewarding. Some of these places harbour small numbers of Levant Sparrowhawks, Scops Owls, Syrian Woodpeckers, Sombre Tits, Olivaceous, Olive-tree, Orphean, Subalpine and Bonelli's Warblers, Nightingales, Woodchats and Golden Orioles. Many of these species are scarce and local, and some will be found only by the persistent searcher. Rufous Bush Chats are found mainly in oleander scrub along watercourses, and Masked Shrikes should be sought in overgrown valleys in the north and east. White Storks nest commonly as far south as Lamia, and their nests usually hold colonies of Spanish Sparrows between April and August. In the migration seasons Collared Flycatchers are quite common and other eastern species should be watched for.

A special word should be said about the archaeological sites, since the trees planted around them provide shelter for birds as well as shade for tourists. Some of these places, isolated in the barren countryside, are as good as anywhere in Greece for seeing such local species as Sombre Tits, Subalpine Warblers and Serins. In Athens itself Blue Rock Thrushes and Lesser Grey Shrikes have been seen even on the Acropolis, and Mount Lykabetos harbours southern warblers and is an excellent place for many species of northern migrants.

The best marshes in Greece for birds are in the north-east. The outstanding place is the delta of the river Evros, more than half of which has been drained since 1960, but which still retains extensive marshes along the river and in the coastal strip between the river and Alexandroupolis. The reclaimed area is becoming accessible by car, but the remoter marshes can be penetrated only by boat, from Pherrai or Alexandroupolis. Breeding birds of this area include Squacco Herons, Glossy Ibises, Ruddy Shelducks, White-tailed Eagles (nesting in winter), Spur-winged Plovers, Black-winged Stilts, Avocets and Pratincoles. Other species which have been reported in summer, and whose status needs further investigation, include Dalmatian Pelican, Pygmy Cormorant, Great White Egret, Greylag Goose and Black-winged Pratincole. In winter there are thousands of geese and other waterfowl, including a regular flock of Red-breasted Geese and sometimes large numbers of Mute and Whooper Swans; White-tailed, Imperial, Spotted and Steppe Eagles are numerous and a few Sakers and Pallid Harriers occur. On migration there occur a large number of herons, Glossy Ibises, pelicans, waterfowl, waders and gulls; at least in spring, large numbers of White Storks, Black Kites, Levant Sparrowhawks and Sparrowhawks migrate overhead; Cranes and other marsh birds should be expected. Our knowledge of the birds of this unique area is still fragmentary, and further investigation is urgently needed before drainage and disturbance take their full toll.

Although the Evros delta has many species which breed in few or no other places in Greece, and a unique winter population of geese and raptors, its most interesting areas are wild and inaccessible and many of the birds can be more easily seen farther to the west. Passage migrant waders, for example, are easily approached in the Axios delta (along the coast west of Thessaloniki), at the west end of Lake Koronia and in the coastal lagoons at Porto Lago. May, August and September are the best months: then Kentish and Little Ringed Plovers, Black-tailed Godwits, Little Stints and Avocets are amongst the most common species; Marsh Sandpipers, Curlew Sandpipers, Temminck's Stints and Black-winged Pratincoles have been recorded several times in recent years, and other eastern species should be watched for. Spur-winged Plovers breed on sandy margins in the Axios delta, the Nestos delta and at Porto Lago. Ruddy Shelducks occur from April to July on most lakes and coastal lagoons, and probably breed in several places. Reed beds on the north side of Lake Koronia and around the Nestos delta are the best places to find species such as Marsh Harriers, Little Bitterns and crakes: Spotted, Little and Baillon's Crakes can all be seen by a stealthy watcher in autumn and should be sought in the breeding season. There is a small colony of Fan-tailed Warblers in the Nestos delta, and one of Bearded Tits at Lake Koronia. Pelicans occur in large numbers on migration—and some can be seen in most months. Many species of terns occur in spring and autumn, including a sprinkling of both White-winged Black and Whiskered Terns, and a few Caspian Terns which may breed on offshore islets. Slender-billed Gulls are quite common on the lakes and islets in May and September. Vast numbers of ducks winter on Lake Vistonia and large numbers on the other marshes. The distribution of geese is badly documented, but they are said to be most numerous in the large river deltas and inland in the Strymon valley; the Whitefront is the commonest species and the Greylag probably the second commonest, but Beans and Lesser Whitefronts also occur. Besides the breeding species and the passage migrants, a few winter visitors, such as Pygmy Cormorants, Great White Egrets, Little and Mediterranean Gulls, and Spotted Eagles, stay late into the spring, and the visitor in April or September should see more species than he would in midsummer or midwinter.

In addition to the water-birds, the margins of these marshes are among the best places to see some of the more local land-birds such as Stone Curlews, Calandra and Short-toed Larks, Tawny Pipits, Cetti's Warblers and Spanish Sparrows. Lesser Spotted Eagles, harriers and other birds of prey are more frequently seen here than in other areas. Isabelline Wheatears breed on open sandy plains as far west as Xanthi, and Little Bustards should be sought in the same type of country. Other species peculiar to the north-east include the

Collared Dove (in the towns and Moslem villages), Rock Partridge (on low hills west to Xanthi) and Black Stork (which probably breeds in some of the valleys but is a rare migrant elsewhere in Greece).

On the west coast there are two large areas of coastal marshes and lagoons—the region west of Mesolonghion and the margins of the Gulf of Arta. Their birds appear to be similar to those of the north-eastern marshes, but the breeding species are fewer in number and they lack some of the eastern species which give the marshes of Thrace their peculiar interest. Dalmatian Pelicans, however, occur on migration and may still breed somewhere in the Gulf of Arta; Ruddy Shelducks have been seen at Mesolonghion and Fan-tailed Warblers and Penduline Tits are common; Great White Egrets winter, and Marsh Sandpipers and other eastern waders occur on passage. Most of the other coastal marshes in Greece are smaller, but all are worth visiting in the migration seasons and in winter: an interesting area is the head of the Gulf of Evvia, easily accessible from the national road to the west of Thermopylae.

Of the inland lakes, the most interesting is Karla near Larissa, now partially drained but still retaining many birds of interest: ducks, herons, White Storks and pelicans in spring; geese, ducks, and Little Gulls in winter. Over 200,000 ducks and Coots have been counted there but it is not known whether such numbers occur regularly. Many of the smaller lakes are stony and barren, but those with shallow margins and reed beds (for instance, Stymphalos and Ioannina) support breeding colonies of Black-necked Grebes, Little Bitterns, Ferruginous Ducks and Spotted Crakes, and perhaps Pygmy Cormorants, Squacco Herons, Little Egrets and Black Terns, and most attract waterfowl, waders and marshbirds on passage and in winter. Few of these lakes have been thoroughly explored by ornithologists: Lakes Trichonis, Ozeros, Kastoria, Dysthos and Prasias would probably be the most interesting to investigate, but some of the best marshes are being drained.

The Greek Islands

Except for Crete in the south and a few wooded islands in the north, the Aegean islands are dry, barren and rugged, with a very limited variety of birds, but they do support a few species of out-standing interest. Rüppell's Warbler is a widespread summer visitor to hillside scrub, and Black-headed and Cretzschmar's Buntings breed on most islands. The Chukar breeds on hillsides on most of the larger islands, replacing the closely related Rock Partridge of mainland Greece. The Cinereous Bunting has been found nesting in the easternmost of the Aegean islands. Eleonora's Falcon breeds in July and August on various rocky islets in the Cyclades, the Spo-rades, and probably the Dodecanese, and can often be seen in the morning and evening hunting over the larger islands. Audouin's Gulls have been found breeding on one or two sloping islands in the northern Sporades since 1961 and may nest elsewhere in the Aegean. During journeys from island to island, Cory's Shearwaters are constantly in sight, Manx Shearwaters are common but more patchy in distribution, and Storm Petrels are seen occasionally, although their breeding place is still unknown. Ruddy Shelducks nest on Rhodes and Kos, and marshes on Skyros, Lesbos and Limnos are also worth investigating for migrants and winter visitors. Migration through the islands is little known, but there are records of phenome-nal falls of migrants on some islands in September, and the Eleonora's Falcons litter their islets with the remains of small birds in August. Especially in the eastern islands, visitors at the migration season should keep close watch for Asiatic vagrants.

The birds of Crete, with its more varied habitats, are in some ways more similar to those of the mainland than to those of the impover-ished Aegean islands. The mountains hold three species of vultures, Bonelli's Eagles, Choughs, and a few mountain birds such as Alpine Swifts and Alpine Accentors. The more fertile valleys support warblers, shrikes, Bee-eaters and Tawny Pipits, and there is a forest of oaks and ilexes on the south side of Mount Ida which deserves investigation. However, some of the Aegean specialities are found also, including the Chukar which is common on the hillsides, and Eleonora's Falcon which breeds on the islets of Dia, Paximandi and Theodorou.

The Ionian islands are little known ornithologically, but Corfu has a rich avifauna: with a variety of habitats and a history of exploration by ornithologists, it has a bird list at least as long as that of comparable areas on the adjacent mainland.

European Turkey

The migration of hawks and storks over the Bosphorus is an outstanding spectacle. In autumn the commonest species is the White Stork, which passes in thousands in the latter half of August, but five other species can be seen daily in hundreds at the appropriate times: Black Kites in late August and early September, Levant Sparrowhawks in early September, Lesser Spotted Eagles during September, and Black Storks at the end of September. In late September up to twenty-five species of raptors have been seen in a day and almost every raptor on the European list has been recorded occasionally. The birds may be seen from any high point in the city of Istanbul or in the hills overlooking the Bosphorus, but the best observation points are the Çamlidža hills on the Asiatic side. In strong north-east winds few birds cross the Bosphorus, and the migration should be sought farther south-west, over Yesilköy and the Princes' Islands. Spring migration is also spectacular, extending from mid-March (Black Kites) to late May (Honey Buzzards), but has been little studied.

In Istanbul city there is an enormous summer colony of Alpine Swifts, and Palm Doves are common in the old streets. In the city parks and the wooded areas along the Bosphorus Syrian Woodpeckers are fairly common and migrants abound in season: Collared and Red-breasted Flycatchers are among the dozen commonest species in autumn and other eastern species should be looked for. A formidable list of Asiatic rarities was compiled by nineteenth-century collectors in the surrounding area, and many of these could turn up again.

Turkish Thrace is an outstanding area in autumn for such open country migrants as storks, eagles, falcons, Bee-eaters, Rollers, shrikes and wagtails. Many storks migrate directly over the Sea of Marmara, from Tekirdağ to Marmara Island, and most of the falcons (including Sakers and Red-footed Falcons) probably migrate across the Sea of Marmara or over the Dardanelles. Cranes migrate in large numbers over the Dardanelles in October, and probably again in March. Little is known of the breeding birds of this area, but Isabelline Wheatears have been recorded on the Gelibolu peninsula and other Asiatic species should be looked for on the Black Sea coast and in wooded areas.

In the west, part of the Evros delta lies in Turkey: this part has been studied less by ornithologists, but may now include the best areas for geese and other species which are persecuted in Greece. The Çekmece and Terkos lakes near Istanbul also attract waterfowl and waders and deserve investigation. The Bosphorus itself, and to a lesser extent the Dardanelles and the Sea of Marmara, teem with Manx Shearwaters, terns, and Mediterranean and Little Gulls at the appropriate seasons.

Many of the best areas for birds in European Turkey are restricted military zones. Prospective visitors should consult their country's consul well in advance.

Albania

Little is known about the birds of Albania except for some long outdated notes in old journals, and it is unlikely that readers of this book will be able to see them in the near future. The avifauna is doubtless similar to that of neighbouring parts of Greece and Yugoslavia, including characteristically Balkan species such as Cretzschmar's and Black-headed Buntings, Olive-tree Warbler, Rock Nuthatch, Rock Partridge and Levant Sparrowhawk. The marshes contain (or used to contain) colonies of Dalmatian Pelicans, Pygmy Cormorants, Great White Egrets and Cranes. Pallid Swifts, Great Spotted Cuckoos and Spectacled Warblers might occur.

Tables of Status

James Ferguson-Lees and Quentin Hockliffe

The sequence of these tables of 432 European species has been drawn up to accord with the completely revised and enlarged edition of *A Field Guide to the Birds of Britain and Europe* (1974) by Roger Peterson, Guy Mountfort and P. A. D. Hollom. Thus it follows the sequence of the *Check-List of Birds of the World* by J. L. Peters down to familial level; within the families it largely follows the sequence of species adopted in *The Birds of the Palearctic Fauna* by Charles Vaurie, and also his scientific nomenclature. It includes all species for which there are 50 or more records each year in at least one country, indicating vagrant status where appropriate, but it excludes species which are purely rare vagrants to Europe as a whole. Each species in each country is put into one of twelve status categories: in any attempt at such rigid categorisation there are bound to be some subjective and arbitrary decisions, and large birds clearly have to be classified on different criteria of frequency from small ones, but our aim has been to indicate the likelihood of the visitor seeing the species concerned.

Excluded from the table are five species which have recently been added to the British list on account of small feral populations in England. These are the Egyptian Goose *Alopochen aegyptiaca*, Mandarin *Aix galericulata*, Ruddy Duck *Oxyura jamaicensis*, Golden Pheasant *Chrysolophus pictus* and Lady Amherst's Pheasant *Chrysolophus amherstiae*, each of which is r in the United Kingdom only.

	United Kingdom	Ireland	Iceland	Norway	Sweden	Finland	Denmark	Poland	Czechoslovakia	Germany	Netherlands	Belgium	Luxembourg	France	Spain
Red-throated Diver	R	Ws	R	Sw	Sw	Sw	WP	p	V	w	WP	w	V	WP	w
Black-throated Diver	r	V		Sw	Sw	Sw	WP	w	p	w	WP	w	V	WP	w
Great Northern Diver	WP	WP	R	w	V	V	w	V	V	w	w	V	V	WP	w
White-billed Diver	V			w	V	V	w	V	V	V	V				
Little Grebe	R	R		V	r	V	R	R	r	r	R	r	r	R	R
Black-necked Grebe	r	w		V	s	V	Sw	SP	s	s	Sw	r	p	R	r
Slavonian Grebe	r	w	Sw	R	Sw	Sw	w	w	p	w	w	w	V	w	w
Red-necked Grebe	w	V		V	Sw	SP	R	s	s	r	r	w	V	w	V
Great Crested Grebe	R	R		R	R	SP	R	Sw	Sw	R	R	r	w	R	R
Fulmar	R	R	R	r	w	V	w	V	V	V	w	V		r	p
Cory's Shearwater	V	p						V	V	V	V	V		p	R
Great Shearwater	p	p	p	w	V		V			V	V			p	p
Sooty Shearwater	p	P	p	V	V		V			V	V	V		p	p
Manx/Balearic Shearwater	Sw	Sw	s	s	V		V			V	p	V		R	R
Storm Petrel	Sw	Sw	s	w	V		V	V		p	p	V		Sw	r
Leach's Petrel	s	p	s	V	V	V	V	V		p	p	V		p	p
White Pelican						V		V		V					V
Dalmatian Pelican										V	V				V
Gannet	Sw	Sw	R	Ws	w	V	P	V		w	w	w	V	Ws	WP
Cormorant	R	R	R	R	r	P	R	SP	SP	r	R	r	V	r	WP
Shag	R	R	R	R	w	V	w			V	V	V		r	R
Pygmy Cormorant					V			V	V	V					V
Bittern	r	V		V	s	r	r	s	SP	r	R	r	V	R	r
Little Bittern	V	V		V	V	V	V	SP	SP	s	SP	s	s	SP	SP

R *Common throughout year* in at least part of the country.

Sw *Common in summer* in suitable habitats but *very scarce to scarce in winter*.

Ws *Common in winter* in suitable habitats but *very scarce to scarce in summer*.

SP *Common in summer* only or *present in summer and common on passage*.

WP *Common in winter* only or *present in winter and common on passage*.

P *Common on passage* only.

Balearic Is.	Portugal	Switzerland	Austria	Italy	Corsica	Sardinia	Sicily	Hungary	Rumania	Bulgaria	Yugoslavia	Albania	Greece	Greek Is.	Eur. Turkey	
w	w	V	w	w				p	w	w	V		V			*Gavia stellata*
w	w	w	w	w				p	w	w	w	w	WP	w	w	*Gavia arctica*
w	w	V	w					V	V							*Gavia immer*
		V	V													*Gavia adamsii*
R	R	R	r	R	R	R	w	Sw	Sw	Ws	R	r	R	w	r	*Podiceps ruficollis*
w	w	r	SP	R		w	r	Sw	Sw	Ws	R	R	R		w	*Podiceps nigricollis*
		w	w	w				V	V	V	V		V			*Podiceps auritus*
w	w	p	w					s	Sw	r	w	w	w		w	*Podiceps griseigena*
w	r	R	Sw	R	r	r	r	Sw	Sw	R	R	R	R	w	R	*Podiceps cristatus*
V											V					*Fulmarus glacialis*
R	Sw	V	V	R	R	R	R				R	R	R	R	R	*Procellaria diomedea*
	p					V										*Puffinus gravis*
	p			V	V	V										*Puffinus griseus*
R	P	V	V	R	R	R	R		V	Sw	R	R	R	R	R	*Puffinus puffinus*
w	w	V	V	r	Sw	Sw	Sw			s	s		r	r		*Hydrobates pelagicus*
	p	V	V	V		V	V									*Oceanodroma leucorhoa*
		V	V	V			V	V	SP	SP	p	p	P	p	P	*Pelecanus onocrotalus*
		V		V			V	s	s	p	s	r	p	p		*Pelecanus crispus*
	WP	V	V			w	w						V			*Sula bassana*
w	WP	WP	r	p		r	r	Sw	R	r	r	r	R	WP	R	*Phalacrocorax carbo*
R	R	V	V	w	R	R	w		V	r	R	r	R	R	WP	*Phalacrocorax aristotelis*
		V	V	V			s	SP	r	r	r	R	WP	w		*Phalacrocorax pygmaeus*
r	r	w	Sw	R		r	r	s	SP	s	r	r	WP		w	*Botaurus stellaris*
s	s	SP	SP	SP		s	s	Sw	SP	SP	s	s	SP	SP	SP	*Ixobrychus minutus*

r *Scarce throughout year* though not necessarily breeding.
s *Scarce in summer* only or largely.
w *Scarce in winter* only or largely.
p *Scarce on passage* only.
V *Vagrant* or casual visitor.
? More information needed.

	United Kingdom	Ireland	Iceland	Norway	Sweden	Finland	Denmark	Poland	Czechoslovakia	Germany	Netherlands	Belgium	Luxembourg	France	Spain
Night Heron	V	V		V	V	V	V	s	SP	s	s	p	V	SP	SP
Squacco Heron	V	V			V	V	V	V	s	p	V	V	V	s	s
Cattle Egret	V						V				V		V	p	R
Great White Egret	V				V		V	V	s	p	V	V		p	V
Little Egret	V	V			V		V	V	SP	p	V	V	V	SP	R
Grey Heron	R	R	V	R	R	s	R	SP	SP	R	R	r	r	R	Ws
Purple Heron	V	V		V	V	V	V	s	SP	s	SP	p	V	SP	SP
White Stork	V	V		V	V	V	s	SP	SP	s	SP	p	p	s	Sw
Black Stork	V			V	V	V	V	s	s	p	p	V	V	p	r
Spoonbill	p	w		V	V		s	V	s	p	SP	p	V	s	s
Glossy Ibis	V	V		V	V	V	V	V	V	p	V	V		p	p
Greater Flamingo	V	V		V	V	V	V	V	V	V	V	V		s	R
Canada Goose	R	r		r	R	V	p			V	V	V		V	V
Barnacle Goose	WP	WP	P	p	P	P	WP	V		V	w	WP	w	w	V
Brent Goose	WP	WP	P	p	P	P	WP	V	p	w	WP	p	V	WP	V
Red-breasted Goose	V	V			V	V	V	V	V	p	V	V			
Greylag Goose	R	w	SP	r	s	s	Sw	s	s	r	Ws	p	p	w	WP
White-fronted Goose	WP	WP	P	V	w	p	WP	p	P	w	Ws	w	V	w	V
Lesser White-fronted Goose	V	V		s	s	s	V	p	p	p	V	V		p	V
Bean Goose	w	V		r	r	SP	WP	P	P	w	w	w	w	WP	WP
Pink-footed Goose	WP	w	SP	p	w	V	P	V	V	w	WP	w	V	w	V
Mute Swan	R	R		r	R	s	R	R	p	R	r	p	V	w	V
Whooper Swan	WP	WP	Sw	r	Ws	s	WP	p	p	WP	WP	p	V	w	V
Bewick's Swan	WP	WP		V	p	p	WP	V		w	WP	p	V	w	V

R *Common throughout year* in at least part of the country.

Sw *Common in summer* in suitable habitats but *very scarce to scarce in winter.*

Ws *Common in winter* in suitable habitats but *very scarce to scarce in summer.*

SP *Common in summer* only or *present in summer and common on passage.*

WP *Common in winter* only or *present in winter and common on passage.*

P *Common on passage* only.

Balearic Is.	Portugal	Switzerland	Austria	Italy	Corsica	Sardinia	Sicily	Hungary	Rumania	Bulgaria	Yugoslavia	Albania	Greece	Greek Is.	Eur. Turkey	
	s	s	s	SP	p	p	p	SP	SP	SP	s	s	SP	p	p	*Nycticorax nycticorax*
	s	p	s	s	p	p	p	s	SP	SP	SP	SP	SP	P	P	*Ardeola ralloides*
V	R		V					V	V	V	V		V			*Bubulcus ibis*
V		V	s	w			p	s	s	r	p	s	P	WP	w	*Egretta alba*
?	R	p	s	SP	s	P	s	SP	SP	SP	SP	SP	SP	P	P	*Egretta garzetta*
WP	WP	R	R	R	r	P	r	Sw	SP	Sw	R	R	R	w	r	*Ardea cinerea*
SP	SP	s	s	SP	p	p	SP	SP	SP	SP	SP	SP	SP	p	p	*Ardea purpurea*
V	Sw	P	s	s				Sw	SP	SP	SP	SP	SP	P	SP	*Ciconia ciconia*
V	s	p	p					s	s	s	s	s	r	p	P	*Ciconia nigra*
V	s	V	SP					SP	s	s	s	s	SP		p	*Platalea leucorodia*
V	r	V	p	s			p	s	SP	s	s	s	SP	p	SP	*Plegadis falcinellus*
V	V	V	V			p		V	V	V			V	V		*Phoenicopterus ruber*
																Branta canadensis
		V	V	V				p	V							*Branta leucopsis*
	w	V	p					p	V	V	V		V			*Branta bernicla*
		V	V					w	w	w	V		w		w	*Branta ruficollis*
	w	p	SP	w		w		SP	SP	Ws	r	w	R	WP	WP	*Anser anser*
		w	P	WP			w	WP	P	WP	WP	WP	WP	w	WP	*Anser albifrons*
		V	p	V				WP	p	w	w	w	w		w	*Anser erythropus*
	w	w	WP	WP	w	w	w	WP	w	w	WP	WP	WP		w	*Anser fabalis*
		V	V	V				V	V		V					*Anser brachyrhynchus*
		R	R	r				V	s	r	w	w	Sw	w	WP	*Cygnus olor*
	V	V	p					V	V	WP	w	w	w	w	w	*Cygnus cygnus*
		V	V	V				V			V					*Cygnus bewickii*

r *Scarce throughout year* though not necessarily breeding.
s *Scarce in summer* only or largely.
w *Scarce in winter* only or largely.
p *Scarce on passage* only.
V *Vagrant* or casual visitor.
? More information needed.

	United Kingdom	Ireland	Iceland	Norway	Sweden	Finland	Denmark	Poland	Czechoslovakia	Germany	Netherlands	Belgium	Luxembourg	France	Spain
Ruddy Shelduck	V	V		V	V	V	V	V		V	V	V		V	w
Shelduck	R	R		r	Sw	s	R	s		R	R	r	V	r	w
Mallard	R	R	R	R	R	R	R	R	R	R	R	R	R	R	R
Teal	R	R	Sw	Sw	Sw	SP	Sw	SP	R	R	Ws	r		Ws	WP
Gadwall	r	r	SP	V	s	V	p	s	s	r	r	WP	w	r	r
Wigeon	Ws	WP	R	Sw	Sw	SP	WP	s		r	WP	Ws	WP	w	WP
Pintail	Ws	WP	SP	SP	SP	SP	r	s		s	WP	Ws	r	w	WP
Garganey	s	V		V	s	s	SP	SP	SP	SP	SP	s	r	Sw	s
Shoveler	R	R	s	s	SP	SP	SP	s	s	r	R	s	P	R	Ws
Marbled Teal									V	V				V	s
Red-crested Pochard	V	V		V	V	V	s	s	p	r	r	p	p	r	R
Pochard	R	Ws	Ws	s	Sw	SP	R	SP	p	R	Ws	r	P	Ws	Ws
Ferruginous Duck	V	V		V	V	V	V	s	s	r	V	p	V	s	r
Tufted Duck	R	R	Sw	R	R	SP	R	SP	s	R	R	r	P	WP	WP
Scaup	Ws	WP	Sw	R	Sw	s	WP	p		WP	WP	w	p	WP	V
Eider	R	R	R	R	R	Sw	R	w		r	R	r	V	r	V
King Eider	V	V	r	WP	V	w	V	V		V				V	
Steller's Eider	V			w	V	V	V	V		V				V	
Common Scoter	R	Ws	SP	R	Sw	s	WP	WP	V	WP	WP	WP	V	WP	WP
Velvet Scoter	Ws	w		R	Sw	SP	R	WP	V	WP	WP	WP	V	WP	w
Harlequin	V		R	V	V		V			V					
Long-tailed Duck	w	w	R	R	r	r	WP	WP	V	w	w	w		w	V
Goldeneye	Ws	WP	r	R	R	Sw	Ws	r	w	r	WP	WP	w	WP	V
Barrow's Goldeneye			R	V	V	V			V						V

R *Common throughout year* in at least part of the country.

Sw *Common in summer* in suitable habitats but *very scarce to scarce in winter.*

Ws *Common in winter* in suitable habitats but *very scarce to scarce in summer.*

SP *Common in summer* only or *present in summer and common on passage.*

WP *Common in winter* only or *present in winter and common on passage.*

P *Common on passage* only.

Balearic Is.	Portugal	Switzerland	Austria	Italy	Corsica	Sardinia	Sicily	Hungary	Rumania	Bulgaria	Yugoslavia	Albania	Greece	Greek Is.	Eur. Turkey	
		V	V	V	V	w	w	V	s	s	V		Sw	w	p	*Tadorna ferruginea*
V	w	w	p	w		r	w	p	s	r	w		WP	R	w	*Tadorna tadorna*
R	R	R	R	R	r	R	R	R	R	R	R	R	R	WP	R	*Anas platyrhynchos*
WP	WP	Ws	P	Ws	w	WP	WP	WP	WP	WP	WP	WP	WP	w	WP	*Anas crecca*
V	w	r	SP	P	w	w	WP	SP	R	r	r	r	R	WP	r	*Anas strepera*
WP	WP	w	P	WP	w	WP	WP	P	WP	WP	WP	WP	WP	w	WP	*Anas penelope*
WP	w	WP	s	WP	w	WP	WP	SP	P	WP	WP	WP	WP	w	WP	*Anas acuta*
P	p	SP	SP	s	P	P	P	SP	SP	Sw	SP	SP	R	P	P	*Anas querquedula*
WP	WP	r	SP	P	P	P	P	SP	r	r	WP	WP	WP	WP	WP	*Anas clypeata*
V	p			V	V	V	V	V	V				V	V		*Marmaronetta angustirostris*
V	V	r	s	r		r	r	V	s	r	p	p	R	w	p	*Netta rufina*
w	WP	Ws	R	WP	P	P	WP	Sw	Sw	Ws	WP	WP	Ws	WP	WP	*Aythya ferina*
w	WP	w	r	R	s	Sw	WP	Sw	Sw	Sw	R	R	R	WP	p	*Aythya nyroca*
w	WP	Ws	WP	WP	P	WP	WP	WP	Ws	WP	WP	WP	WP	w	WP	*Aythya fuligula*
V	V	w	w	WP	WP	V		p	w	w	w	w	V			*Aythya marila*
	V	w	p	V				w	V	V	V		V			*Somateria mollissima*
		V	V					V								*Somateria spectabilis*
																Polysticta stelleri
V	WP	w	w	w	w	w		V	V	V			V			*Melanitta nigra*
V	w	w	w	w				w	w	V			V			*Melanitta fusca*
		V		V												*Histrionicus histrionicus*
	V	V	w	w		V		w	w			V	V			*Clangula hyemalis*
	V	Ws	WP	WP		w		WP	w	w	w	w	w		w	*Bucephala clangula*
																Bucephala islandica

r *Scarce throughout year* though not necessarily breeding.
s *Scarce in summer* only or largely.
w *Scarce in winter* only or largely.
p *Scarce on passage* only.
V *Vagrant* or casual visitor.
? More information needed.

	United Kingdom	Ireland	Iceland	Norway	Sweden	Finland	Denmark	Poland	Czechoslovakia	Germany	Netherlands	Belgium	Luxembourg	France	Spain
Smew	w	V		r	r	s	w	WP	p	w	WP	w	p	w	w
Red-breasted Merganser	R	R	R	R	R	SP	R	s		p	r	WP	w	V	WP	WP
Goosander	r	w	R	R	R	SP	Ws	SP	p		r	WP	w	V	WP	w
White-headed Duck								V	V	V	V			V	r
Osprey	s	V		s	SP	SP	P	s		p	s	p	p	p	p	r
Black-winged Kite									V	V	V				V	r
Honey Buzzard	s	V		s	SP	SP	s		SP	SP	s	s	s	s	SP	P
Red Kite	r	V		V	s	V	p		s	SP	s	V	s	s	s	R
Black Kite	V			V	p	s		p	SP	SP	s	V	s	s	SP	SP
White-tailed Eagle	V	V	r	R	r	r	w	r	r	r	w	V	V	w	V
Goshawk	V	V		R	R	R	r		R	R	r	r	R	r	r	r
Levant Sparrowhawk										V					
Sparrowhawk	R	R		Sw	Sw	Sw	R	r		R	R	r	R	R	R	WP
Rough-legged Buzzard	w	V		SP	Sw	SP	WP	WP	w		w	w	w	w	p	V
Long-legged Buzzard								V	V			V	V		V	
Buzzard	R	r		s	Sw	SP	R	R		R	R	r	R	R	R	R
Booted Eagle					V			V	s	V		V		s	SP
Bonelli's Eagle					V	V				V	V	V		r	r
Tawny Eagle					V									V	V
Spotted Eagle	V	V			p	V	V	s	s	s	V	V		w	V
Lesser Spotted Eagle					V	V	V	s	SP	s	V	V	V	V	V
Imperial Eagle					V		V	V	s	V	V			V	r
Golden Eagle	R	V		R	r	r	w	r	r	r	V	V		r	r
Egyptian Vulture	V							V	V	V				s	SP

R *Common throughout year* in at least part of the country.

Sw *Common in summer* in suitable habitats but *very scarce to scarce in winter*.

Ws *Common in winter* in suitable habitats but *very scarce to scarce in summer*.

SP *Common in summer* only or *present in summer and common on passage*.

WP *Common in winter* only or *present in winter and common on passage*.

P *Common on passage* only.

Balearic Is.	Portugal	Switzerland	Austria	Italy	Corsica	Sardinia	Sicily	Hungary	Rumania	Bulgaria	Yugoslavia	Albania	Greece	Greek Is.	Eur. Turkey	
V	V	w	WP	p				WP	w	w	w	w	w		w	*Mergus albellus*
w	w	p	w	w	p	p	w	w	w	w	WP	WP	WP	WP	w	*Mergus serrator*
w	V	r	WP	p			V	WP	WP	w	w	w	w		w	*Mergus merganser*
	V		p	r	r	r	p	s	r	w		p	w		p	*Oxyura leucocephala*
r	r	p	p	s	r	r	r	P	s	p	p	p	w	w	p	*Pandion haliaetus*
	r		V													*Elanus caeruleus*
p	s	SP	SP	P	p	p	p	s	s	s	s	p	s	p	P	*Pernis apivorus*
r	r	s	s	s	R	s	R	s	s	p	s	s	w		w	*Milvus milvus*
p	SP	SP	SP	SP	p	p	p	SP	SP	SP	SP	SP	SP	p	SP	*Milvus migrans*
V	V	r						r	r	Ws	s	r	r	r	WP	*Haliaeetus albicilla*
V	r	r	R	r	R	R	r	R	R	R	r	r	r	w	r	*Accipiter gentilis*
		V	V					s	s	s	s	s	Sw	P	SP	*Accipiter brevipes*
p	r	R	R	R	R	R	r	R	Ws	Ws	R	r	r	P	P	*Accipiter nisus*
V		w	WP	w				WP	WP	WP	w	w	V		w	*Buteo lagopus*
		V		V				V	p	s	V	V	Sw	Sw	R	*Buteo rufinus*
p	r	R	R	R	R	R	R	R	R	r	R	R	R	w	R	*Buteo buteo*
SP	s	V	p	V				s	s	s	s	s	r	w	p	*Hieraaetus pennatus*
r	r		V	r	R	r	r	V	V	V		p	r	w	p	*Hieraaetus fasciatus*
							V		V	p	V		V		w	*Aquila rapax*
	V	V	p	w			V	p	s	p	p	p	w		w	*Aquila clanga*
		V	p	V				s	SP	s	s	s	Sw	P	P	*Aquila pomarina*
V	r		V	V				r	r	p	r	r	r	r	r	*Aquila heliaca*
r	r	R	r	R	r	r	r	V	r	r	r	r	r	r	p	*Aquila chrysaetos*
SP	s	V	V	s		V	SP	V	s	s	s	r	Sw	Sw	SP	*Neophron percnopterus*

r *Scarce throughout year* though not necessarily breeding.
s *Scarce in summer* only or largely.
w *Scarce in winter* only or largely.
p *Scarce on passage* only.
V *Vagrant* or casual visitor.
? More information needed.

	United Kingdom	Ireland	Iceland	Norway	Sweden	Finland	Denmark	Poland	Czechoslovakia	Germany	Netherlands	Belgium	Luxembourg	France	Spain
Lammergeier										V				r	r
Black Vulture							V	V		V	V				r
Griffon Vulture	V	V					V	V	V	V	V	V	V	r	R
Short-toed Eagle					V	V	V	s	s	s	V	V	V	s	s
Hen Harrier	R	r		s	Sw	Sw	WP	s	s	r	r	r	r	r	r
Pallid Harrier	V			V	V	V	V	p	p	p	V	V	V	p	V
Montagu's Harrier	s	V		V	s	V	s	s	s	s	s	s	p	SP	SP
Marsh Harrier	s	V		V	Sw	s	s	s	s	s	s	s	s	R	R
Gyr Falcon	V	V	r	r	r	r	V	V		V	V	V		V	
Saker					V			V	s	V				V	
Lanner										V				V	V
Peregrine	r	r		r	r	s	r	r	s	r	w	r	r	R	R
Hobby	s	V		p	s	SP	s	SP	SP	SP	s	s	s	SP	SP
Eleonora's Falcon										V				V	p
Merlin	r	r	Sw	Sw	SP	SP	WP	p	p	w	w	w	p	w	w
Red-footed Falcon	V	V		V	p	V	V	s	s	p	V	V	V	p	V
Lesser Kestrel	V	V			V		V	s	s	p		V		s	SP
Kestrel	R	R		Sw	Sw	SP	R	R	R	R	R	R	R	R	R
Willow/Red Grouse	R	R		R	R	R		V		V		r			
Ptarmigan	R		R	R	R	R				r				R	r
Hazel Grouse				r	r	R		r	R	r		V	r	r	
Black Grouse	R			R	R	R	R	r	R	r	r	r	r	R	
Capercaillie	R			R	R	R	V	r	R	r			V	R	r
Rock Partridge										r				R	

R *Common throughout year* in at least part of the country.
Sw *Common in summer* in suitable habitats but *very scarce in winter.*
Ws *Common in winter* in suitable habitats but *very scarce to scarce in summer.*
SP *Common in summer* only or *present in summer and common on passage.*
WP *Common in winter* only or *present in winter and common on passage.*
P *Common on passage* only.

Balearic Is.	Portugal	Switzerland	Austria	Italy	Corsica	Sardinia	Sicily	Hungary	Rumania	Bulgaria	Yugoslavia	Albania	Greece	Greek Is.	Eur. Turkey	
		V	V	V	r	r	?			V	r	?	r	r		Gypaetus barbatus
R	r	V	V			r	?	V	r	?	r	r	r	r	r	Aegypius monachus
V	r	V	s	r	V	r	r	V	r	r	r	r	r	R	R	Gyps fulvus
s	s	s	s	s	p	p	s	s	s	s	s	s	SP	SP	P	Circaetus gallicus
p	r	WP	r	r	w	w	p	WP	WP	w	w	w	WP	p	w	Circus cyaneus
V		V	p				p	P	r	w	w	p	WP	p	w	Circus macrourus
p	s	SP	s	s				s	s	r	s	p	p		p	Circus pygargus
r	R	P	R	R	r	r	R	Sw	SP	Sw	SP	SP	R	w	P	Circus aeruginosus
	V		V	V												Falco rusticolus
		s	V					s	s	r			p	p	w	Falco cherrug
V	V			r			r		V	V	r	r	r	r		Falco biarmicus
R	r	r	Ws	r	r	r	r	R	r	r	r	r	r	r	w	Falco peregrinus
p	s	SP	SP	s	SP	p	s	SP	SP	SP	s	s	SP	p	P	Falco subbuteo
SP				s	SP	p							Sw	Sw		Falco eleonorae
w	w	p	WP	w	w	p		WP	w	w	w	w	P		w	Falco columbarius
p		V	s	p	p	p	p	SP	SP	s	s	p	P	p	P	Falco vespertinus
p	s	V	s	s	p	s	s	s	s	s	SP	SP	Sw	Sw	SP	Falco naumanni
R	R	R	R	R	R	R	R	R	R	Sw	Sw	R	R	R	R	Falco tinnunculus
																Lagopus lagopus
		R	R	R												Lagopus mutus
		r	R	r				r	R	r	R	r				Tetrastes bonasia
		R	R	R					r		r	r	V			Lyrurus tetrix
		r	R	r				V	R	r	R	r				Tetrao urogallus
		R	r	R		R		?	R	R	R	R				Alectoris graeca

r *Scarce throughout year* though not necessarily breeding.
s *Scarce in summer* only or largely.
w *Scarce in winter* only or largely.
p *Scarce on passage* only.
V *Vagrant* or casual visitor.
? More information needed.

	United Kingdom	Ireland	Iceland	Norway	Sweden	Finland	Denmark	Poland	Czechoslovakia	Germany	Netherlands	Belgium	Luxembourg	France	Spain
Chukar															
Barbary Partridge															r
Red-legged Partridge	R									V	V		V	R	R
Partridge	R	R		r	r	r	R	R	R	R	R	R	R	R	r
Quail	s	s		V	s	s	V	s	SP	s	s	s	SP	SP	Sw
Pheasant	R	R		r	R	r	R	r	R	R	R	R	R	R	r
Andalusian Hemipode															r
Crane	V	V		s	SP	SP	s	s	p	s	p	p	p	p	WP
Demoiselle Crane				V	V	V	V			V					V
Water Rail	R	R	r	r	Sw	s	R	SP	SP	r	R	R	r	R	R
Spotted Crake	r	V		s	s	s	s		SP	SP	s	Sw	s	SP	P
Little Crake	V	V			V	V	s	s	s	s	s	p	V	s	r
Baillon's Crake	V	V				V	V	s	s	s	V			s	s
Corncrake	SP	SP		s	s	s	s	s	SP	SP	s	SP	s	SP	p
Moorhen	R	R	V	Sw	Sw	s	R	SP	SP	R	R	R	R	R	R
Purple Gallinule				V					V						r
Coot	R	R	V	r	R	SP	R	SP	SP	R	R	R	R	R	R
Crested Coot															r
Great Bustard	V	V			V	V	V	r	Sw	r	V	V	V		r
Little Bustard	V	V			V	V	V	V	V	p	V	V	V	SP	R
Houbara Bustard	V				V	V	V	V	V	V	V	V			V
Oystercatcher	R	R	R	R	Sw	Sw	Sw	p	V	R	R	r	V	R	r
Ringed Plover	R	R	SP	SP	SP	SP	SP	s	p	s	Sw	s	p	Ws	WP
Little Ringed Plover	s	V		s	s	s	s	s	SP	SP	s	s	s	SP	SP

R *Common throughout year* in at least part of the country.

Sw *Common in summer* in suitable habitats but *very scarce to scarce in winter.*

Ws *Common in winter* in suitable habitats but *very scarce to scarce in summer.*

SP *Common in summer* only or *present in summer and common on passage.*

WP *Common in winter* only or *present in winter and common on passage.*

P *Common on passage* only.

Balearic Is.	Portugal	Switzerland	Austria	Italy	Corsica	Sardinia	Sicily	Hungary	Rumania	Bulgaria	Yugoslavia	Albania	Greece	Greek Is.	Eur. Turkey	
										R			R	R	R	*Alectoris chukar*
						R										*Alectoris barbara*
R	R			R	R											*Alectoris rufa*
	r	r	R	R				R	r	r	R	r	r			*Perdix perdix*
Sw	Sw	SP	SP	Sw	Sw	Sw	Sw	SP	SP	Sw	SP	Sw	Sw	Sw	SP	*Coturnix coturnix*
r		R	R	R	r		r	R	R	r	r	r	r		r	*Phasianus colchicus*
	r															*Turnix sylvatica*
V	V	p	p	w				p	p	P	P	P	P	p	P	*Grus grus*
	V							V	V	p			V		p	*Anthropoides virgo*
R	r	R	R	R	r	R	R	Sw	Sw	r	r	r	R	P	r	*Rallus aquaticus*
	w	SP	SP	Sw	s	Sw	w	Sw	s	s	s	s	p	p	p	*Porzana porzana*
	s		SP	s		p	p	Sw	SP	s	s	p	P	P		*Porzana parva*
	s	s	s	s		p	p	s	s	?	s	p	p	p	p	*Porzana pusilla*
	w	s	SP	s		w	w	SP	SP	SP	SP	s	p	p	p	*Crex crex*
R	R	R	R	R	R	R	R	Sw	Sw	Sw	R	R	R	p	R	*Gallinula chloropus*
	?		V			r	R						V			*Porphyrio porphyrio*
R	R	R	R	R	R	R	R	R	Sw	R	R	R	R	Ws	R	*Fulica atra*
	w			V		V	V									*Fulica cristata*
	r	V	r	V			V	R	r	r	V	V	V			*Otis tarda*
V	R	V	r	Ws	p	Ws	R	s	p	r	Ws	Ws	Ws		Ws	*Otis tetrax*
	V	V		V			V	V	V							*Chlamydotis undulata*
	Ws	V	p	r	V	V		p	s	p	r	r	Sw		r	*Haematopus ostralegus*
WP	WP	P	P	P	p	WP	WP	P	p	p	p	p	P	p	p	*Charadrius hiaticula*
SP	SP	s	SP	SP	s	s	s	s	SP	SP	SP	s	SP	s	s	*Charadrius dubius*

r *Scarce throughout year* though not necessarily breeding.
s *Scarce in summer* only or largely.
w *Scarce in winter* only or largely.
p *Scarce on passage* only.
V *Vagrant* or casual visitor.
? More information needed.

	United Kingdom	Ireland	Iceland	Norway	Sweden	Finland	Denmark	Poland	Czechoslovakia	Germany	Netherlands	Belgium	Luxembourg	France	Spain
Kentish Plover	V	V		V	s	V	s	V		s	SP	s		Sw	R
Dotterel	s	V		SP	SP	SP	p	p	s	p	r	p	V	p	w
Golden Plover	R	Ws	SP	SP	SP	SP	r	P	p	s	WP	WP	P	P	WP
Grey Plover	WP	WP	V	P	P	P	P	p	p	w	WP	WP		P	w
Lapwing	R	R	V	Sw	Sw	SP	R	SP	SP	R	R	R	R	R	Ws
Spur-winged Plover															
Turnstone	Ws	Ws	Ws	Sw	SP	SP	s	p	V	r	Ws	WP		WP	WP
Little Stint	p	p		s	P	P	P	P	P	p	P	P	P	P	WP
Temminck's Stint	s	V		SP	SP	SP	P	P	p	P	p	p	V	w	
Pectoral Sandpiper	V	V	V	V	V	V	V	V			V			V	
Purple Sandpiper	WP	WP	R	r	r	s	w	V		w	w	w		w	p
Dunlin	R	R	Sw	Sw	SP	s	r	s	p	R	Ws	Ws	p	WP	WP
Curlew Sandpiper	p	p		P	P	P	P	p	p	P	p	p	V	p	p
Knot	Ws	Ws	P	P	P	P	P	p	p	R	Ws	WP	V	WP	WP
Sanderling	Ws	Ws	P	P	p	p	P	p		P	WP	WP	V	WP	WP
Ruff	r	p	V	SP	SP	SP	SP	s	s	s	Sw	s	P	r	WP
Broad-billed Sandpiper	V	V		s	s	s	p	p	p	p	V	V		V	V
Spotted Redshank	P	p		SP	SP	SP	P	p	p	P	P	P	p	WP	WP
Redshank	R	R	Sw	SP	SP	SP	SP	SP	SP	SP	R	R	P	R	R
Marsh Sandpiper	V				V	V		V		p	V	V	V	p	p
Greenshank	r	w		SP	SP	SP	P	P	P	P	P	p	p	WP	WP
Green Sandpiper	P	p		SP	SP	SP	P	s	SP	s	P	P	P	WP	WP
Wood Sandpiper	s	p		SP	SP	SP	s	s	s	s	P	P	p	P	P
Common Sandpiper	Sw	Sw		SP	SP	SP	P	SP	SP	SP	P	r	P	Sw	R

R   Common throughout year in at least part of the country.

Sw   Common in summer in suitable habitats but very scarce to scarce in winter.

Ws   Common in winter in suitable habitats but very scarce to scarce in summer.

SP   Common in summer only or present in summer and common on passage.

WP   Common in winter only or present in winter and common on passage.

P   Common on passage only.

Balearic Is.	Portugal	Switzerland	Austria	Italy	Corsica	Sardinia	Sicily	Hungary	Rumania	Bulgaria	Yugoslavia	Albania	Greece	Greek Is.	Eur. Turkey	
R	R	V	SP	R	r	R	r	SP	SP	SP	SP	SP	Sw	P	s	*Charadrius alexandrinus*
	p	SP	p		p	p	p	s	p	p	p	p	p		p	*Eudromias morinellus*
w	WP	P	p	WP	w	w	WP	p	P	p	WP	WP	WP	p	WP	*Pluvialis apricaria*
w	WP	P	P	w	p	w	p	p	p	p	w	w	w		w	*Pluvialis squatarola*
WP	WP	SP	R	Ws	w	WP	w	Sw	Sw	Sw	R	R	Sw	WP	R	*Vanellus vanellus*
								V	V				Sw	p	s	*Vanellus spinosus*
p	w	p	p	w	p	p	p	p	p	p	p	p	P	p	p	*Arenaria interpres*
WP	WP	p	P	WP	p	WP	WP	P	P	P	P	P	WP	p	P	*Calidris minuta*
p	p	p	P	P	p	p	p	P	P	p	P	P	P	p	P	*Calidris temminckii*
		V														*Calidris melanotos*
	V	V	p	V			V						V			*Calidris maritima*
WP	WP	P	P	WP	w	w	WP	P	P	P	WP	WP	WP	p	w	*Calidris alpina*
p	p	p	p	P	p	p	P	P	P	P	P	P	P	P	P	*Calidris ferruginea*
p	WP	p	p	p	p	p	p	p								*Calidris canutus*
p	WP	p	p	p	p	p	p	p	p	WP	p		p			*Calidris alba*
P	WP	P	P	WP	WP	WP	WP	SP	P	P	P	P	P	p	P	*Philomachus pugnax*
V		V	p	p				p	p	p	p	p	p		p	*Limicola falcinellus*
WP	WP	P	P	WP	WP	WP	WP	P	p	p	p	p	WP	p	p	*Tringa erythropus*
WP	r	P	SP	Ws	WP	WP	WP	SP	Sw	SP	P	R	R	r	R	*Tringa totanus*
p		V	p	p			p	p	s	s	p	p	p	p	p	*Tringa stagnatilis*
P	WP	P	P	WP	WP	WP	WP	P	P	P	p	p	P	p	p	*Tringa nebularia*
WP	WP	P	P	WP	WP	WP	WP	P	P	SP	w	w	WP	w	w	*Tringa ochropus*
P	p	P	P	P	P	P	P	P	P	P	p	P	P	p	P	*Tringa glareola*
WP	r	SP	SP	R	s	R	WP	SP	SP	SP	R	R	P	p	WP	*Tringa hypoleucos*

r *Scarce throughout year* though not necessarily breeding.
s *Scarce in summer* only or largely.
w *Scarce in winter* only or largely.
p *Scarce on passage* only.
V *Vagrant* or casual visitor.
? More information needed.

	United Kingdom	Ireland	Iceland	Norway	Sweden	Finland	Denmark	Poland	Czechoslovakia	Germany	Netherlands	Belgium	Luxembourg	France	Spain
Terek Sandpiper	V				V	s	V	V		V	V			V	V
Black-tailed Godwit	Ws	Ws	SP	V	s	V	SP	s	SP	SP	Sw	s	p	P	WP
Bar-tailed Godwit	Ws	Ws	V	s	s	s	P	p		P	WP	WP	V	WP	WP
Curlew	R	R	w	Sw	SP	SP	Ws	s	SP	R	R	R	P	R	WP
Slender-billed Curlew								V	V	V	V	V		V	p
Whimbrel	SP	P	SP	SP	SP	SP	P	p	p	p	P	P	V	P	P
Woodcock	R	R	V	Sw	Sw	SP	SP	SP	SP	SP	R	R	s	R	Ws
Snipe	R	R	Sw	SP	SP	SP	SP	SP	SP	R	R	Ws	r	Ws	Ws
Great Snipe	V	V		s	s	s	p	s	p	p	p	V	V	p	V
Jack Snipe	WP	WP		s	SP	SP	p	p	p	p	WP	WP	p	WP	WP
Black-winged Stilt	V	V			V		V	V	p	p	V	V	V	SP	SP
Avocet	r	w		V	s	V	SP	V	s	s	SP	s	V	Sw	R
Grey Phalarope	p	p	s	p	V	V	V	V		p	p	p		p	p
Red-necked Phalarope	s	s	SP	SP	SP	s	p	p		p	p	p	V	p	p
Stone Curlew	s	V			V		V	s	SP	s	V	V	V	Sw	R
Pratincole	V	V			V		V	V	p	V	V	V		SP	SP
Black-winged Pratincole	V	V		V	V	V	V	V			V				
Great Skua	SP	P	SP	V	V	V	V	V		V	p	p	V	p	p
Pomarine Skua	p	p	p	p	p	p	p	p	V	p	p	p	V	p	p
Arctic Skua	SP	p	SP	SP	s	s	P	P	p	p	P	P	V	P	p
Long-tailed Skua	p	V	p	SP	SP	SP	p	p		p	p	p		p	p
Mediterranean Gull	r	V			V		V	V	p	s	V	V		w	w
Little Gull	r	p	V	V	s	s	r	s		r	p	p	V	w	w
Black-headed Gull	R	R	R	r	Sw	SP	R	Sw	Sw	R	R	R	WP	R	Ws

R *Common throughout year* in at least part of the country.

Sw *Common in summer* in suitable habitats but *very scarce to scarce in winter*.

Ws *Common in winter* in suitable habitats but *very scarce to scarce in summer*.

SP *Common in summer* only or *present in summer and common on passage*.

WP *Common in winter* only or *present in winter and common on passage*.

P *Common on passage* only.

Switzerland	Austria	Italy	Corsica	Sardinia	Sicily	Hungary	Rumania	Bulgaria	Yugoslavia	Albania	Greece	Greek Is.	Eur. Turkey	
V	V		V	V							V	V		*Xenus cinereus*
VP	P	s	P	p	p	P	SP	P	P	P	WP	p	WP	*Limosa limosa*
VP	V	p	p		p		p	V	V		p	p		*Limosa lapponica*
VP	SP	SP	WP	w		WP	WP	SP	SP	WP	WP	WP	w	*Numenius arquata*
V	V	V	p					p	p	p	WP	P		*Numenius tenuirostris*
VP	p	p	p	p	p	p	P	V	V	p	p	P	P	*Numenius phaeopus*
VP	SP	P	Ws	Ws	WP	WP	SP	SP	SP	r	w	WP	w	*Scolopax rusticola*
Ws	SP	R	Ws	w	WP	WP	SP	SP	WP	Ws	WP	WP	w	*Gallinago gallinago*
V	p	P			p	r	p	P	P	p	p	p		*Gallinago media*
VP	w	p	WP	w	WP	WP	p	P	P	p	WP	w	w	*Lymnocryptes minimus*
SP	V	p	s	p	p	p	s	s	SP	p	Sw	p	SP	*Himantopus himantopus*
Ws	V	SP	s	p	p	w	s	s	SP	s	s	SP	s	*Recurvirostra avosetta*
V	V					V	V	V			V			*Phalaropus fulicarius*
V	p					p	p	V			p			*Phalaropus lobatus*
Ws	V	s	R	Sw	Sw	R	s	s	s	s	r	Sw	WP r	*Burhinus oedicnemus*
SP	V	p	s	P	P	P	s	SP	SP	s	s	SP	P SP	*Glareola pratincola*
		V				V	s	s	V		p	p	p	*Glareola nordmanni*
V	V	V				V			V		V			*Stercorarius skua*
V	V	V				V	p	p	V		V	V		*Stercorarius pomarinus*
p	V	p				p	V	p			p			*Stercorarius parasiticus*
V	V	p				p	V							*Stercorarius longicaudus*
V	p	V	w		w	w	s	s	Sw	w	Sw	WP	P	*Larus melanocephalus*
w	P	P	WP	w	w	w	P	P	Sw	WP	WP	w	WP	*Larus minutus*
Ws	R	R	Ws	w	w	WP	R	R	R	Ws	WP	WP	w	WP *Larus ridibundus*

r *Scarce throughout year* though not necessarily breeding.
s *Scarce in summer* only or largely.
w *Scarce in winter* only or largely.
p *Scarce on passage* only.
V *Vagrant* or casual visitor.
? More information needed.

	United Kingdom	Ireland	Iceland	Norway	Sweden	Finland	Denmark	Poland	Czechoslovakia	Germany	Netherlands	Belgium	Luxembourg	France	Spain
Slender-billed Gull	V													s	r
Lesser Black-backed Gull	Sw	Sw	SP	SP	SP	SP	Sw	P	p	Sw	Sw	P	V	Sw	WP
Herring Gull	R	R	R	R	R	R	R	R	p	R	R	R	V	R	R
Iceland Gull	w	w	WP	w	V	V	V			V	V	V		V	V
Glaucous Gull	w	w	R	w	w	w	V	V		w	V	V		w	V
Great Black-backed Gull	R	R	R	R	R	SP	Ws	r		Ws	Ws	Ws	V	R	w
Common Gull	R	R	r	R	R	SP	R	r	p	R	R	WP	w	WP	w
Audouin's Gull															r
Sabine's Gull	p	p	p	V	V	V	V	V		V	V	V		p	p
Kittiwake	R	R	R	R	w	V	r	V	V	r	w	w	V	r	w
Ivory Gull	V	V	V	V	V	V	V				V			V	
Black Tern	P	p	V	V	s	p	s	SP	s	s	SP	s	p	SP	SP
White-winged Black Tern	V	V		V			V	s	p	p	V	V	p	p	p
Whiskered Tern	V	V					s		V	V	V	V	V	SP	SP
Gull-billed Tern	V	V		V	V		s	V	V	s	p	V	V	s	s
Caspian Tern	V	V		p	SP	SP	s	p	V	p	V	V		p	p
Sandwich Tern	SP	SP		V	s	V	SP	p	V	s	s	p		SP	P
Common Tern	SP	SP		SP	SP	SP	SP	SP	s	SP	SP	SP	p	SP	SP
Arctic Tern	SP	SP	SP	SP	SP	SP	SP	p		SP	s	p	V	s	P
Roseate Tern	s	SP			V		V			p	V			s	p
Little Tern	SP	SP		V	s	s	SP	s	s	s	s	s	V	SP	SP
Little Auk	w	w	r	WP	w	V	w	V		w	w	w		w	w
Razorbill	R	R	R	R	r	s	r	w		w	w	w		Ws	WP
Guillemot	R	R	R	R	r	s	r	w		r	w	w		Ws	R

R *Common throughout year* in at least part of the country.

Sw *Common in summer* in suitable habitats but *very scarce to scarce in winter.*

Ws *Common in winter* in suitable habitats but *very scarce to scarce in summer.*

SP *Common in summer* only or *present in summer and common on passage.*

WP *Common in winter* only or *present in winter and common on passage.*

P *Common on passage* only.

...c Is.	Portugal	Switzerland	Austria	Italy	Corsica	Sardinia	Sicily	Hungary	Rumania	Bulgaria	Yugoslavia	Albania	Greece	Greek Is.	Eur. Turkey	
				w	w	w	w		s	p	w	w	r		p	*Larus genei*
	WP	w	w	w	w	w	w	p	r	p	w	w	WP	WP	w	*Larus fuscus*
R	R	r	p	R	R	R	R	SP	R	R	R	R	R	R	R	*Larus argentatus*
	V	V	V	V				V								*Larus glaucoides*
	V		V	V		V		V	V							*Larus hyperboreus*
	w	V	V	V				V					V			*Larus marinus*
	w	w	p	w	w	w		WP	WP	w	w	w	Ws			*Larus canus*
		V		r	r	r	V			V	V		r	r		*Larus audouinii*
	p	V	V					V								*Larus sabini*
	w	V	V	w		w		w	V				w	V		*Rissa tridactyla*
		V	V	V												*Pagophila eburnea*
	s	P	s	SP	P	P	P	SP	SP	SP	SP	SP	r	P	P	*Chlidonias niger*
	p	V	s	p	p	p	p	s	SP	s	p	p	P	V	p	*Chlidonias leucopterus*
	s	V	V	s	p	p	p	s	SP	SP	s	s	p		p	*Chlidonias hybrida*
	s	V	s	s	p	p	p	V	SP	s	s	p	r	p	p	*Gelochelidon nilotica*
	p	V	V	p	p	p	p	P	s	p	p	p	SP	p	p	*Hydroprogne caspia*
	P	V		p	p	p	p	V	s	p	p	p	WP		p	*Sterna sandvicensis*
	SP	s	SP	s	P	s	P	SP	SP	SP	SP	SP	SP	p	P	*Sterna hirundo*
	P	V	V										p			*Sterna paradisaea*
	p	V	V	V		V										*Sterna dougallii*
	SP	V	s	SP	SP	SP	P		SP	SP	SP	s	SP	P	s	*Sterna albifrons*
	w			V												*Plautus alle*
w	w	V		w	w	w		V								*Alca torda*
	Ws	V	V													*Uria aalge*

r *Scarce throughout year* though not necessarily breeding.
s *Scarce in summer* only or largely.
w *Scarce in winter* only or largely.
p *Scarce on passage* only.
V *Vagrant* or casual visitor.
? More information needed.

	United Kingdom	Ireland	Iceland	Norway	Sweden	Finland	Denmark	Poland	Czechoslovakia	Germany	Netherlands	Belgium	Luxembourg	France	Spain
Brünnich's Guillemot	V	V	R	Ws	V	V	V	V	V	V	V			V	V
Black Guillemot	R	R	R	R	R	SP	r	w		w	V	V		V	
Puffin	Sw	Sw	Sw	R	r	V	w	V		p	p	w		r	WP
Black-bellied Sandgrouse										V		V			R
Pin-tailed Sandgrouse										V				r	R
Woodpigeon	R	R	V	Sw	Sw	SP	R	SP	Sw	R	R	R	R	R	R
Stock Dove	R	R		s	s	s	s	s	SP	r	R	R	r	R	R
Rock Dove	R	R							?		r			r	R
Collared Dove	R	R		r	r	V	R	R	R	R	R	R	R	R	
Turtle Dove	SP	s	V	V	V	V	s		SP	SP	SP	SP	SP	SP	SP
Laughing or Palm Dove															
Cuckoo	SP	SP		SP	SP	SP	SP	SP	SP	SP	SP	SP	SP	SP	SP
Great Spotted Cuckoo	V	V				V	V			V	V	V		s	SP
Barn Owl	R	R		V	r		V	R	r	R	R	R	R	R	R
Snowy Owl	r	V	r	V	V	V	V	w	V	V	V	V	V		
Eagle Owl	V			r	r	r	V	r	r	r	V	V	V	r	r
Long-eared Owl	r	R	V	r	R	SP	R	R	R	R	R	R	R	r	r
Short-eared Owl	Ws	w	r	SP	SP	SP	r	s	SP	r	R	Ws	w	Ws	w
Scops Owl	V	V		V	V		V	V	s	V	V	V	V	SP	Sw
Tengmalm's Owl	V			R	R	R	V	r	R	r		V	V	r	V
Little Owl	R	V			V		R	r	R	R	R	R	R	R	R
Pygmy Owl				R	R	R	V	r	r	r		V		r	
Hawk Owl	V			r	r	R	V	V	p	w	V	V	V	V	
Tawny Owl	R			R	R	R	R	R	R	R	R	R	R	R	R

R *Common throughout year* in at least part of the country.

Sw *Common in summer* in suitable habitats but *very scarce to scarce in winter.*

Ws *Common in winter* in suitable habitats but *very scarce to scarce in summer.*

SP *Common in summer* only or *present in summer and common on passage.*

WP *Common in winter* only or *present in winter and common on passage.*

P *Common on passage* only.

	Portugal	Switzerland	Austria	Italy	Corsica	Sardinia	Sicily	Hungary	Rumania	Bulgaria	Yugoslavia	Albania	Greece	Greek Is.	Eur. Turkey	
			V													*Uria lomvia*
																Cepphus grylle
w	w		V	V		V		V			V					*Fratercula arctica*
r			V													*Pterocles orientalis*
r			V			V										*Pterocles alchata*
	R	Sw	R	R	R	R	R	Sw	SP	SP	R	r	r	R	R	*Columba palumbus*
	w	SP	R	r	?	r	r	SP	SP	s	r	r	r	WP	r	*Columba oenas*
	R	?	R	R	R	R				R	R	r	R	R	r	*Columba livia*
		R	R	r				R	R	R	R	R	R	r	R	*Streptopelia decaocto*
P	SP	SP	SP	SP	SP	SP	SP	Sw	SP	SP	SP	SP	SP	SP	SP	*Streptopelia turtur*
													V		r	*Streptopelia senegalensis*
P	SP	SP	SP	SP	SP	SP	SP	SP	SP	SP	SP	SP	SP	s	SP	*Cuculus canorus*
	s	V	V	?		V	V				V		s	V		*Clamator glandarius*
	R	R	R	R	R	R	R	R	r	r	SP	r	r	r		*Tyto alba*
			V					V			V					*Nyctea scandiaca*
	r	r	r	r			r	r	r	r	r	r	R	V		*Bubo bubo*
	w	R	R	r	w	w	r	R	R	R	r	r	Sw		w	*Asio otus*
	w	V	r	Ws	w	w	w	Ws	Ws	Ws	WP	w	WP	w	w	*Asio flammeus*
w	SP	s	s	Sw	R	R	R	s	SP	SP	SP	s	Sw	s	s	*Otus scops*
		R	R	r				V	r	V	r		r			*Aegolius funereus*
	R	R	R	R	R	R	R	R	R	R	R	R	R	R	R	*Athene noctua*
		r	r	r					r	V	r					*Glaucidium passerinum*
		V	V					V	V		V					*Surnia ulula*
	R	R	R	r			R	R	R	R	R	r	R	r	r	*Strix aluco*

r *Scarce throughout year* though not necessarily breeding.
s *Scarce in summer* only or largely.
w *Scarce in winter* only or largely.
p *Scarce on passage* only.
V *Vagrant* or casual visitor.
? More information needed.

	United Kingdom	Ireland	Iceland	Norway	Sweden	Finland	Denmark	Poland	Czechoslovakia	Germany	Netherlands	Belgium	Luxembourg	France	Spain
Ural Owl				r	R	R		r	r	r					
Great Grey Owl				V	r	r			s		V				
Nightjar	SP	SP		s	SP	SP	SP	SP	SP	s	SP	SP	s	SP	SP
Red-necked Nightjar	V													V	SP
White-rumped Swift															s
Pallid Swift														s	s
Swift	SP	SP	V	SP	SP	SP	SP	SP	SP	SP	SP	SP	SP	SP	SP
Alpine Swift	V	V		V			V			s	V	V		SP	SP
Kingfisher	R	R		V	r	s	r	R	R	r	r	R	R	R	R
Bee-eater	V	V		V	V	V	V	s	SP	s	V	V	V	SP	SP
Blue-cheeked Bee-eater	V				V									V	
Roller	V	V		V	s	V	V	s	SP	s	V	V	V	s	s
Hoopoe	p	p		V	p	p	p	SP	SP	s	s	s	s	SP	Sw
Wryneck	s	V		SP	SP	s	s	SP	SP	SP	s	s	SP	s	SP
Green Woodpecker	R	V		R	R	V	R	R	R	R	R	R	R	R	R
Grey-headed Woodpecker				r	r	r		r	R	R	V	V	r	R	
Black Woodpecker				R	R	R	w	r	R	R	r	r	r	R	r
Great Spotted Woodpecker	R	V		R	R	R	R	R	R	R	R	R	R	R	R
Syrian Woodpecker									R						
Middle Spotted Woodpecker					r	V	r	r	R	r	r	V	r	R	r
White-backed Woodpecker				r	r	r		r	r	r			V	r	r
Lesser Spotted Woodpecker	R			R	R	r	V	R	R	R	R	R	r	R	r
Three-toed Woodpecker				r	R	R	V	r	r	r				r	
Short-toed Lark	V	V		V	V	V	V		V	V			V	SP	SP

R *Common throughout year* in at least part of the country.

Sw *Common in summer* in suitable habitats but *very scarce to scarce in winter.*

Ws *Common in winter* in suitable habitats but *very scarce to scarce in summer.*

SP *Common in summer* only or *present in summer and common on passage.*

WP *Common in winter* only or *present in winter and common on passage.*

P *Common on passage* only.

Balearic Is.	Portugal	Switzerland	Austria	Italy	Corsica	Sardinia	Sicily	Hungary	Rumania	Bulgaria	Yugoslavia	Albania	Greece	Greek Is.	Eur. Turkey	
			r	V				w	r		r	r	V			*Strix uralensis*
																Strix nebulosa
	SP	s	SP	SP	SP	SP	SP	SP	SP	SP	SP	SP	SP	SP	s	*Caprimulgus europaeus*
	s						V				V					*Caprimulgus ruficollis*
r																*Apus caffer*
SP	s			SP	SP	SP	?			s		s	s			*Apus pallidus*
SP	SP	SP	SP	SP	SP	SP	SP	SP	SP	SP	SP	SP	SP	SP	SP	*Apus apus*
SP	s	SP	s	SP	SP	SP	SP	V	s	SP	SP	s	Sw	SP	SP	*Apus melba*
v	R	r	R	R	r	R	R	r	r	r	R	r	R	w	r	*Alcedo atthis*
SP	SP	V	s	SP	SP	SP	SP	SP	SP	SP	SP	SP	SP	SP	SP	*Merops apiaster*
			V										V	p		*Merops superciliosus*
	s	V	s	SP	SP	SP	SP	SP	SP	SP	SP	SP	SP	SP	SP	*Coracias garrulus*
Sw	Sw	SP	SP	SP	SP	SP	SP	SP	SP	SP	SP	s	s	SP	SP	*Upupa epops*
	s	SP	SP	Sw	r		Sw	Sw	SP	SP	SP	SP	w	SP	P	w	*Jynx torquilla*
V	R	R	R	R	V		?	R	R	R	R	r	R		r	*Picus viridis*
		R	R	r				r	R	R	r	r	?			*Picus canus*
		R	R	r				r	r	r	r	r	R		r	*Dryocopus martius*
	R	R	R	R	R	R	R	R	R	R	R	r	r		r	*Dendrocopos major*
			r					R	R	R	R	R	R	r	R	*Dendrocopos syriacus*
	V	r	R	r				r	R	r	r	r	R	R	r	*Dendrocopos medius*
		r	r					r	R	r	r	r	r	r	R	*Dendrocopos leucotos*
	r	r	R	R	?	r	r	R	R	R	R	r	r	r	r	*Dendrocopos minor*
		r	r	V				r	V	r	r	r				*Picoides tridactylus*
SP	SP	V	V	SP	SP	SP	SP	SP	s		SP	SP	SP	SP	SP	*Calandrella cinerea*

r *Scarce throughout year* though not necessarily breeding.
s *Scarce in summer* only or largely.
w *Scarce in winter* only or largely.
p *Scarce on passage* only.
V *Vagrant* or casual visitor.
? More information needed.

	United Kingdom	Ireland	Iceland	Norway	Sweden	Finland	Denmark	Poland	Czechoslovakia	Germany	Netherlands	Belgium	Luxembourg	France	Spain
Lesser Short-toed Lark		V				V				V					r
Calandra Lark	V			V		V		V	V	V	V	V	V	r	R
White-winged Lark	V			V				V		V		V			
Shore Lark	w	V		s	r	s	WP	w	p	w	w	w		w	V
Crested Lark	V			r	r	V	R	R	R	R	R	R	r	R	R
Thekla Lark														r	R
Woodlark	r	V		s	SP	s	r	Sw	SP	SP	r	r	Sw	R	R
Skylark	R	R	V	Sw	Sw	SP	R	Sw	SP	R	R	R	R	R	R
Sand Martin	SP	SP		SP	SP	SP	SP	SP	SP	SP	SP	SP	SP	SP	SP
Crag Martin										s				Sw	Sw
Swallow	SP	SP	s	SP	SP	SP	SP	SP	SP	SP	SP	SP	SP	SP	SP
Red-rumped Swallow	V	V		V		V	V			V	V			s	SP
House Martin	SP	SP	s	SP	SP	SP	SP	SP	SP	SP	SP	SP	SP	SP	SP
Richard's Pipit	p	V		p	V	p		V		p	V	V	V	V	V
Tawny Pipit	V	V		V	s	V	s	s	SP	s	s	s	s	SP	SP
Tree Pipit	SP	s		SP	SP	SP	SP	SP	SP	SP	SP	SP	SP	SP	P
Meadow Pipit	R	R	SP	SP	SP	SP	R	SP	s	Sw	R	R	R	R	WP*
Red-throated Pipit	V	V		SP	s	s	p	p	p	p	V	V	V	V	V
Water/Rock Pipit	R	R		R	Sw	s	r	s	SP	r	w	w	V	R	R
Blue-headed/Yellow Wagtail	SP	s		SP	SP	SP	SP	SP	SP	SP	SP	SP	SP	SP	SP
Grey Wagtail	R	R		r	s	V	r	s	SP	R	r	r	R	R	R
White/Pied Wagtail	R	R	SP	SP	SP	SP	SP	SP	SP	SP	Sw	Sw	Sw	R	R
Red-backed Shrike	s	V		SP	SP	s		SP	SP	SP	SP	s	s	SP	s
Masked Shrike														V	V

R   *Common throughout year* in at least part of the country.

Sw   *Common in summer* in suitable habitats but *very scarce to scarce in winter.*

Ws   *Common in winter* in suitable habitats but *very scarce to scarce in summer.*

SP   *Common in summer* only or *present in summer and common on passage.*

WP   *Common in winter* only or *present in winter and common on passage.*

P   *Common on passage* only.

Balearic Is	Portugal	Switzerland	Austria	Italy	Corsica	Sardinia	Sicily	Hungary	Rumania	Bulgaria	Yugoslavia	Albania	Greece	Greek Is.	Eur. Turkey	
V			V												r	*Calandrella rufescens*
V	R	V		R	R	R	R	V	R	R	R	R	R	R		*Melanocorypha calandra*
		V		V				V		V		V			p	*Melanocorypha leucoptera*
		V	V	V			V	w	r	r	r	r	R			*Eremophila alpestris*
V	R	r	R	R				R	R	R	R	R	R	R	R	*Galerida cristata*
R	R															*Galerida theklae*
w	R	SP	s	R	R	R	R	SP	SP	SP	R	R	R	R	r	*Lullula arborea*
WP	R	Sw	SP	R	R	R	R	Sw	Sw	R	R	R	R	R	R	*Alauda arvensis*
SP	SP	SP	SP	SP	SP	SP	SP	SP	SP	SP	SP	SP	SP	P	SP	*Riparia riparia*
R	r	SP	s	R	R	R	R			SP	Sw	r	R	r	r	*Hirundo rupestris*
SP	SP	SP	SP	SP	SP	SP	SP	SP	SP	SP	SP	SP	SP	SP	SP	*Hirundo rustica*
V	s	V	V	?	s	s	?			s	s	s	SP	SP	p	*Hirundo daurica*
SP	SP	SP	SP	SP	SP	SP	SP	SP	SP	SP	SP	SP	SP	SP	SP	*Delichon urbica*
p	V		V	V		V							V	V		*Anthus novaeseelandiae*
SP	SP	P	s	SP	SP	SP	SP	s	SP	SP	SP	SP	SP	SP	SP	*Anthus campestris*
p	P	SP	SP	SP	P	P	P	SP	SP	SP	SP	s	SP	P	SP	*Anthus trivialis*
WP	WP	P		R	Ws	WP	WP	WP	WP	WP	WP	WP	WP	WP	WP	*Anthus pratensis*
p	V		p	p				p	P	P	p	p	P	p	p	*Anthus cervinus*
p	WP	Sw	R	R	R	R	R	WP	WP	SP	R	Ws	Ws	R	w	w	*Anthus spinoletta*
SP	SP	P	SP	SP	SP	SP	SP	Sw	SP	SP	SP	SP	SP	SP	SP	*Motacilla flava*
w	R	R	R	R	R	R	R	Ws	Sw	Sw	R	r	R	w	WP	*Motacilla cinerea*
WP	R	Sw	R	R	Ws	R	R	Sw	SP	Sw	R	R	R	WP	R	*Motacilla alba*
V	s	SP	SP	SP	SP	SP	P	Sw	SP	SP	SP	SP	Sw	SP	SP	*Lanius collurio*
									s	s	?	r	r		s	*Lanius nubicus*

r *Scarce throughout year* though not necessarily breeding.
s *Scarce in summer* only or largely.
w *Scarce in winter* only or largely.
p *Scarce on passage* only.
V *Vagrant* or casual visitor.
? More information needed.

	United Kingdom	Ireland	Iceland	Norway	Sweden	Finland	Denmark	Poland	Czechoslovakia	Germany	Netherlands	Belgium	Luxembourg	France	Spain
Woodchat Shrike	V	V		V	V	V	V	s	s	s	V	V	SP	SP	SP
Lesser Grey Shrike	V	V		V	V	V	V	s	SP	s	V	V	V	SP	s
Great Grey Shrike	w	V		r	r	r	r	r	r	r	r	r	r	R	R
Waxwing	w	w	V	r	Ws	Ws	WP	w	WP	WP	w	w	V	w	V
Dipper	R	R		R	Sw	Sw	w	r	R	r	V	r	R	R	R
Wren	R	R	R	R	r	r	R	R	R	R	R	R	R	R	R
Alpine Accentor	V				V		V	r	r	r				r	R
Dunnock	R	R		Sw	R	s	R	r	Sw	R	R	R	R	R	R
Cetti's Warbler	r	V								V	p	r		R	R
Savi's Warbler	s				V	V		SP	s	s	SP	s		SP	SP
River Warbler	V			V	s		V	V	s	SP	s	V	V	V	
Grasshopper Warbler	SP	SP		V	s	s	s	s	SP	SP	SP	s	s	SP	s
Moustached Warbler	V						V		s	V				r	Sw
Aquatic Warbler	V	V			V		V	s	s	s	s	V	V	p	p
Sedge Warbler	SP	SP		SP	SP	SP	SP	SP	SP	SP	SP	SP	s	SP	P
Blyth's Reed Warbler	V	V			V	s									
Marsh Warbler	s			V	s	s	SP	SP	SP	SP	SP	SP	SP	s	p
Reed Warbler	SP	V			s	SP	SP	SP	SP	SP	SP	SP	SP	SP	SP
Great Reed Warbler	V	V		V	s	s	s	SP	SP	SP	SP	s	s	SP	SP
Icterine Warbler	p	p		SP	SP	s	SP	SP	SP	SP	SP	SP	s	SP	V
Melodious Warbler	V	V								V	V	V		SP	SP
Olive-tree Warbler															
Olivaceous Warbler	V	V			V					V				V	SP
Barred Warbler	p	V		p	s	s	s	s	SP	s	V	V		V	

R *Common throughout year* in at least part of the country.

Sw *Common in summer* in suitable habitats but *very scarce to scarce in winter*.

Ws *Common in winter* in suitable habitats but *very scarce to scarce in summer*.

SP *Common in summer* only or *present in summer and common on passage*.

WP *Common in winter* only or *present in winter and common on passage*.

P *Common on passage* only.

Balearic Is.	Portugal	Switzerland	Austria	Italy	Corsica	Sardinia	Sicily	Hungary	Rumania	Bulgaria	Yugoslavia	Albania	Greece	Greek Is.	Eur. Turkey	
SP	SP	s	s	SP	SP	SP	SP	s	s	s	s	s	Sw	p	r	*Lanius senator*
s			SP	SP	p	p	?	SP	SP	SP	SP	SP	Sw	P	SP	*Lanius minor*
V	R	R	R	r	V	V	w	WP	r	w	r	w	w		w	*Lanius excubitor*
	V	V	WP	w				WP	w	w	w	w	w	V	w	*Bombycilla garrulus*
r	R	R	R	R	R	R	?	r	R	R	R	r	R	V	r	*Cinclus cinclus*
r	R	R	R	R	R	R	R	R	R	R	R	R	R	R	R	*Troglodytes troglodytes*
V	V	R	R	r	?	?	w	R	R	R	r	R	R		r	*Prunella collaris*
w	R	Sw	R	R	?	?	WP	WP	SP	R	R	WP	WP	w	w	*Prunella modularis*
R	R	V		R	R	R	R		r	r	R	R	R	r	r	*Cettia cetti*
SP	SP	s	SP	s	V	V	s	SP	SP	s	s	s	s	s	p	*Locustella luscinioides*
		V	s					SP	s	p	s	?	p			*Locustella fluviatilis*
p	w	s	SP	s			s	SP	V	s			p	V		*Locustella naevia*
R		V	SP	R	?	?	R	SP	s	p	r	w	r		p	*Lusciniola melanopogon*
p	p	p	s	s		?	s	p	s	V	s	s	V	V		*Acrocephalus paludicola*
p	P	P	SP	SP	P	P	P	SP	SP	SP	SP	s	P	p	p	*Acrocephalus schoenobaenus*
																Acrocephalus dumetorum
		SP	SP	s		V	V	SP	SP	SP	s	s	SP		s	*Acrocephalus palustris*
SP	SP	SP	SP	SP	s	SP	s	SP	SP	SP	SP	SP	SP	p	SP	*Acrocephalus scirpaceus*
SP	SP	SP	SP	SP	?	p	SP	SP	SP	SP	SP	SP	SP	P	p	*Acrocephalus arundinaceus*
p		SP	SP	s	p	p		SP	SP	SP	s	p	P	p	p	*Hippolais icterina*
p	SP	s		SP	p	p	SP					s	?			*Hippolais polyglotta*
			V						s	s	s		SP	p		*Hippolais olivetorum*
p		s	V					s	s	SP	SP	s	SP	s	SP	*Hippolais pallida*
		V	SP	s				SP	SP	SP	SP	s	s		p	*Sylvia nisoria*

r *Scarce throughout year* though not necessarily breeding.
s *Scarce in summer* only or largely.
w *Scarce in winter* only or largely.
p *Scarce on passage* only.
V *Vagrant* or casual visitor.
? More information needed.

	United Kingdom	Ireland	Iceland	Norway	Sweden	Finland	Denmark	Poland	Czechoslovakia	Germany	Netherlands	Belgium	Luxembourg	France	Spain
Orphean Warbler	V									p		V	V	SP	SP
Garden Warbler	SP	s	V	SP	SP	SP	SP	SP	SP	SP	SP	SP	SP	SP	SP
Blackcap	Sw	r	V	SP	SP	SP	SP	SP	SP	SP	Sw	Sw	SP	Sw	R
Whitethroat	SP	SP	V	SP	SP	SP	SP	SP	SP	SP	SP	SP	SP	SP	SP
Lesser Whitethroat	SP	p		SP	SP	SP	SP	SP	SP	SP	SP	SP	SP	SP	V
Rüppell's Warbler					V	V									V
Sardinian Warbler	V									V				R	R
Subalpine Warbler	V	V		V						V	V			Sw	SP
Spectacled Warbler	V													s	s
Dartford Warbler	r	V									V			R	R
Marmora's Warbler														V	r
Willow Warbler	SP	SP	p	SP	SP	SP	SP	SP	SP	SP	SP	SP	SP	SP	P
Chiffchaff	Sw	Sw	p	SP	SP	SP	SP	SP	SP	SP	SP	Sw	SP	Sw	R
Bonelli's Warbler	V	V			V			V	V	SP	V	V		SP	SP
Wood Warbler	SP	s	V	SP	SP	s		SP	SP	SP	SP	SP	s	SP	p
Yellow-browed Warbler	p	p		V	V	V	V	V	V	p	V			V	V
Arctic Warbler	V	V		s	s	s				V	V				
Greenish Warbler	V	V			p	V	s	s		s	V				
Goldcrest	R	R	V	R	R	R	R	R	R	R	R	R	R	R	Ws
Firecrest	r	V		V	V		V	s		Sw	SP	R	R	Sw	R
Fan-tailed Warbler		V												r	R
Pied Flycatcher	SP	p	V	SP	SP	SP	SP	SP	s	SP	SP	s	s	SP	SP
Collared Flycatcher	V				SP	V	V	s	SP	s	V	V	V	s	
Red-breasted Flycatcher	p	p		p	s	s	p	s	SP	s	p	V		p	V

R   *Common throughout year* in at least part of the country.

Sw *Common in summer* in suitable habitats but *very scarce to scarce in winter*.

Ws *Common in winter* in suitable habitats but *very scarce to scarce in summer*.

SP *Common in summer* only or *present in summer and common on passage*.

WP *Common in winter* only or *present in winter and common on passage*.

P   *Common on passage* only.

Balearic Is.	Portugal	Switzerland	Austria	Italy	Corsica	Sardinia	Sicily	Hungary	Rumania	Bulgaria	Yugoslavia	Albania	Greece	Greek Is.	Eur. Turkey	
p	SP	s	V	SP	s		p			s	s	s	SP	SP	s	*Sylvia hortensis*
p	SP	SP	SP	s	p	p	p	SP	SP	s	s	p	P	P	p	*Sylvia borin*
R	R	Sw	SP	R	R	R	R	SP	SP	SP	Sw	R	R	WP	r	*Sylvia atricapilla*
P	SP	SP	SP	SP	P	P	SP	SP	SP	SP	SP	SP	SP	SP	SP	*Sylvia communis*
p		SP	SP	s			p	SP	SP	SP	s	s	s	P	P	*Sylvia curruca*
			V				V						s	SP		*Sylvia rueppelli*
R	R	V		R	R	R	R			r	R	R	R	R	R	*Sylvia melanocephala*
P	s	V		SP	s	s	SP			s	s	s	Sw	Sw		*Sylvia cantillans*
p	s			s	s	s	s				?	?	V	V		*Sylvia conspicillata*
w	R			R	R	R	?						V	V		*Sylvia undata*
R				r	R	R	?									*Sylvia sarda*
WP	P	SP	SP	s	P	P	P	SP	s	P	s	P	WP	P	P	*Phylloscopus trochilus*
WP	R	SP	SP	R	WP	WP	R	SP	SP	R	R	R	Ws	WP	WP	*Phylloscopus collybita*
p	s	SP	s	SP	SP	?	?		V	s	s	s	SP	P	p	*Phylloscopus bonelli*
p		SP	SP	SP	?		?	SP	SP	P	s	s	P	P	p	*Phylloscopus sibilatrix*
		V	V	V			V						V			*Phylloscopus inornatus*
V				V									V			*Phylloscopus borealis*
																Phylloscopus trochiloides
WP	WP	R	R	R	R	r	WP	Ws	R	R	R	r	r	w	w	*Regulus regulus*
R	Ws	SP	SP	R	R	R	R	p	Sw	SP	R	R	R	r	r	*Regulus ignicapillus*
R	R			R	R	R	R				?	r	R	r		*Cisticola juncidis*
P	SP	SP	SP	s	p	p	p	P	s	P	P	P	P	p	p	*Ficedula hypoleuca*
V	V	s	s	s			s	SP	SP	SP	s	s	P	p	P	*Ficedula albicollis*
V		V	s	V			s			SP	SP	s		p	P	*Ficedula parva*

r *Scarce throughout year* though not necessarily breeding.

s *Scarce in summer* only or largely.

w *Scarce in winter* only or largely.

p *Scarce on passage* only.

V *Vagrant* or casual visitor.

? More information needed.

	United Kingdom	Ireland	Iceland	Norway	Sweden	Finland	Denmark	Poland	Czechoslovakia	Germany	Netherlands	Belgium	Luxembourg	France	Spain
Spotted Flycatcher	SP	SP		SP	SP	SP	SP	SP	SP	SP	SP	SP	SP	SP	SP
Whinchat	SP	s		SP	SP	SP	SP	SP	SP	SP	SP	SP	SP	SP	SP
Stonechat	R	R		V	V	V	s	s	SP	SP	Sw	Sw	Sw	Sw	R
Wheatear	SP	SP	SP	SP	SP	SP	SP	SP	SP	SP	SP	SP	SP	SP	SP
Pied Wheatear	V								V						
Black-eared Wheatear	V	V								V	V			s	SP
Isabelline Wheatear	V														
Black Wheatear	V	V								V				r	R
Rufous Bush Chat or Robin	V	V								V				V	s
Rock Thrush	V	V			V			s	SP	p	V	V	V	SP	SP
Blue Rock Thrush									V	V				R	R
Black Redstart	r	w		V	V	V	s	SP	SP	SP	Sw	Sw	Sw	Sw	R
Redstart	SP	s		SP	SP	SP	SP	SP	SP	SP	SP	SP	SP	SP	SP
Robin	R	R	V	Sw	Sw	SP	R	SP	Sw	R	R	R	R	R	R
Nightingale	SP	V						V	SP	SP	SP	SP	s	SP	SP
Thrush Nightingale	V			p	SP	s	SP	SP	s	s					
Bluethroat	p	V		SP	SP	SP	p	s	s	s	s	s	p	s	r
Red-flanked Bluetail	V				s					V	V				
Fieldfare	Ws	WP	w	Sw	Sw	Sw	WP	SP	R	R	WP	WP	Ws	Ws	WP
Ring Ouzel	SP	s		SP	SP	s	p	s	SP	s	p	p	p	R	r
Blackbird	R	R	w	R	R	Sw	R	R	R	R	R	R	R	R	R
Redwing	Ws	WP	Sw	Sw	Sw	SP	WP	s	P		WP	WP	WP	WP	WP
Song Thrush	R	R		Sw	SP	SP	Sw	SP	SP	SP	R	R	Sw	R	Ws
Mistle Thrush	R	R		r	Sw	Sw	r	r	R	R	R	R	R	R	R

R *Common throughout year* in at least part of the country.

Sw *Common in summer* in suitable habitats but *very scarce to scarce in winter.*

Ws *Common in winter* in suitable habitats but *very scarce to scarce in summer.*

SP *Common in summer* only or *present in summer and common on passage.*

WP *Common in winter* only or *present in winter and common on passage.*

P *Common on passage* only.

Balearic Is.	Portugal	Switzerland	Austria	Italy	Corsica	Sardinia	Sicily	Hungary	Rumania	Bulgaria	Yugoslavia	Albania	Greece	Greek Is.	Eur. Turkey	
SP	s	SP	SP	SP	SP	SP	?	SP	SP	SP	SP	SP	SP	P	SP	*Muscicapa striata*
P	s	SP	SP	s	SP	P	P	SP	SP	SP	SP	SP	Sw	r	P	*Saxicola rubetra*
R	R	SP	SP	R	R	R	R	SP	SP	SP	R	R	R	R	R	*Saxicola torquata*
SP	SP	SP	SP	SP	SP	SP	?	SP	SP	SP	SP	SP	SP	SP	SP	*Oenanthe oenanthe*
			V					s	s				V	V		*Oenanthe pleschanka*
p	SP	V	V	SP	p	p	SP	V	s	s	SP	SP	SP	SP	SP	*Oenanthe hispanica*
									V				s	s	s	*Oenanthe isabellina*
	R	V		r		r	?			V			V		V	*Oenanthe leucura*
p	s		V							V	s	s	s	s	s	*Cercotrichas galactotes*
s	SP	SP	s	SP	SP	SP	P	s	s	SP	SP	s	s	s	p	*Monticola saxatilis*
R	R	r	V	R	R	R	R			r	r	r	R	r	r	*Monticola solitarius*
WP	R	SP	SP	R	?	R	R	R	SP	Sw	R	r	R	r	r	*Phoenicurus ochruros*
P	s	SP	SP	SP	P	P	SP	SP	SP	SP	SP	s	Sw	P	P	*Phoenicurus phoenicurus*
WP	R	R	R	R	R	R	R	R	R	R	R	R	R	WP	R	*Erithacus rubecula*
SP	SP	SP	SP	SP	SP	s	SP	SP	SP	SP	SP	SP	Sw	Sw	SP	*Luscinia megarhynchos*
		s	V					SP	SP	p	p		p	p	p	*Luscinia luscinia*
p	s	P	s	p	p	p	p	s	s	p	s	p	p	p	p	*Luscinia svecica*
			V													*Tarsiger cyanurus*
w	w	R	R	WP	w	w	w	WP	Ws	WP	WP	WP	WP	w	WP	*Turdus pilaris*
p		SP	P	r	w	w	w	p	SP	R	R	r	w	w	P	*Turdus torquatus*
R	R	R	R	R	R	R	R	R	R	R	R	R	R	R	R	*Turdus merula*
WP	WP	P	WP	WP	w	w	WP	P	p	WP	WP	WP	WP	w	WP	*Turdus iliacus*
WP	w	Sw	SP	Ws	WP	WP	WP	SP	SP	SP	R	R	Ws	WP	WP	*Turdus philomelos*
w	R	R	R	R	R	R	R	Sw	R	R	R	R	R	r	R	*Turdus viscivorus*

r *Scarce throughout year* though not necessarily breeding.
s *Scarce in summer* only or largely.
w *Scarce in winter* only or largely.
p *Scarce on passage* only.
V *Vagrant* or casual visitor.
? More information needed.

	United Kingdom	Ireland	Iceland	Norway	Sweden	Finland	Denmark	Poland	Czechoslovakia	Germany	Netherlands	Belgium	Luxembourg	France	Spain
Bearded Tit or Reedling	r	V				V	V	r	r	r	R	V	V	r	R
Long-tailed Tit	R	R		R	R	r	R	R	R	R	R	R	R	R	R
Marsh Tit	R			R	R	V	R	R	R	R	R	R	R	R	r
Willow Tit	R			R	R	R		r	R	R	R	R	R		
Sombre Tit															
Siberian Tit				R	R	R									
Crested Tit	r			R	R	R	R	R	R	R	R	R	R	R	R
Coal Tit	R	R		R	R	R	R	R	R	R	R	R	R	R	R
Blue Tit	R	R		R	R	R	R	R	R	R	R	R	R	R	R
Great Tit	R	R		R	R	R	R	R	R	R	R	R	R	R	R
Penduline Tit	V				V	V	V	SP	SP	r	V	V	V	r	R
Nuthatch	R			R	R	V	R	R	R	R	R	R	R	R	R
Corsican Nuthatch															
Krüper's Nuthatch															
Rock Nuthatch															
Wallcreeper	V								r	s	r	V	V	r	r
Treecreeper	R	R		R	R	R	R	R	R	R		r	r	r	r
Short-toed Treecreeper	?					V	r	r	R	R	R	R	R	R	R
Corn Bunting	R	r		V	r	V	R	R	Sw	R	R	R	Sw	Sw	R
Yellowhammer	R	R		R	R	R	R	R	R	R	R	R	R	R	R
Rock Bunting	V							V	s	s	V	V	V	R	R
Cinereous Bunting															
Ortolan Bunting	p	V		SP	SP	SP	P	SP	s	SP	s	s	V	SP	SP
Cretzschmar's Bunting	V									V	V			V	V

R *Common throughout year* in at least part of the country.

Sw *Common in summer* in suitable habitats but *very scarce to scarce in winter.*

Ws *Common in winter* in suitable habitats but *very scarce to scarce in summer.*

SP *Common in summer* only or *present in summer and common on passage.*

WP *Common in winter* only or *present in winter and common on passage.*

P *Common on passage* only.

Balearic Is.	Portugal	Switzerland	Austria	Italy	Corsica	Sardinia	Sicily	Hungary	Rumania	Bulgaria	Yugoslavia	Albania	Greece	Greek Is.	Eur. Turkey	
V		V	r	r			r	r	R	r	r	r	R		r	*Panurus biarmicus*
	R	R	R	R	R		R	R	R	r	r	r	r	w	r	*Aegithalos caudatus*
	R	R	R	R	r	r	R	R	R	R	r	r	r			*Parus palustris*
	R	R	r	V				r	r	R	r	r	r			*Parus montanus*
			V						r	r	r	r	r	r	r	*Parus lugubris*
																Parus cinctus
	R	R	R	r				r	R	r	r	r	r	r	r	*Parus cristatus*
	R	R	R	R	R	R	r	Ws	R	R	R	R	R	r	r	*Parus ater*
R	R	R	R	R	R	R	R	R	R	R	R	R	R	R	R	*Parus caeruleus*
R	R	R	R	R	R	R	R	R	R	R	R	R	R	R	R	*Parus major*
V		r	R	R				r	r	R	r	r	r	r	r	*Remiz pendulinus*
	r	R	R	R			R	R	R	R	R	r	R	r	R	*Sitta europaea*
					r											*Sitta whiteheadi*
													r			*Sitta krueperi*
										r	r	r	R	r	r	*Sitta neumayer*
V	V	R	R	r	?	?		w	r	r	R	r	r			*Tichodroma muraria*
		R	R	r	r	r	?	R	R	r	R	r	r			*Certhia familiaris*
	R	R	R	R	?		R	R	r	R	R	r	R	r	r	*Certhia brachydactyla*
R	R	Sw	R	R	R	r	R	R	R	R	R	R	R	R	R	*Emberiza calandra*
V	r	R	R	R	w	w	V	R	R	R	R	R	R	r	w	*Emberiza citrinella*
	R	R	s	R	V	w	w	r	r	r	r	r	R	w	r	*Emberiza cia*
														r		*Emberiza cineracea*
p	s	SP	s	SP	p	?	p	s	SP	SP	SP	SP	SP	SP	SP	*Emberiza hortulana*
		V	V								s	s	SP	SP		*Emberiza caesia*

r *Scarce throughout year* though not necessarily breeding.
s *Scarce in summer* only or largely.
w *Scarce in winter* only or largely.
p *Scarce on passage* only.
V *Vagrant* or casual visitor.
? More information needed.

	United Kingdom	Ireland	Iceland	Norway	Sweden	Finland	Denmark	Poland	Czechoslovakia	Germany	Netherlands	Belgium	Luxembourg	France	Spain
Cirl Bunting	r	V						V		r	V	V	s	R	R
Little Bunting	V	V		V	s	s	V	V		V	V	V		V	V
Rustic Bunting	V	V		V	s	SP	V	V		V	V	V		V	
Yellow-breasted Bunting	V	V		V	V	s		V	V	V	V	V		V	
Black-headed Bunting	V	V			V	V		V	V	V	V			V	V
Reed Bunting	R	R		Sw	Sw	SP	R	R	SP	R	Sw	Sw	Sw	R	Ws
Lapland Bunting	w	p	p	SP	SP	SP	w	w	V	w	w	w		w	
Snow Bunting	Ws	WP	R	R	Sw	Sw	WP	w	p	WP	w	w	V	w	w
Chaffinch	R	R	p	R	R	SP	R	Sw	R	R	R	R	R	R	R
Brambling	WP	WP	p	Sw	Sw	SP	WP	WP	WP	WP	WP	WP	WP	WP	WP
Citril Finch	V									r		V		r	r
Serin	r	V		V	V	V	V	SP	SP	SP	s	r	SP	Sw	R
Greenfinch	R	R		R	R	R	R	R	R	R	R	R	R	R	R
Siskin	Ws	R		R	R	R	Ws	R	R	R	Ws	Ws	WP	Ws	WP
Goldfinch	R	R		r	r	r	r	R	R	R	r	r	R	R	R
Twite	R	r		R	p	p	WP	w	w	WP	WP	w	V	w	w
Linnet	R	R		Sw	Sw	s	Sw	R	R	R	R	R	R	R	R
Redpoll	R	R	R	R	Sw	Sw	WP	r	r	WP	r	w	p	r	w
Arctic Redpoll	V			V	r	r	w	V	V	V	V			V	
Trumpeter Finch	V														?r
Scarlet or Common Rosefinch	V	V		V	s	SP	V	s	s	s	V	V		V	V
Pine Grosbeak	V			Sw	Sw	r		V	w	p	w	V	V	V	
Parrot Crossbill	V	V		r	r	r	V	r	w	w	V	V		V	
Crossbill	r	s		R	R	R	R	r	R	R	w	r	V	R	r

R *Common throughout year* in at least part of the country.
Sw *Common in summer* in suitable habitats but *very scarce in winter.*
Ws *Common in winter* in suitable habitats but *very scarce to scarce in summer.*
SP *Common in summer* only or *present in summer and common on passage.*
WP *Common in winter* only or *present in winter and common on passage.*
P *Common on passage* only.

Balearic Is.	Portugal	Switzerland	Austria	Italy	Corsica	Sardinia	Sicily	Hungary	Rumania	Bulgaria	Yugoslavia	Albania	Greece	Greek Is.	Eur. Turkey	
R	R	SP	s	R	R	R	R	V	r	R	R	r	R	r	R	*Emberiza cirlus*
		V	V	V	V								V			*Emberiza pusilla*
		V	V	V									V			*Emberiza rustica*
													V			*Emberiza aureola*
		V	V	s			V	V		SP	SP	SP	SP	SP	SP	*Emberiza melanocephala*
Ws	r	Sw	SP	R	?	r	Ws	R	R	Ws	R	r	r	w	s	*Emberiza schoeniclus*
		V	V	V				V		V						*Calcarius lapponicus*
	V	V	w	w		V		w	w	V	w					*Plectrophenax nivalis*
R	R	R	R	R	R	R	R	R	R	R	R	R	R	R	R	*Fringilla coelebs*
w	w	P	WP	WP	w	w	w	WP	WP	WP	WP	WP	w	w	WP	*Fringilla montifringilla*
?		SP	r	r	r	r		V								*Serinus citrinella*
R	R	Sw	SP	R	R	R	R	Sw	Sw	r	R	r	Sw	w	r	*Serinus serinus*
R	R	R	R	R	R	R	R	R	R	R	R	R	R	r	R	*Carduelis chloris*
w	WP	R	R	Ws	w		w	WP	Ws	Ws	r	r	r	w	w	*Carduelis spinus*
R	R	Sw	R	R	R	R	R	R	R	R	R	R	R	R	R	*Carduelis carduelis*
			w	V				WP								*Acanthis flavirostris*
R	R	Sw	R	R	R	R	R	R	R	R	R	R	R	R	R	*Acanthis cannabina*
		R	R	r				w	WP	WP	w	w				*Acanthis flammea*
								V								*Acanthis hornemanni*
			V										V			*Rhodopechys githaginea*
		V	V	V				V								*Carpodacus erythrinus*
			V	V				V			V					*Pinicola enucleator*
			w	V				V			V					*Loxia pytyopsittacus*
R	r	R	R	r	r	?	w	Ws	R	R	R	r	R	w	r	*Loxia curvirostra*

r *Scarce throughout year* though not necessarily breeding.
s *Scarce in summer* only or largely.
w *Scarce in winter* only or largely.
p *Scarce on passage* only.
V *Vagrant* or casual visitor.
? More information needed.

	United Kingdom	Ireland	Iceland	Norway	Sweden	Finland	Denmark	Poland	Czechoslovakia	Germany	Netherlands	Belgium	Luxembourg	France	Spain
Two-barred Crossbill	V	V		V	w	r	V	V	p	p	V	V		V	
Bullfinch	R	R		R	R	R	R	R	R	R	r		r	R	r
Hawfinch	R	V		V	r	V	r	r	R	R	r		r	R	r
Waxbill															
House Sparrow	R	R	V	R	R	R	R	R	R	R	R	R	R	R	R
Spanish Sparrow	V													V	r
Tree Sparrow	R	r		R	R	R	R	R	R	R	R	R	R	R	R
Rock Sparrow								V			V	V	V	r	R
Snow Finch								V	V	r	V		V	r	r
Rose-coloured Starling	V	V		V	V	V	V	V	V	V	V	V			
Starling	R	R	R	R	Sw	SP	R	SP	SP	R	R	R	R	R	WP
Spotless Starling														V	R
Golden Oriole	s	V		V	s	s	s	SP	SP	SP	SP	SP	s	SP	SP
Siberian Jay				R	R	R		V	V	V					
Jay	R	R		R	R	R	R	R	R	R	R	R	R	R	R
Azure-winged Magpie															R
Magpie	R	R		R	R	R	R	R	R	R	R	R	R	R	R
Nutcracker	V			r	r	r	V	r	R	r	V	V	V	r	V
Chough	r	R									V			r	R
Alpine Chough									V	r	V			r	R
Jackdaw	R	R	V	R	R	R	R	R	R	R	R	R	R	R	R
Rook	R	R	V	r	r	s	R	R	R	R	R	R	R	R	Ws
Carrion/Hooded Crow	R	R	V	R	R	R	R	R	R	R	R	R	R	R	R
Raven	R	R	R	R	R	r	r	r	R	r	V	V	V	r	R

R *Common throughout year* in at least part of the country.

Sw *Common in summer* in suitable habitats but *very scarce to scarce in winter*.

Ws *Common in winter* in suitable habitats but *very scarce to scarce in summer*.

SP *Common in summer* only or *present in summer and common on passage*.

WP *Common in winter* only or *present in winter and common on passage*.

P *Common on passage* only.